PRODIGY PLANNER

Your Workbook To Success

One Year Edition, Revision One

AF820897

Belongs To:_______

This Workbook Offers One Year Worth Of Planning, Based On A 28 Day, 13 Month System.

Publisher, Author, & Book Design By:
Draven Xarcell Vestatt

On Behalf Of Xarchology

Neither I or the publisher guarantee results, or any warranties, or claim any responsibility for any adverse effects resulting directly or indirectly from the information or practices contained within this book.

Published By: **XarBooks.**

INTRODUCTION

This planner to success will help you track your daily & monthly challenges, and ultimately help you achieve your goals. Time is the most important thing that you can't get back or replace. This planner will be an excellent tracker on how you spend that time.

No one should be looking at this planner, but you. Not your friends, not your spouse or significant other, not your parents, and not your children. You should also not be viewing someone else's planner.

This planner keeps track of everything just like a score. Some of you may require calculators, especially at the end of the month. However, instead of calling it a "score", will call it money and refer to it in the currency terms. This will ensure that it effect you subconsciously, improving your results.

Your challenges have been divided into five categories: Mental, Financial, Physical, Social, and Spiritual. By dividing your challenges into these five categories, you will be able to track and determine how you spend your time and energy.

Challenges can anything you have to force yourself to do. If you like shaving everyday, and do it out of habit, then it's not a challenge. However, if you dread shaving, and have to force yourself to do it, it should be considered a daily challenge until it becomes a habit and effortless.

When you do your challenges, you pay yourself an hourly rate, multiplied by the number of hours that challenge took to complete, rounded up to the nearest whole number. In some cases a challenge can't be measured in terms of an hour. In these instances, just pay yourself a flat rate equal to one hour.

To determine your hourly rate for each year, you divide your real annual salary by 1,000 and then round up to the nearest whole number. If you do not have a salary, I recommend starting at an annual salary of $20,000. Meaning your hourly rate should be $20.

In addition each year, you give yourself a %5 hourly rate bonus, regardless if your real annual salary went up. So your first year is a 0% bonus, your second year is a %5 bonus, and your third year a 10% bonus, so on and so forth.

Once you pay yourself for a challenge, you "deposit" that amount. So if you did a challenge for 2 hours, and your hourly rate is $20, then you deposit $40. You add up all your deposits for that category, then subtract all of your withdrawals.

A withdrawal is when you plan a challenge, but do not follow through with it. For example, in your financial category, you have planned 8 hours of work at your job, but you left 3 hours early due to an unforeseen illness. That means you still pay yourself for 5 hours of work and deposit that, then you withdrawal 3 hours worth of work because you didn't complete the challenge. At an hourly rate of $20; leaving 3 hours early means you have a withdrawal $60.

At the bottom of the category, you add up your all deposits and withdrawals, then round up to the nearest whole number. This determines your total for that category. You can use this information to track your progress in a specific category from month to month, or even year to year.

It is important to understand that there needs to be a daily challenge for each category, regardless if you are able to complete it or not.

The Challenges you add are completely up to you, depending on what your goals are. Your financial goals could be a hourly wage job, and/or commission goal. Your physical challenge could be exercise and/or diet. So on and so forth. You can put as many challenges as you want for each category, as long at there is at least 1 daily challenge per category.

After filling out your challenges, you will see a section for notes and a section for affirmations.

Notes is to be used like a brief journal, or dairy. Be sure to jot down any usual happenings, so that you will have a record of it

Affirmations is to be used in instances when you feel your planner is working. Be sure to write out your pay in long-hand.

At the end of every month, you will do a "Wealth" Assessment. This will give you a monthly bonus. If you met the criteria of the challenge, you pay yourself for 1 hour, and write it in the deposit box.

WEALTH INTRODUCTION
What is it?

You may be wondering what does wealth have to do with personal development. The truth is: "everything". Every repair on your body or your property, the tools you need to complete other tasks, or even an event you may try to attend, is going to cost you money. The whole world evolves around it, so there is no point in trying to avoid it. So let's get your finances under control, so you can maximize your personal development in other areas.

There is a lot to cover in terms of wealth and it may seem over-whelming or even unattainable at times, but you have to keeping reaching for it. You don't have to follow all of these these guidelines in the proper order, but the more goals you reach, the more secure you'll feel.

Reaching these goals just isn't about trying to get rich. It's also about getting financial relief. Most people stay under constant stress worrying about their financial responsibility. This prodigy planner will resolve these issues, giving you some satisfaction knowing that your covered and prepared.

Now, in the beginning you may feel like your losing all of your financial freedoms and you will be tempted to just ignore or cheat your wealth sections. Mainly because most of your extra cash will go towards saving, but stick with it, because in the long run you'll be glad you did! If your really in a hurry, my may be necessary to take up more than one job.

WEALTH LEVEL ONE
The Essentials

There are many types of income that can be acquired, and they normally fall under one of these first four categories:

1.| Earned Income: this is compensation of your time involved in the form of wages, salaries, tips, and commissions because of your efforts.

2.| Investment Income: this is derived from capital gains & dividends from the purchase and sale of securities. Such as the buying & selling of stocks, bonds, money markets, real estate, and other investments. Do it yourself, or you can hire an company to manage it for you.

3.| Leveraged Income: this is income gained in conjunction with the combined efforts of others with very little effort to maintain. Such as affiliate pay, referral pay, or gains from percentages on the bottom-line. Also such as third party web-page ads, chain letters, and contractors who earn a profit-margin from sub-contractors.

4.| Residual Income: these are gains from a product that is re-occurring, but without re-occurring effort. Such as royalties from the sale of your music, books, photos, video, and inventions, but is not classified as "investment income".

5.| Have More Than One Type Of Income: The more types of income earn at once, the better off financially you'll be...

WEALTH LEVEL TWO
The Fundamentals

1.| 10% Of Income Saved Upon Payment: ten percent of your income should be saved upon every payment to you. Doing this upon every payment you receive will seem to add up quicker than you would expect, and creates great saving & spending habits.

This money saved can be used towards setting up emergency funds, investments, unexpected repairs, and taxes.

2.| 6-Month Emergency Cash Fund Reserved: A six month emergency cash fund should be saved in an event of a REAL emergency. Such job loss or missed work due to bereavement, sickness, disability, injury, car or house repair, but not unnecessary remodeling.

How much you should save depends on how much your monthly bills are. For a six month emergency fund, you want to add up all your monthly bills, including food and gas if you drive, then multiply that by six. That is how you determine the amount that should be saved for your 6-month emergency fund.

Since the funds are in cash, it is preferred that you store your cash in a place that will make it more difficult to obtain. This helps against impulse spending and even theft. You could try freezing it in ice, which requires you to thaw it to obtain it, or placing in sealed glass picture frame, which requires you to break it to obtain it, or by other difficult means.

3.| 1-Year Emergency Electronic Fund Reserved: once you have a six month emergency fund, you should consider creating a one year electronic emergency fund. Use this emergency fund for emergencies instead of your six month cash fund. This way your will have a fall back if something happens and your electronic funds become inaccessible.

4.| All Monthly Bills Paid On Time: for credit reasons and down right good character, all of your bills should be paid on time. Including money burrowed from friends & family. If you are having trouble paying your monthly bills on time, it's time to re-consider your spending priorities and/or monthly services. Debt always haunt you until it's paid, and that is unnecessary stress you don't need.

5.| Bills Do Not Exceed 50% Of Monthly Income: to avoid debt, it's important that you are not living above your means. So things like your rent/mortgage, power, water, insurance, and things of that nature should not exceed fifty percent of your monthly income. If you follow this rule, you will always have money to save, invest, and spend to ensure your quality of life during the meantime.

6.| No Debt - With Exception Of Mortgage: having no debt is a lot harder to achieve than you think. Owing a $15 late fee to your local video store doesn't count as debt free, nor does owing your parents $300 for that car repair. Being debt free comes with a feeling of freedom that cannot be substituted by anything other than being absolutely debt free.

WEALTH LEVEL 3
The Safety Net

Once you have your emergency funds, you should build a safety net to help keep you from dipping into your emergency funds. Best way to do this is with insurance, where in some cases it is even required by law.

1.| Life Insurance: this is important because it costs hundreds if not thousands to bury or cremate you. It may vary depending your your needs, but would also be irresponsible to dump the financial burden of dealing with your remains to your spouse or next of kin without financial restitution.

2.| Medical Insurance: nowadays expensive, you still cannot risk going without it. One year you may find yourself only needing a simple flu shot, and ask why do you bother paying this expensive premium, but then the next year you may require minor emergency surgery and it could cost you up to ten thousand dollars. At that point, you'll realize your glad you stuck with it.

3.| Disability Insurance: this is an inexpensive policy that will continue to pay your other insurance premiums in the event that you cannot work due to temporary disability.

4.| Dental Insurance: is sometime everyone needs at some point in his or her life. This insurance is often worth it's weight in gold and is usually fairly cheap.

5.| **Optical Insurance**: this isn't something everyone needs, or ever will need. However, these expenses can add up, and it's better to be safe than sorry.

6.| **Long Term Care Insurance**: or retirement insurance as some call it. This assures you get the qualified assistance and support for basic living needs when you are too old to perform them yourself.

7.| **Umbrella Insurance**: this policy is often overlooked and is one of the most important insurance policies that you can have. Umbrella insurance in most cases will cover you in a situation where your being sued for whatever reason. Your premiums may vary, depending on what you due for a living.

8.| **Property Insurance**: most people don't need this until they acquire expense items in his or her household. This inexpensive policy will reimburse you in case of fire, water damage, and in some cases theft. Considering how cheap this is to have, it wouldn't make much sense not to have it.

9.| **Auto Insurance**: required in most states and countries in order to drive, it's understandable why. Most accidents occur on the road. If your driving, this is simply one you cannot due without.

10.| **File All Bills & Receipts**: you should have some kind of filing system in which you save all your bills, receipts, and even warranties. This will help you prove your costs and expenses in case you are audited by the government, need to return an item that's broken, or show proof of payment.

WEALTH LEVEL FOUR

Look Good On Paper

1.| Have A Credit Score Above 760: today, the standard for good credit is a 760 FICO score. This is a credit score determined by 3 credit agencies. This is the score you need to get great interest rates on mortgages, car loans, and credit cards.

2.| Have Secured Credit Cards Only: get yourself at least one credit card to help build your credit, with a maximum of three credit cards. Each credit card should be a secured credit card. This means there should be an equal amount of funds saved compared to limit. For example, if you have a credit card with a $1000 limit, you should also have a $1000 saved in an account somewhere to cover it in case financial ruin. There are several companies that will do this automatically if requested, regardless of credit score.

3.| 10% Of Income Invested Upon Payment: if you are keeping your bills at 50% of monthly income, then investing an additional 10% shouldn't be a problem. You can invest in 401k, stocks, money markets, gold, or whatever the heart desires. After a few years it really begins to add up.

4.| Monitor Your Credit Report Monthly: it takes years to build good credit, and only months to ruin it. Most companies do not report payments made on time, only payments not made or paid late. Also, most people have discrepancies and do not know it. If you catch it as soon as it happens, it can be an easy fix.

WEALTH LEVEL FIVE
Sustainability

The goal here is to be self-sustaining in case of economic collapse or natural disaster. You want to eliminate as much as your bills as possible, and not have to depend on third party services in order to survive.

1.| **Sustainable Power Supply**: eliminate your power bill as much as possible by installing solar panels, wind mills, or other means. The goal is to not have a power bill, and it is certainly possible.

2.| **Sustainable Water Supply**: well water and septic tank will eliminate the monthly city water and sewage bill.

3.| **Recycle & Eliminate Own Waste**: recycling materials will bring in extra income and creating compost with your waste can save you money.

4.| **Have No Mortgage Or Rent Bill**: have no mortgage or rent bill, this means your house should be owned and paid for. This saves you massive amounts of cash monthly.

5.| **20-Year Property Tax Funds Reserved**: make sure you have enough money reserved to pay your property taxes for your retirement. Some people who have paid their house off, end up losing it due to not having enough money to pay the annual taxes on it.

6.| **Homestead**: grow your own food. You'll have fresher, more nutritious food without having to run to the store and buy it.

PROCESS REVIEW
Looking at Examples

Let's take a look at what an example would look like. In the following example on the next pages, you will see that at the beginning of a month, a "Wealth" category is to be completed first. NOTE: the wealth category will only appear once at the beginning of each month, based on a 28 day, 13 month year.

In this wealth category, you can see that the John Doe has paid himself a flat rate of $20 for things like: multiple types of income, bills are paid on time, and auto insurance.

Next, you can see where the John Doe as paid himself for working at a local job as a cashier. Because he worked 8 hours, he paid himself his hourly rate of $20, which equals out to be a deposit of $160(8 x $20 = $160).

Furthermore you can see where John Doe withdrew his flat rate because he planned on exercising, but did not. However, he did not eat junk food, and he took vitamins, so he paid himself a flat rate for each.

In the end you can see that John Doe wrote in each of the categories totals, plus his wealth bonus, and then added it up.

Lastly, you can see he wrote down some notes, and his affirmations. He even remembered to write out his earnings under affirmations in long hand. By writing it out long-hand, it re-enforces the feeling of progress, which is a very important step.

SEE EXAMPLES

WEALTH LEVEL 1 - Essentials		
#	**Description**	**Deposit**
1	Have Earned Income	$20.00
2	Have Investment Income	$20.00
3	Have Leveraged Income	/
4	Have Residual Income	/
5	Have More Than One Type Of Income	$20.00

WEALTH LEVEL 2 - Fundamentals		
#	**Description**	**Deposit**
1	10% Of Income Saved Upon Payment	$20.00
2	6-Month Emergency Cash Fund Reserved	/
3	1-Year Emergency Electronic Fund Reserved	/
4	All Monthly Bills Are Paid On Time	$20.00
5	Bills Do Not Exceed 50% Of Monthly Income	/
6	No Debt – With Exception Of Mortgage	/

WEALTH LEVEL 3 - Safety Net		
#	**Description**	**Deposit**
1	Life Insurance – All Dependents	/
2	Medical Insurance – All Dependents	/
3	Disability Insurance – If Not Retired	/
4	Dental Insurance – All Dependents	/
5	Optical Insurance - All Dependents	/
6	Long Term Care Insurance – If Retired	/
7	Umbrella Insurance	/
8	Property Insurance – Homeowner/Renters	/
9	Auto Insurance	$20.00
10	Filed All Bills & Receipts	$20.00

Prodigy Planner Workbook

WEALTH LEVEL 4 - Look Good On Paper		
#	**Description**	**Deposit**
1	Have A Credit Score Above 760	/
2	Have A Secured Credit Cards Only	/
3	10% Of Income Invested Upon Payment	/
4	Monitor Your Credit Report Monthly	/
WEALTH LEVEL 5 - Sustainability		
#	**Description**	**Deposit**
1	Sustainable Power Supply – No Bill	/
2	Sustainable Water Supply – No Bill	/
3	Recycle & Eliminate Own Waste	/
4	Have No Mortgage Or Rent Bill	/
5	20-Year Property Tax Funds Reserved	/
6	Homestead	/
	Total	$140.00

NOTES:

I have $190 saved, once I have $200
I can open a secured credit card.

AFFIRMATIONS:

Lately I have had a stronger sense of accomplishment, and have given me more confidence in myself. My friends and family have also noticed that I'm more confident!

SIGNATURE: John Doe DATE: 1-1-2012

FINANCIAL CHALLENGES					
#	Description	Hours	Rate	Deposit	Withdrawal
1	Cashier	8	$20.00	$160.00	
2	Online Trading	1	$20.00	$20.00	
3					
4					
5					
		Total:		$180.00	

MENTAL CHALLENGES					
#	Description	Hours	Rate	Deposit	Withdrawal
1	Studied For Exam	2	$20.00	$40.00	
2	Practice Spanish	1	$20.00	$20.00	
3					
4					
5					
		Total:		$60.00	

PHYSICAL CHALLENGES					
#	Description	Hours	Rate	Deposit	Withdrawal
1	Exercise	1	$20.00		-$20.00
2	No Junk Food	/	$20.00	$20.00	
3	Take Vitamins	/	$20.00	$20.00	
4					
5					
		Total:		$20.00	

SOCIAL CHALLENGES					
#	Description	Hours	Rate	Deposit	Withdrawal
1	Call Mother	1	$20.00		-$20.00
2	Visit Grandma	1	$20.00	$20.00	
3	Niece's B-day Party	3	$20.00	$60.00	
4					
5					
		Total:		$60.00	

Prodigy Planner Workbook

SPIRITUAL CHALLENGES					
#	Description	Hours	Rate	Deposit	Withdrawal
1	Meditate	1	$20.00	$20.00	
2	Pray Before Meals	/	$20.00	$20.00	
3					
4					
5					
			Total:	$40.00	

DAILY SUMMARY			
#	Description	Yesterday's Balance	Add Today's Balance
1	Financial	$480.00	$660.00
2	Mental	$200.00	$260.00
3	Physical	$360.00	$380.00
4	Social	$180.00	$240.00
5	Spiritual	$230.00	$270.00
	Monthly Wealth Bonus		$140.00
	Total		$1,950.00

NOTES:

I didn't have a chance to call mom due to busier plan than expected. I was also too lazy to work out. I'll get it done tomorrow!

AFFIRMATIONS:

I have one thousand nine hundred and thirty dollars this year so far!

SIGNATURE: John Doe DATE: 1-1-2012

GOALS & CHALLRNGES

A Reference

Now write down some ideas for challenges you would like to do in order to reach your goals. This can act as a reference, in case later on you forget some goals or challenges you would like to perform.

At the end of the year, you can come back and see what challenges and goals you had, and what you followed.

Goals	Challenge Ideas
______________________	______________________
______________________	______________________
______________________	______________________
______________________	______________________
______________________	______________________
______________________	______________________
______________________	______________________
______________________	______________________
______________________	______________________
______________________	______________________
______________________	______________________
______________________	______________________
______________________	______________________
______________________	______________________
______________________	______________________
______________________	______________________
______________________	______________________
______________________	______________________
______________________	______________________
______________________	______________________

GETTING IT DONE

When To Do It

The single most important thing about this planner is doing it. You may have had a long day, you may exhausted, and you may have a headache. Regardless of how you feel, you just have to do it. If your struggling with doing this every night, then make it a challenge out of it and pay yourself for it.

The best time, and pretty much only time to write in your planner is at bedtime. Almost everyday something happens unexpectedly that we have to deal with and dread doing it. By doing this at bedtime, you can write it in unexpected challenges and pay yourself for it.

So keep this planner and a pen dedicated to it beside or near your bed in a safe place. You may even need a calculator, especially for the monthly bonuses.

In the lines below, I want you to write "*This planner to success belongs to* YOUR NAME HERE. *I will challenge myself everyday, to reach my goals, and I will succeed.*" Then sign & date.

____

____

____

____

____

____

____

NOW YOUR ARE READY TO BEGIN!

WEALTH LEVEL 1 - Essentials		
#	**Description**	**Deposit**
1	Have Earned Income	
2	Have Investment Income	
3	Have Leveraged Income	
4	Have Residual Income	
5	Have More Than One Type Of Income	
WEALTH LEVEL 2 - Fundamentals		
#	**Description**	**Deposit**
1	10% Of Income Saved Upon Payment	
2	6-Month Emergency Cash Fund Reserved	
3	1-Year Emergency Electronic Fund Reserved	
4	All Monthly Bills Are Paid On Time	
5	Bills Do Not Exceed 50% Of Monthly Income	
6	No Debt – With Exception Of Mortgage	
WEALTH LEVEL 3 - Safety Net		
#	**Description**	**Deposit**
1	Life Insurance – All Dependents	
2	Medical Insurance – All Dependents	
3	Disability Insurance – If Not Retired	
4	Dental Insurance – All Dependents	
5	Optical Insurance - All Dependents	
6	Long Term Care Insurance – If Retired	
7	Umbrella Insurance	
8	Property Insurance – Homeowner/Renters	
9	Auto Insurance	
10	Filed All Bills & Receipts	

Prodigy Planner Workbook

#	Description	Deposit
	WEALTH LEVEL 4 - Look Good On Paper	
#	**Description**	**Deposit**
1	Have A Credit Score Above 760	
2	Have A Secured Credit Cards Only	
3	10% Of Income Invested Upon Payment	
4	Monitor Your Credit Report Monthly	
	WEALTH LEVEL 5 - Sustainability	
#	**Description**	**Deposit**
1	Sustainable Power Supply – No Bill	
2	Sustainable Water Supply – No Bill	
3	Recycle & Eliminate Own Waste	
4	Have No Mortgage Or Rent Bill	
5	20-Year Property Tax Funds Reserved	
6	Homestead	
	Total:	

NOTES:____

AFFIRMATIONS:__________________________________

SIGNATURE:________________________ DATE:______________

FINANCIAL CHALLENGES					
#	Description	Hours	Rate	Deposit	Withdrawal
1					
2					
3					
4					
5					
		Total:			

MENTAL CHALLENGES					
#	Description	Hours	Rate	Deposit	Withdrawal
1					
2					
3					
4					
5					
		Total:			

PHYSICAL CHALLENGES					
#	Description	Hours	Rate	Deposit	Withdrawal
1					
2					
3					
4					
5					
		Total:			

SOCIAL CHALLENGES					
#	Description	Hours	Rate	Deposit	Withdrawal
1					
2					
3					
4					
5					
		Total:			

SPIRITUAL CHALLENGES					
#	**Description**	**Hours**	**Rate**	**Deposit**	**Withdrawal**
1					
2					
3					
4					
5					
		Total:			

DAILY SUMMARY			
#	**Description**	**Yesterday's Balance**	**Add Today's Balance**
1	Financial		
2	Mental		
3	Physical		
4	Social		
5	Spiritual		
Monthly Wealth Bonus			
Total			

NOTES:____

____

____

____

____

____

AFFIRMATIONS:____

____

____

____

____

____

SIGNATURE:______________________________ DATE:________________

FINANCIAL CHALLENGES					
#	Description	Hours	Rate	Deposit	Withdrawal
1					
2					
3					
4					
5					
		Total:			

MENTAL CHALLENGES					
#	Description	Hours	Rate	Deposit	Withdrawal
1					
2					
3					
4					
5					
		Total:			

PHYSICAL CHALLENGES					
#	Description	Hours	Rate	Deposit	Withdrawal
1					
2					
3					
4					
5					
		Total:			

SOCIAL CHALLENGES					
#	Description	Hours	Rate	Deposit	Withdrawal
1					
2					
3					
4					
5					
		Total:			

Prodigy Planner Workbook

SPIRITUAL CHALLENGES					
#	Description	Hours	Rate	Deposit	Withdrawal
1					
2					
3					
4					
5					
		Total:			

DAILY SUMMARY			
#	Description	Yesterday's Balance	Add Today's Balance
1	Financial		
2	Mental		
3	Physical		
4	Social		
5	Spiritual		
Total			

NOTES:______________________________________

AFFIRMATIONS:________________________________

SIGNATURE:________________________ DATE:____________

FINANCIAL CHALLENGES					
#	Description	Hours	Rate	Deposit	Withdrawal
1					
2					
3					
4					
5					
		Total:			

MENTAL CHALLENGES					
#	Description	Hours	Rate	Deposit	Withdrawal
1					
2					
3					
4					
5					
		Total:			

PHYSICAL CHALLENGES					
#	Description	Hours	Rate	Deposit	Withdrawal
1					
2					
3					
4					
5					
		Total:			

SOCIAL CHALLENGES					
#	Description	Hours	Rate	Deposit	Withdrawal
1					
2					
3					
4					
5					
		Total:			

Prodigy Planner Workbook

SPIRITUAL CHALLENGES					
#	**Description**	**Hours**	**Rate**	**Deposit**	**Withdrawal**
1					
2					
3					
4					
5					
		Total:			

DAILY SUMMARY			
#	**Description**	**Yesterday's Balance**	**Add Today's Balance**
1	Financial		
2	Mental		
3	Physical		
4	Social		
5	Spiritual		
Total			

NOTES:____

____

____

____

____

____

AFFIRMATIONS:______________________________________

____

____

____

____

____

____

SIGNATURE:____________________________ DATE:______________

FINANCIAL CHALLENGES					
#	Description	Hours	Rate	Deposit	Withdrawal
1					
2					
3					
4					
5					
		Total:			

MENTAL CHALLENGES					
#	Description	Hours	Rate	Deposit	Withdrawal
1					
2					
3					
4					
5					
		Total:			

PHYSICAL CHALLENGES					
#	Description	Hours	Rate	Deposit	Withdrawal
1					
2					
3					
4					
5					
		Total:			

SOCIAL CHALLENGES					
#	Description	Hours	Rate	Deposit	Withdrawal
1					
2					
3					
4					
5					
		Total:			

Prodigy Planner Workbook

SPIRITUAL CHALLENGES					
#	Description	Hours	Rate	Deposit	Withdrawal
1					
2					
3					
4					
5					
		Total:			

DAILY SUMMARY			
#	Description	Yesterday's Balance	Add Today's Balance
1	Financial		
2	Mental		
3	Physical		
4	Social		
5	Spiritual		
Total			

NOTES:____

AFFIRMATIONS:__________________________________

SIGNATURE:________________________ DATE:______________

FINANCIAL CHALLENGES					
#	Description	Hours	Rate	Deposit	Withdrawal
1					
2					
3					
4					
5					
		Total:			

MENTAL CHALLENGES					
#	Description	Hours	Rate	Deposit	Withdrawal
1					
2					
3					
4					
5					
		Total:			

PHYSICAL CHALLENGES					
#	Description	Hours	Rate	Deposit	Withdrawal
1					
2					
3					
4					
5					
		Total:			

SOCIAL CHALLENGES					
#	Description	Hours	Rate	Deposit	Withdrawal
1					
2					
3					
4					
5					
		Total:			

Prodigy Planner Workbook

SPIRITUAL CHALLENGES					
#	**Description**	**Hours**	**Rate**	**Deposit**	**Withdrawal**
1					
2					
3					
4					
5					
		Total:			

DAILY SUMMARY			
#	**Description**	**Yesterday's Balance**	**Add Today's Balance**
1	Financial		
2	Mental		
3	Physical		
4	Social		
5	Spiritual		
Total			

NOTES:____

AFFIRMATIONS:____________________________________

SIGNATURE:__________________________ DATE:________________

Prodigy Planner Workbook

FINANCIAL CHALLENGES					
#	**Description**	**Hours**	**Rate**	**Deposit**	**Withdrawal**
1					
2					
3					
4					
5					
		Total:			

MENTAL CHALLENGES					
#	**Description**	**Hours**	**Rate**	**Deposit**	**Withdrawal**
1					
2					
3					
4					
5					
		Total:			

PHYSICAL CHALLENGES					
#	**Description**	**Hours**	**Rate**	**Deposit**	**Withdrawal**
1					
2					
3					
4					
5					
		Total:			

SOCIAL CHALLENGES					
#	**Description**	**Hours**	**Rate**	**Deposit**	**Withdrawal**
1					
2					
3					
4					
5					
		Total:			

Prodigy Planner Workbook

SPIRITUAL CHALLENGES					
#	Description	Hours	Rate	Deposit	Withdrawal
1					
2					
3					
4					
5					
		Total:			

DAILY SUMMARY			
#	Description	Yesterday's Balance	Add Today's Balance
1	Financial		
2	Mental		
3	Physical		
4	Social		
5	Spiritual		
Total			

NOTES:____

AFFIRMATIONS:__________________________________

SIGNATURE:________________________ DATE:____________

FINANCIAL CHALLENGES					
#	Description	Hours	Rate	Deposit	Withdrawal
1					
2					
3					
4					
5					
		Total:			

MENTAL CHALLENGES					
#	Description	Hours	Rate	Deposit	Withdrawal
1					
2					
3					
4					
5					
		Total:			

PHYSICAL CHALLENGES					
#	Description	Hours	Rate	Deposit	Withdrawal
1					
2					
3					
4					
5					
		Total:			

SOCIAL CHALLENGES					
#	Description	Hours	Rate	Deposit	Withdrawal
1					
2					
3					
4					
5					
		Total:			

Prodigy Planner Workbook

SPIRITUAL CHALLENGES					
#	Description	Hours	Rate	Deposit	Withdrawal
1					
2					
3					
4					
5					
			Total:		

DAILY SUMMARY			
#	Description	Yesterday's Balance	Add Today's Balance
1	Financial		
2	Mental		
3	Physical		
4	Social		
5	Spiritual		
Total			

NOTES:____

____

____

____

____

____

AFFIRMATIONS:______________________________________

____

____

____

____

____

____

SIGNATURE:_____________________________ DATE:_______________

FINANCIAL CHALLENGES					
#	Description	Hours	Rate	Deposit	Withdrawal
1					
2					
3					
4					
5					
		Total:			

MENTAL CHALLENGES					
#	Description	Hours	Rate	Deposit	Withdrawal
1					
2					
3					
4					
5					
		Total:			

PHYSICAL CHALLENGES					
#	Description	Hours	Rate	Deposit	Withdrawal
1					
2					
3					
4					
5					
		Total:			

SOCIAL CHALLENGES					
#	Description	Hours	Rate	Deposit	Withdrawal
1					
2					
3					
4					
5					
		Total:			

SPIRITUAL CHALLENGES					
#	**Description**	**Hours**	**Rate**	**Deposit**	**Withdrawal**
1					
2					
3					
4					
5					
		Total:			

DAILY SUMMARY			
#	**Description**	**Yesterday's Balance**	**Add Today's Balance**
1	Financial		
2	Mental		
3	Physical		
4	Social		
5	Spiritual		
Total			

NOTES:____

____

____

____

____

____

AFFIRMATIONS:______________________________________

____

____

____

____

____

____

SIGNATURE:______________________________ DATE:________________

FINANCIAL CHALLENGES					
#	Description	Hours	Rate	Deposit	Withdrawal
1					
2					
3					
4					
5					
		Total:			

MENTAL CHALLENGES					
#	Description	Hours	Rate	Deposit	Withdrawal
1					
2					
3					
4					
5					
		Total:			

PHYSICAL CHALLENGES					
#	Description	Hours	Rate	Deposit	Withdrawal
1					
2					
3					
4					
5					
		Total:			

SOCIAL CHALLENGES					
#	Description	Hours	Rate	Deposit	Withdrawal
1					
2					
3					
4					
5					
		Total:			

Prodigy Planner Workbook

SPIRITUAL CHALLENGES					
#	Description	Hours	Rate	Deposit	Withdrawal
1					
2					
3					
4					
5					
		Total:			

DAILY SUMMARY			
#	Description	Yesterday's Balance	Add Today's Balance
1	Financial		
2	Mental		
3	Physical		
4	Social		
5	Spiritual		
Total			

NOTES:____

____

____

____

____

____

AFFIRMATIONS:____

____

____

____

____

____

____

SIGNATURE:______________________________ DATE:________________

FINANCIAL CHALLENGES					
#	Description	Hours	Rate	Deposit	Withdrawal
1					
2					
3					
4					
5					
		Total:			

MENTAL CHALLENGES					
#	Description	Hours	Rate	Deposit	Withdrawal
1					
2					
3					
4					
5					
		Total:			

PHYSICAL CHALLENGES					
#	Description	Hours	Rate	Deposit	Withdrawal
1					
2					
3					
4					
5					
		Total:			

SOCIAL CHALLENGES					
#	Description	Hours	Rate	Deposit	Withdrawal
1					
2					
3					
4					
5					
		Total:			

SPIRITUAL CHALLENGES					
#	**Description**	**Hours**	**Rate**	**Deposit**	**Withdrawal**
1					
2					
3					
4					
5					
		Total:			

DAILY SUMMARY			
#	**Description**	**Yesterday's Balance**	**Add Today's Balance**
1	Financial		
2	Mental		
3	Physical		
4	Social		
5	Spiritual		
Total			

NOTES:____

AFFIRMATIONS:______________________________________

SIGNATURE:__________________________ DATE:_______________

FINANCIAL CHALLENGES					
#	Description	Hours	Rate	Deposit	Withdrawal
1					
2					
3					
4					
5					
		Total:			

MENTAL CHALLENGES					
#	Description	Hours	Rate	Deposit	Withdrawal
1					
2					
3					
4					
5					
		Total:			

PHYSICAL CHALLENGES					
#	Description	Hours	Rate	Deposit	Withdrawal
1					
2					
3					
4					
5					
		Total:			

SOCIAL CHALLENGES					
#	Description	Hours	Rate	Deposit	Withdrawal
1					
2					
3					
4					
5					
		Total:			

Prodigy Planner Workbook

SPIRITUAL CHALLENGES					
#	**Description**	**Hours**	**Rate**	**Deposit**	**Withdrawal**
1					
2					
3					
4					
5					
		Total:			

DAILY SUMMARY			
#	**Description**	**Yesterday's Balance**	**Add Today's Balance**
1	Financial		
2	Mental		
3	Physical		
4	Social		
5	Spiritual		
Total			

NOTES:____

AFFIRMATIONS:__________________________________

SIGNATURE:________________________ DATE:____________

FINANCIAL CHALLENGES					
#	Description	Hours	Rate	Deposit	Withdrawal
1					
2					
3					
4					
5					
		Total:			

MENTAL CHALLENGES					
#	Description	Hours	Rate	Deposit	Withdrawal
1					
2					
3					
4					
5					
		Total:			

PHYSICAL CHALLENGES					
#	Description	Hours	Rate	Deposit	Withdrawal
1					
2					
3					
4					
5					
		Total:			

SOCIAL CHALLENGES					
#	Description	Hours	Rate	Deposit	Withdrawal
1					
2					
3					
4					
5					
		Total:			

SPIRITUAL CHALLENGES					
#	Description	Hours	Rate	Deposit	Withdrawal
1					
2					
3					
4					
5					
		Total:			

DAILY SUMMARY			
#	Description	Yesterday's Balance	Add Today's Balance
1	Financial		
2	Mental		
3	Physical		
4	Social		
5	Spiritual		
Total			

NOTES:____

____

____

____

____

____

AFFIRMATIONS:______________________________________

____

____

____

____

____

____

SIGNATURE:______________________________ DATE:________________

FINANCIAL CHALLENGES					
#	Description	Hours	Rate	Deposit	Withdrawal
1					
2					
3					
4					
5					
		Total:			

MENTAL CHALLENGES					
#	Description	Hours	Rate	Deposit	Withdrawal
1					
2					
3					
4					
5					
		Total:			

PHYSICAL CHALLENGES					
#	Description	Hours	Rate	Deposit	Withdrawal
1					
2					
3					
4					
5					
		Total:			

SOCIAL CHALLENGES					
#	Description	Hours	Rate	Deposit	Withdrawal
1					
2					
3					
4					
5					
		Total:			

SPIRITUAL CHALLENGES					
#	Description	Hours	Rate	Deposit	Withdrawal
1					
2					
3					
4					
5					
		Total:			

DAILY SUMMARY			
#	Description	Yesterday's Balance	Add Today's Balance
1	Financial		
2	Mental		
3	Physical		
4	Social		
5	Spiritual		
Total			

NOTES:______________________________

AFFIRMATIONS:______________________________

SIGNATURE:____________________ DATE:____________

FINANCIAL CHALLENGES					
#	Description	Hours	Rate	Deposit	Withdrawal
1					
2					
3					
4					
5					
		Total:			

MENTAL CHALLENGES					
#	Description	Hours	Rate	Deposit	Withdrawal
1					
2					
3					
4					
5					
		Total:			

PHYSICAL CHALLENGES					
#	Description	Hours	Rate	Deposit	Withdrawal
1					
2					
3					
4					
5					
		Total:			

SOCIAL CHALLENGES					
#	Description	Hours	Rate	Deposit	Withdrawal
1					
2					
3					
4					
5					
		Total:			

SPIRITUAL CHALLENGES					
#	Description	Hours	Rate	Deposit	Withdrawal
1					
2					
3					
4					
5					
		Total:			

DAILY SUMMARY			
#	Description	Yesterday's Balance	Add Today's Balance
1	Financial		
2	Mental		
3	Physical		
4	Social		
5	Spiritual		
Total			

NOTES:____

AFFIRMATIONS:______________________________________

SIGNATURE:__________________________ DATE:______________

FINANCIAL CHALLENGES					
#	Description	Hours	Rate	Deposit	Withdrawal
1					
2					
3					
4					
5					
		Total:			

MENTAL CHALLENGES					
#	Description	Hours	Rate	Deposit	Withdrawal
1					
2					
3					
4					
5					
		Total:			

PHYSICAL CHALLENGES					
#	Description	Hours	Rate	Deposit	Withdrawal
1					
2					
3					
4					
5					
		Total:			

SOCIAL CHALLENGES					
#	Description	Hours	Rate	Deposit	Withdrawal
1					
2					
3					
4					
5					
		Total:			

SPIRITUAL CHALLENGES					
#	**Description**	**Hours**	**Rate**	**Deposit**	**Withdrawal**
1					
2					
3					
4					
5					
		Total:			

DAILY SUMMARY			
#	**Description**	**Yesterday's Balance**	**Add Today's Balance**
1	Financial		
2	Mental		
3	Physical		
4	Social		
5	Spiritual		
	Total		

NOTES:____

AFFIRMATIONS:____________________________________

SIGNATURE:________________________ DATE:______________

FINANCIAL CHALLENGES					
#	Description	Hours	Rate	Deposit	Withdrawal
1					
2					
3					
4					
5					
		Total:			

MENTAL CHALLENGES					
#	Description	Hours	Rate	Deposit	Withdrawal
1					
2					
3					
4					
5					
		Total:			

PHYSICAL CHALLENGES					
#	Description	Hours	Rate	Deposit	Withdrawal
1					
2					
3					
4					
5					
		Total:			

SOCIAL CHALLENGES					
#	Description	Hours	Rate	Deposit	Withdrawal
1					
2					
3					
4					
5					
		Total:			

Prodigy Planner Workbook

SPIRITUAL CHALLENGES					
#	Description	Hours	Rate	Deposit	Withdrawal
1					
2					
3					
4					
5					
			Total:		

DAILY SUMMARY			
#	Description	Yesterday's Balance	Add Today's Balance
1	Financial		
2	Mental		
3	Physical		
4	Social		
5	Spiritual		
	Total		

NOTES:______________________________

AFFIRMATIONS:______________________________

SIGNATURE:______________________ DATE:______________

FINANCIAL CHALLENGES					
#	Description	Hours	Rate	Deposit	Withdrawal
1					
2					
3					
4					
5					
		Total:			

MENTAL CHALLENGES					
#	Description	Hours	Rate	Deposit	Withdrawal
1					
2					
3					
4					
5					
		Total:			

PHYSICAL CHALLENGES					
#	Description	Hours	Rate	Deposit	Withdrawal
1					
2					
3					
4					
5					
		Total:			

SOCIAL CHALLENGES					
#	Description	Hours	Rate	Deposit	Withdrawal
1					
2					
3					
4					
5					
		Total:			

SPIRITUAL CHALLENGES					
#	**Description**	**Hours**	**Rate**	**Deposit**	**Withdrawal**
1					
2					
3					
4					
5					
		Total:			

DAILY SUMMARY			
#	**Description**	**Yesterday's Balance**	**Add Today's Balance**
1	Financial		
2	Mental		
3	Physical		
4	Social		
5	Spiritual		
Total			

NOTES:____

AFFIRMATIONS:_______________________________________

SIGNATURE:____________________________ DATE:________________

FINANCIAL CHALLENGES					
#	Description	Hours	Rate	Deposit	Withdrawal
1					
2					
3					
4					
5					
		Total:			

MENTAL CHALLENGES					
#	Description	Hours	Rate	Deposit	Withdrawal
1					
2					
3					
4					
5					
		Total:			

PHYSICAL CHALLENGES					
#	Description	Hours	Rate	Deposit	Withdrawal
1					
2					
3					
4					
5					
		Total:			

SOCIAL CHALLENGES					
#	Description	Hours	Rate	Deposit	Withdrawal
1					
2					
3					
4					
5					
		Total:			

Prodigy Planner Workbook

SPIRITUAL CHALLENGES					
#	Description	Hours	Rate	Deposit	Withdrawal
1					
2					
3					
4					
5					
		Total:			

DAILY SUMMARY			
#	Description	Yesterday's Balance	Add Today's Balance
1	Financial		
2	Mental		
3	Physical		
4	Social		
5	Spiritual		
Total			

NOTES:____

AFFIRMATIONS:____

SIGNATURE:________________________ DATE:______________

FINANCIAL CHALLENGES					
#	Description	Hours	Rate	Deposit	Withdrawal
1					
2					
3					
4					
5					
		Total:			

MENTAL CHALLENGES					
#	Description	Hours	Rate	Deposit	Withdrawal
1					
2					
3					
4					
5					
		Total:			

PHYSICAL CHALLENGES					
#	Description	Hours	Rate	Deposit	Withdrawal
1					
2					
3					
4					
5					
		Total:			

SOCIAL CHALLENGES					
#	Description	Hours	Rate	Deposit	Withdrawal
1					
2					
3					
4					
5					
		Total:			

Prodigy Planner Workbook

SPIRITUAL CHALLENGES					
#	**Description**	**Hours**	**Rate**	**Deposit**	**Withdrawal**
1					
2					
3					
4					
5					
		Total:			

DAILY SUMMARY			
#	**Description**	**Yesterday's Balance**	**Add Today's Balance**
1	Financial		
2	Mental		
3	Physical		
4	Social		
5	Spiritual		
Total			

NOTES:____

AFFIRMATIONS:____

SIGNATURE:______________________________ DATE:________________

FINANCIAL CHALLENGES					
#	Description	Hours	Rate	Deposit	Withdrawal
1					
2					
3					
4					
5					
		Total:			

MENTAL CHALLENGES					
#	Description	Hours	Rate	Deposit	Withdrawal
1					
2					
3					
4					
5					
		Total:			

PHYSICAL CHALLENGES					
#	Description	Hours	Rate	Deposit	Withdrawal
1					
2					
3					
4					
5					
		Total:			

SOCIAL CHALLENGES					
#	Description	Hours	Rate	Deposit	Withdrawal
1					
2					
3					
4					
5					
		Total:			

Prodigy Planner Workbook

SPIRITUAL CHALLENGES					
#	**Description**	**Hours**	**Rate**	**Deposit**	**Withdrawal**
1					
2					
3					
4					
5					
			Total:		

DAILY SUMMARY			
#	**Description**	**Yesterday's Balance**	**Add Today's Balance**
1	Financial		
2	Mental		
3	Physical		
4	Social		
5	Spiritual		
Total			

NOTES:____

AFFIRMATIONS:____________________________________

SIGNATURE:________________________ DATE:______________

FINANCIAL CHALLENGES					
#	Description	Hours	Rate	Deposit	Withdrawal
1					
2					
3					
4					
5					
		Total:			

MENTAL CHALLENGES					
#	Description	Hours	Rate	Deposit	Withdrawal
1					
2					
3					
4					
5					
		Total:			

PHYSICAL CHALLENGES					
#	Description	Hours	Rate	Deposit	Withdrawal
1					
2					
3					
4					
5					
		Total:			

SOCIAL CHALLENGES					
#	Description	Hours	Rate	Deposit	Withdrawal
1					
2					
3					
4					
5					
		Total:			

SPIRITUAL CHALLENGES					
#	Description	Hours	Rate	Deposit	Withdrawal
1					
2					
3					
4					
5					
		Total:			

DAILY SUMMARY			
#	Description	Yesterday's Balance	Add Today's Balance
1	Financial		
2	Mental		
3	Physical		
4	Social		
5	Spiritual		
Total			

NOTES:____

AFFIRMATIONS:______________________________________

SIGNATURE:__________________________ DATE:______________

FINANCIAL CHALLENGES					
#	Description	Hours	Rate	Deposit	Withdrawal
1					
2					
3					
4					
5					
		Total:			

MENTAL CHALLENGES					
#	Description	Hours	Rate	Deposit	Withdrawal
1					
2					
3					
4					
5					
		Total:			

PHYSICAL CHALLENGES					
#	Description	Hours	Rate	Deposit	Withdrawal
1					
2					
3					
4					
5					
		Total:			

SOCIAL CHALLENGES					
#	Description	Hours	Rate	Deposit	Withdrawal
1					
2					
3					
4					
5					
		Total:			

SPIRITUAL CHALLENGES					
#	Description	Hours	Rate	Deposit	Withdrawal
1					
2					
3					
4					
5					
		Total:			

DAILY SUMMARY			
#	Description	Yesterday's Balance	Add Today's Balance
1	Financial		
2	Mental		
3	Physical		
4	Social		
5	Spiritual		
Total			

NOTES:____

____

____

____

____

____

AFFIRMATIONS:____

____

____

____

____

____

____

SIGNATURE:______________________________ DATE:________________

FINANCIAL CHALLENGES					
#	Description	Hours	Rate	Deposit	Withdrawal
1					
2					
3					
4					
5					
		Total:			

MENTAL CHALLENGES					
#	Description	Hours	Rate	Deposit	Withdrawal
1					
2					
3					
4					
5					
		Total:			

PHYSICAL CHALLENGES					
#	Description	Hours	Rate	Deposit	Withdrawal
1					
2					
3					
4					
5					
		Total:			

SOCIAL CHALLENGES					
#	Description	Hours	Rate	Deposit	Withdrawal
1					
2					
3					
4					
5					
		Total:			

Prodigy Planner Workbook

SPIRITUAL CHALLENGES					
#	Description	Hours	Rate	Deposit	Withdrawal
1					
2					
3					
4					
5					
		Total:			

DAILY SUMMARY			
#	Description	Yesterday's Balance	Add Today's Balance
1	Financial		
2	Mental		
3	Physical		
4	Social		
5	Spiritual		
Total			

NOTES:____

AFFIRMATIONS:____

SIGNATURE:______________________ DATE:____________

FINANCIAL CHALLENGES					
#	Description	Hours	Rate	Deposit	Withdrawal
1					
2					
3					
4					
5					
		Total:			

MENTAL CHALLENGES					
#	Description	Hours	Rate	Deposit	Withdrawal
1					
2					
3					
4					
5					
		Total:			

PHYSICAL CHALLENGES					
#	Description	Hours	Rate	Deposit	Withdrawal
1					
2					
3					
4					
5					
		Total:			

SOCIAL CHALLENGES					
#	Description	Hours	Rate	Deposit	Withdrawal
1					
2					
3					
4					
5					
		Total:			

SPIRITUAL CHALLENGES					
#	Description	Hours	Rate	Deposit	Withdrawal
1					
2					
3					
4					
5					
		Total:			

DAILY SUMMARY			
#	Description	Yesterday's Balance	Add Today's Balance
1	Financial		
2	Mental		
3	Physical		
4	Social		
5	Spiritual		
Total			

NOTES:____

____

____

____

____

____

AFFIRMATIONS:______________________________________

____

____

____

____

____

____

SIGNATURE:______________________________ DATE:______________

FINANCIAL CHALLENGES					
#	Description	Hours	Rate	Deposit	Withdrawal
1					
2					
3					
4					
5					
		Total:			

MENTAL CHALLENGES					
#	Description	Hours	Rate	Deposit	Withdrawal
1					
2					
3					
4					
5					
		Total:			

PHYSICAL CHALLENGES					
#	Description	Hours	Rate	Deposit	Withdrawal
1					
2					
3					
4					
5					
		Total:			

SOCIAL CHALLENGES					
#	Description	Hours	Rate	Deposit	Withdrawal
1					
2					
3					
4					
5					
		Total:			

SPIRITUAL CHALLENGES					
#	**Description**	**Hours**	**Rate**	**Deposit**	**Withdrawal**
1					
2					
3					
4					
5					
		Total:			

DAILY SUMMARY			
#	**Description**	**Yesterday's Balance**	**Add Today's Balance**
1	Financial		
2	Mental		
3	Physical		
4	Social		
5	Spiritual		
Total			

NOTES:____

____

____

____

____

____

AFFIRMATIONS:____

____

____

____

____

____

____

SIGNATURE:______________________________ DATE:________________

FINANCIAL CHALLENGES					
#	Description	Hours	Rate	Deposit	Withdrawal
1					
2					
3					
4					
5					
		Total:			

MENTAL CHALLENGES					
#	Description	Hours	Rate	Deposit	Withdrawal
1					
2					
3					
4					
5					
		Total:			

PHYSICAL CHALLENGES					
#	Description	Hours	Rate	Deposit	Withdrawal
1					
2					
3					
4					
5					
		Total:			

SOCIAL CHALLENGES					
#	Description	Hours	Rate	Deposit	Withdrawal
1					
2					
3					
4					
5					
		Total:			

Prodigy Planner Workbook

SPIRITUAL CHALLENGES					
#	Description	Hours	Rate	Deposit	Withdrawal
1					
2					
3					
4					
5					
			Total:		

DAILY SUMMARY			
#	Description	Yesterday's Balance	Add Today's Balance
1	Financial		
2	Mental		
3	Physical		
4	Social		
5	Spiritual		
Total			

NOTES:______________________________________

AFFIRMATIONS:________________________________

SIGNATURE:______________________ DATE:____________

FINANCIAL CHALLENGES					
#	Description	Hours	Rate	Deposit	Withdrawal
1					
2					
3					
4					
5					
		Total:			

MENTAL CHALLENGES					
#	Description	Hours	Rate	Deposit	Withdrawal
1					
2					
3					
4					
5					
		Total:			

PHYSICAL CHALLENGES					
#	Description	Hours	Rate	Deposit	Withdrawal
1					
2					
3					
4					
5					
		Total:			

SOCIAL CHALLENGES					
#	Description	Hours	Rate	Deposit	Withdrawal
1					
2					
3					
4					
5					
		Total:			

Prodigy Planner Workbook

SPIRITUAL CHALLENGES					
#	Description	Hours	Rate	Deposit	Withdrawal
1					
2					
3					
4					
5					
			Total:		

DAILY SUMMARY			
#	Description	Yesterday's Balance	Add Today's Balance
1	Financial		
2	Mental		
3	Physical		
4	Social		
5	Spiritual		
		Total	

NOTES:____

____

____

____

____

____

AFFIRMATIONS:_______________________________________

____

____

____

____

____

____

SIGNATURE:____________________________ DATE:______________

FINANCIAL CHALLENGES					
#	Description	Hours	Rate	Deposit	Withdrawal
1					
2					
3					
4					
5					
		Total:			

MENTAL CHALLENGES					
#	Description	Hours	Rate	Deposit	Withdrawal
1					
2					
3					
4					
5					
		Total:			

PHYSICAL CHALLENGES					
#	Description	Hours	Rate	Deposit	Withdrawal
1					
2					
3					
4					
5					
		Total:			

SOCIAL CHALLENGES					
#	Description	Hours	Rate	Deposit	Withdrawal
1					
2					
3					
4					
5					
		Total:			

SPIRITUAL CHALLENGES					
#	**Description**	**Hours**	**Rate**	**Deposit**	**Withdrawal**
1					
2					
3					
4					
5					
		Total:			

DAILY SUMMARY			
#	**Description**	**Yesterday's Balance**	**Add Today's Balance**
1	Financial		
2	Mental		
3	Physical		
4	Social		
5	Spiritual		
Total			

NOTES:____

____

____

____

____

____

AFFIRMATIONS:______________________________________

____

____

____

____

____

____

SIGNATURE:______________________ DATE:____________

WEALTH LEVEL 1 - Essentials		
#	**Description**	**Deposit**
1	Have Earned Income	
2	Have Investment Income	
3	Have Leveraged Income	
4	Have Residual Income	
5	Have More Than One Type Of Income	

WEALTH LEVEL 2 - Fundamentals		
#	**Description**	**Deposit**
1	10% Of Income Saved Upon Payment	
2	6-Month Emergency Cash Fund Reserved	
3	1-Year Emergency Electronic Fund Reserved	
4	All Monthly Bills Are Paid On Time	
5	Bills Do Not Exceed 50% Of Monthly Income	
6	No Debt – With Exception Of Mortgage	

WEALTH LEVEL 3 - Safety Net		
#	**Description**	**Deposit**
1	Life Insurance – All Dependents	
2	Medical Insurance – All Dependents	
3	Disability Insurance – If Not Retired	
4	Dental Insurance – All Dependents	
5	Optical Insurance - All Dependents	
6	Long Term Care Insurance – If Retired	
7	Umbrella Insurance	
8	Property Insurance – Homeowner/Renters	
9	Auto Insurance	
10	Filed All Bills & Receipts	

WEALTH LEVEL 4 - Look Good On Paper		
#	**Description**	**Deposit**
1	Have A Credit Score Above 760	
2	Have A Secured Credit Cards Only	
3	10% Of Income Invested Upon Payment	
4	Monitor Your Credit Report Monthly	
WEALTH LEVEL 5 - Sustainability		
#	**Description**	**Deposit**
1	Sustainable Power Supply – No Bill	
2	Sustainable Water Supply – No Bill	
3	Recycle & Eliminate Own Waste	
4	Have No Mortgage Or Rent Bill	
5	20-Year Property Tax Funds Reserved	
6	Homestead	
	Total:	

NOTES:____

____

____

____

____

____

AFFIRMATIONS:__________________________________

____

____

____

____

____

____

SIGNATURE:______________________ DATE:____________

FINANCIAL CHALLENGES					
#	Description	Hours	Rate	Deposit	Withdrawal
1					
2					
3					
4					
5					
		Total:			

MENTAL CHALLENGES					
#	Description	Hours	Rate	Deposit	Withdrawal
1					
2					
3					
4					
5					
		Total:			

PHYSICAL CHALLENGES					
#	Description	Hours	Rate	Deposit	Withdrawal
1					
2					
3					
4					
5					
		Total:			

SOCIAL CHALLENGES					
#	Description	Hours	Rate	Deposit	Withdrawal
1					
2					
3					
4					
5					
		Total:			

SPIRITUAL CHALLENGES					
#	**Description**	**Hours**	**Rate**	**Deposit**	**Withdrawal**
1					
2					
3					
4					
5					
		Total:			

DAILY SUMMARY			
#	**Description**	**Yesterday's Balance**	**Add Today's Balance**
1	Financial		
2	Mental		
3	Physical		
4	Social		
5	Spiritual		
Monthly Wealth Bonus			
Total			

NOTES:____

AFFIRMATIONS:__________________________________

SIGNATURE:________________________ DATE:____________

Prodigy Planner Workbook

FINANCIAL CHALLENGES					
#	Description	Hours	Rate	Deposit	Withdrawal
1					
2					
3					
4					
5					
		Total:			

MENTAL CHALLENGES					
#	Description	Hours	Rate	Deposit	Withdrawal
1					
2					
3					
4					
5					
		Total:			

PHYSICAL CHALLENGES					
#	Description	Hours	Rate	Deposit	Withdrawal
1					
2					
3					
4					
5					
		Total:			

SOCIAL CHALLENGES					
#	Description	Hours	Rate	Deposit	Withdrawal
1					
2					
3					
4					
5					
		Total:			

SPIRITUAL CHALLENGES					
#	**Description**	**Hours**	**Rate**	**Deposit**	**Withdrawal**
1					
2					
3					
4					
5					
		Total:			

DAILY SUMMARY			
#	**Description**	**Yesterday's Balance**	**Add Today's Balance**
1	Financial		
2	Mental		
3	Physical		
4	Social		
5	Spiritual		
Total			

NOTES:____

AFFIRMATIONS:__________________________________

SIGNATURE:____________________ DATE:____________

FINANCIAL CHALLENGES					
#	Description	Hours	Rate	Deposit	Withdrawal
1					
2					
3					
4					
5					
		Total:			

MENTAL CHALLENGES					
#	Description	Hours	Rate	Deposit	Withdrawal
1					
2					
3					
4					
5					
		Total:			

PHYSICAL CHALLENGES					
#	Description	Hours	Rate	Deposit	Withdrawal
1					
2					
3					
4					
5					
		Total:			

SOCIAL CHALLENGES					
#	Description	Hours	Rate	Deposit	Withdrawal
1					
2					
3					
4					
5					
		Total:			

SPIRITUAL CHALLENGES					
#	Description	Hours	Rate	Deposit	Withdrawal
1					
2					
3					
4					
5					
		Total:			

DAILY SUMMARY			
#	Description	Yesterday's Balance	Add Today's Balance
1	Financial		
2	Mental		
3	Physical		
4	Social		
5	Spiritual		
Total			

NOTES:____

____

____

____

____

____

AFFIRMATIONS:______________________________________

____

____

____

____

____

____

SIGNATURE:______________________________ DATE:________________

Prodigy Planner Workbook

FINANCIAL CHALLENGES					
#	Description	Hours	Rate	Deposit	Withdrawal
1					
2					
3					
4					
5					
		Total:			

MENTAL CHALLENGES					
#	Description	Hours	Rate	Deposit	Withdrawal
1					
2					
3					
4					
5					
		Total:			

PHYSICAL CHALLENGES					
#	Description	Hours	Rate	Deposit	Withdrawal
1					
2					
3					
4					
5					
		Total:			

SOCIAL CHALLENGES					
#	Description	Hours	Rate	Deposit	Withdrawal
1					
2					
3					
4					
5					
		Total:			

Prodigy Planner Workbook

SPIRITUAL CHALLENGES					
#	Description	Hours	Rate	Deposit	Withdrawal
1					
2					
3					
4					
5					
		Total:			

DAILY SUMMARY			
#	Description	Yesterday's Balance	Add Today's Balance
1	Financial		
2	Mental		
3	Physical		
4	Social		
5	Spiritual		
Total			

NOTES:____

____

____

____

____

____

AFFIRMATIONS:______________________________________

____

____

____

____

____

____

SIGNATURE:______________________________ DATE:________________

FINANCIAL CHALLENGES					
#	Description	Hours	Rate	Deposit	Withdrawal
1					
2					
3					
4					
5					
		Total:			

MENTAL CHALLENGES					
#	Description	Hours	Rate	Deposit	Withdrawal
1					
2					
3					
4					
5					
		Total:			

PHYSICAL CHALLENGES					
#	Description	Hours	Rate	Deposit	Withdrawal
1					
2					
3					
4					
5					
		Total:			

SOCIAL CHALLENGES					
#	Description	Hours	Rate	Deposit	Withdrawal
1					
2					
3					
4					
5					
		Total:			

Prodigy Planner Workbook

SPIRITUAL CHALLENGES					
#	Description	Hours	Rate	Deposit	Withdrawal
1					
2					
3					
4					
5					
		Total:			

DAILY SUMMARY			
#	Description	Yesterday's Balance	Add Today's Balance
1	Financial		
2	Mental		
3	Physical		
4	Social		
5	Spiritual		
Total			

NOTES:____

AFFIRMATIONS:__________________________________

SIGNATURE:________________________ DATE:____________

FINANCIAL CHALLENGES					
#	Description	Hours	Rate	Deposit	Withdrawal
1					
2					
3					
4					
5					
		Total:			

MENTAL CHALLENGES					
#	Description	Hours	Rate	Deposit	Withdrawal
1					
2					
3					
4					
5					
		Total:			

PHYSICAL CHALLENGES					
#	Description	Hours	Rate	Deposit	Withdrawal
1					
2					
3					
4					
5					
		Total:			

SOCIAL CHALLENGES					
#	Description	Hours	Rate	Deposit	Withdrawal
1					
2					
3					
4					
5					
		Total:			

SPIRITUAL CHALLENGES					
#	Description	Hours	Rate	Deposit	Withdrawal
1					
2					
3					
4					
5					
		Total:			

DAILY SUMMARY			
#	Description	Yesterday's Balance	Add Today's Balance
1	Financial		
2	Mental		
3	Physical		
4	Social		
5	Spiritual		
Total			

NOTES:____

____

____

____

____

____

AFFIRMATIONS:____

____

____

____

____

____

____

SIGNATURE:____________________________ DATE:________________

FINANCIAL CHALLENGES					
#	Description	Hours	Rate	Deposit	Withdrawal
1					
2					
3					
4					
5					
		Total:			

MENTAL CHALLENGES					
#	Description	Hours	Rate	Deposit	Withdrawal
1					
2					
3					
4					
5					
		Total:			

PHYSICAL CHALLENGES					
#	Description	Hours	Rate	Deposit	Withdrawal
1					
2					
3					
4					
5					
		Total:			

SOCIAL CHALLENGES					
#	Description	Hours	Rate	Deposit	Withdrawal
1					
2					
3					
4					
5					
		Total:			

Prodigy Planner Workbook

SPIRITUAL CHALLENGES					
#	**Description**	**Hours**	**Rate**	**Deposit**	**Withdrawal**
1					
2					
3					
4					
5					
			Total:		

DAILY SUMMARY			
#	**Description**	**Yesterday's Balance**	**Add Today's Balance**
1	Financial		
2	Mental		
3	Physical		
4	Social		
5	Spiritual		
	Total		

NOTES:____

____

____

____

____

____

AFFIRMATIONS:____

____

____

____

____

____

____

SIGNATURE:______________________________ DATE:________________

FINANCIAL CHALLENGES					
#	Description	Hours	Rate	Deposit	Withdrawal
1					
2					
3					
4					
5					
		Total:			

MENTAL CHALLENGES					
#	Description	Hours	Rate	Deposit	Withdrawal
1					
2					
3					
4					
5					
		Total:			

PHYSICAL CHALLENGES					
#	Description	Hours	Rate	Deposit	Withdrawal
1					
2					
3					
4					
5					
		Total:			

SOCIAL CHALLENGES					
#	Description	Hours	Rate	Deposit	Withdrawal
1					
2					
3					
4					
5					
		Total:			

SPIRITUAL CHALLENGES					
#	Description	Hours	Rate	Deposit	Withdrawal
1					
2					
3					
4					
5					
		Total:			

DAILY SUMMARY			
#	Description	Yesterday's Balance	Add Today's Balance
1	Financial		
2	Mental		
3	Physical		
4	Social		
5	Spiritual		
Total			

NOTES:____

AFFIRMATIONS:____________________________________

SIGNATURE:________________________ DATE:______________

FINANCIAL CHALLENGES					
#	Description	Hours	Rate	Deposit	Withdrawal
1					
2					
3					
4					
5					
		Total:			

MENTAL CHALLENGES					
#	Description	Hours	Rate	Deposit	Withdrawal
1					
2					
3					
4					
5					
		Total:			

PHYSICAL CHALLENGES					
#	Description	Hours	Rate	Deposit	Withdrawal
1					
2					
3					
4					
5					
		Total:			

SOCIAL CHALLENGES					
#	Description	Hours	Rate	Deposit	Withdrawal
1					
2					
3					
4					
5					
		Total:			

Prodigy Planner Workbook

SPIRITUAL CHALLENGES					
#	**Description**	**Hours**	**Rate**	**Deposit**	**Withdrawal**
1					
2					
3					
4					
5					
		Total:			

DAILY SUMMARY			
#	**Description**	**Yesterday's Balance**	**Add Today's Balance**
1	Financial		
2	Mental		
3	Physical		
4	Social		
5	Spiritual		
Total			

NOTES:____

AFFIRMATIONS:______________________________________

SIGNATURE:________________________ DATE:______________

FINANCIAL CHALLENGES					
#	Description	Hours	Rate	Deposit	Withdrawal
1					
2					
3					
4					
5					
		Total:			

MENTAL CHALLENGES					
#	Description	Hours	Rate	Deposit	Withdrawal
1					
2					
3					
4					
5					
		Total:			

PHYSICAL CHALLENGES					
#	Description	Hours	Rate	Deposit	Withdrawal
1					
2					
3					
4					
5					
		Total:			

SOCIAL CHALLENGES					
#	Description	Hours	Rate	Deposit	Withdrawal
1					
2					
3					
4					
5					
		Total:			

Prodigy Planner Workbook

SPIRITUAL CHALLENGES					
#	Description	Hours	Rate	Deposit	Withdrawal
1					
2					
3					
4					
5					
			Total:		

DAILY SUMMARY			
#	Description	Yesterday's Balance	Add Today's Balance
1	Financial		
2	Mental		
3	Physical		
4	Social		
5	Spiritual		
Total			

NOTES:____

AFFIRMATIONS:____________________________________

SIGNATURE:_________________________ DATE:______________

FINANCIAL CHALLENGES					
#	Description	Hours	Rate	Deposit	Withdrawal
1					
2					
3					
4					
5					
		Total:			

MENTAL CHALLENGES					
#	Description	Hours	Rate	Deposit	Withdrawal
1					
2					
3					
4					
5					
		Total:			

PHYSICAL CHALLENGES					
#	Description	Hours	Rate	Deposit	Withdrawal
1					
2					
3					
4					
5					
		Total:			

SOCIAL CHALLENGES					
#	Description	Hours	Rate	Deposit	Withdrawal
1					
2					
3					
4					
5					
		Total:			

Prodigy Planner Workbook

SPIRITUAL CHALLENGES					
#	Description	Hours	Rate	Deposit	Withdrawal
1					
2					
3					
4					
5					
		Total:			

DAILY SUMMARY			
#	Description	Yesterday's Balance	Add Today's Balance
1	Financial		
2	Mental		
3	Physical		
4	Social		
5	Spiritual		
Total			

NOTES:____

AFFIRMATIONS:__________________________________

SIGNATURE:_____________________________ DATE:_______________

FINANCIAL CHALLENGES					
#	Description	Hours	Rate	Deposit	Withdrawal
1					
2					
3					
4					
5					
		Total:			

MENTAL CHALLENGES					
#	Description	Hours	Rate	Deposit	Withdrawal
1					
2					
3					
4					
5					
		Total:			

PHYSICAL CHALLENGES					
#	Description	Hours	Rate	Deposit	Withdrawal
1					
2					
3					
4					
5					
		Total:			

SOCIAL CHALLENGES					
#	Description	Hours	Rate	Deposit	Withdrawal
1					
2					
3					
4					
5					
		Total:			

SPIRITUAL CHALLENGES					
#	**Description**	**Hours**	**Rate**	**Deposit**	**Withdrawal**
1					
2					
3					
4					
5					
		Total:			

DAILY SUMMARY			
#	**Description**	**Yesterday's Balance**	**Add Today's Balance**
1	Financial		
2	Mental		
3	Physical		
4	Social		
5	Spiritual		
Total			

NOTES:____

____

____

____

____

____

AFFIRMATIONS:______________________________________

____

____

____

____

____

____

SIGNATURE:______________________ DATE:______________

FINANCIAL CHALLENGES					
#	Description	Hours	Rate	Deposit	Withdrawal
1					
2					
3					
4					
5					
		Total:			

MENTAL CHALLENGES					
#	Description	Hours	Rate	Deposit	Withdrawal
1					
2					
3					
4					
5					
		Total:			

PHYSICAL CHALLENGES					
#	Description	Hours	Rate	Deposit	Withdrawal
1					
2					
3					
4					
5					
		Total:			

SOCIAL CHALLENGES					
#	Description	Hours	Rate	Deposit	Withdrawal
1					
2					
3					
4					
5					
		Total:			

Prodigy Planner Workbook

SPIRITUAL CHALLENGES					
#	**Description**	**Hours**	**Rate**	**Deposit**	**Withdrawal**
1					
2					
3					
4					
5					
		Total:			

DAILY SUMMARY			
#	**Description**	**Yesterday's Balance**	**Add Today's Balance**
1	Financial		
2	Mental		
3	Physical		
4	Social		
5	Spiritual		
Total			

NOTES:____

AFFIRMATIONS:____

SIGNATURE:______________________ DATE:______________

FINANCIAL CHALLENGES					
#	Description	Hours	Rate	Deposit	Withdrawal
1					
2					
3					
4					
5					
		Total:			

MENTAL CHALLENGES					
#	Description	Hours	Rate	Deposit	Withdrawal
1					
2					
3					
4					
5					
		Total:			

PHYSICAL CHALLENGES					
#	Description	Hours	Rate	Deposit	Withdrawal
1					
2					
3					
4					
5					
		Total:			

SOCIAL CHALLENGES					
#	Description	Hours	Rate	Deposit	Withdrawal
1					
2					
3					
4					
5					
		Total:			

SPIRITUAL CHALLENGES					
#	Description	Hours	Rate	Deposit	Withdrawal
1					
2					
3					
4					
5					
		Total:			

DAILY SUMMARY			
#	Description	Yesterday's Balance	Add Today's Balance
1	Financial		
2	Mental		
3	Physical		
4	Social		
5	Spiritual		
Total			

NOTES:____

AFFIRMATIONS:____________________________________

SIGNATURE:________________________ DATE:______________

FINANCIAL CHALLENGES					
#	Description	Hours	Rate	Deposit	Withdrawal
1					
2					
3					
4					
5					
		Total:			

MENTAL CHALLENGES					
#	Description	Hours	Rate	Deposit	Withdrawal
1					
2					
3					
4					
5					
		Total:			

PHYSICAL CHALLENGES					
#	Description	Hours	Rate	Deposit	Withdrawal
1					
2					
3					
4					
5					
		Total:			

SOCIAL CHALLENGES					
#	Description	Hours	Rate	Deposit	Withdrawal
1					
2					
3					
4					
5					
		Total:			

Prodigy Planner Workbook

SPIRITUAL CHALLENGES					
#	Description	Hours	Rate	Deposit	Withdrawal
1					
2					
3					
4					
5					
		Total:			

DAILY SUMMARY			
#	Description	Yesterday's Balance	Add Today's Balance
1	Financial		
2	Mental		
3	Physical		
4	Social		
5	Spiritual		
Total			

NOTES:____

____

____

____

____

____

AFFIRMATIONS:____

____

____

____

____

____

____

SIGNATURE:_______________________ DATE:______________

FINANCIAL CHALLENGES					
#	Description	Hours	Rate	Deposit	Withdrawal
1					
2					
3					
4					
5					
		Total:			

MENTAL CHALLENGES					
#	Description	Hours	Rate	Deposit	Withdrawal
1					
2					
3					
4					
5					
		Total:			

PHYSICAL CHALLENGES					
#	Description	Hours	Rate	Deposit	Withdrawal
1					
2					
3					
4					
5					
		Total:			

SOCIAL CHALLENGES					
#	Description	Hours	Rate	Deposit	Withdrawal
1					
2					
3					
4					
5					
		Total:			

Prodigy Planner Workbook

SPIRITUAL CHALLENGES					
#	**Description**	**Hours**	**Rate**	**Deposit**	**Withdrawal**
1					
2					
3					
4					
5					
		Total:			

DAILY SUMMARY			
#	**Description**	**Yesterday's Balance**	**Add Today's Balance**
1	Financial		
2	Mental		
3	Physical		
4	Social		
5	Spiritual		
Total			

NOTES:____

AFFIRMATIONS:__________________________________

SIGNATURE:________________________ DATE:____________

FINANCIAL CHALLENGES					
#	Description	Hours	Rate	Deposit	Withdrawal
1					
2					
3					
4					
5					
		Total:			

MENTAL CHALLENGES					
#	Description	Hours	Rate	Deposit	Withdrawal
1					
2					
3					
4					
5					
		Total:			

PHYSICAL CHALLENGES					
#	Description	Hours	Rate	Deposit	Withdrawal
1					
2					
3					
4					
5					
		Total:			

SOCIAL CHALLENGES					
#	Description	Hours	Rate	Deposit	Withdrawal
1					
2					
3					
4					
5					
		Total:			

Prodigy Planner Workbook

SPIRITUAL CHALLENGES					
#	Description	Hours	Rate	Deposit	Withdrawal
1					
2					
3					
4					
5					
		Total:			

DAILY SUMMARY			
#	Description	Yesterday's Balance	Add Today's Balance
1	Financial		
2	Mental		
3	Physical		
4	Social		
5	Spiritual		
Total			

NOTES:____

AFFIRMATIONS:__________________________________

SIGNATURE:______________________ DATE:____________

FINANCIAL CHALLENGES					
#	Description	Hours	Rate	Deposit	Withdrawal
1					
2					
3					
4					
5					
		Total:			

MENTAL CHALLENGES					
#	Description	Hours	Rate	Deposit	Withdrawal
1					
2					
3					
4					
5					
		Total:			

PHYSICAL CHALLENGES					
#	Description	Hours	Rate	Deposit	Withdrawal
1					
2					
3					
4					
5					
		Total:			

SOCIAL CHALLENGES					
#	Description	Hours	Rate	Deposit	Withdrawal
1					
2					
3					
4					
5					
		Total:			

SPIRITUAL CHALLENGES					
#	Description	Hours	Rate	Deposit	Withdrawal
1					
2					
3					
4					
5					
		Total:			

DAILY SUMMARY			
#	Description	Yesterday's Balance	Add Today's Balance
1	Financial		
2	Mental		
3	Physical		
4	Social		
5	Spiritual		
Total			

NOTES:____

AFFIRMATIONS:____

SIGNATURE:____________________ DATE:______________

FINANCIAL CHALLENGES					
#	**Description**	**Hours**	**Rate**	**Deposit**	**Withdrawal**
1					
2					
3					
4					
5					
		Total:			

MENTAL CHALLENGES					
#	**Description**	**Hours**	**Rate**	**Deposit**	**Withdrawal**
1					
2					
3					
4					
5					
		Total:			

PHYSICAL CHALLENGES					
#	**Description**	**Hours**	**Rate**	**Deposit**	**Withdrawal**
1					
2					
3					
4					
5					
		Total:			

SOCIAL CHALLENGES					
#	**Description**	**Hours**	**Rate**	**Deposit**	**Withdrawal**
1					
2					
3					
4					
5					
		Total:			

SPIRITUAL CHALLENGES					
#	**Description**	**Hours**	**Rate**	**Deposit**	**Withdrawal**
1					
2					
3					
4					
5					
		Total:			

DAILY SUMMARY			
#	**Description**	**Yesterday's Balance**	**Add Today's Balance**
1	Financial		
2	Mental		
3	Physical		
4	Social		
5	Spiritual		
Total			

NOTES:____

AFFIRMATIONS:____

SIGNATURE:______________________________ DATE:________________

FINANCIAL CHALLENGES					
#	**Description**	**Hours**	**Rate**	**Deposit**	**Withdrawal**
1					
2					
3					
4					
5					
		Total:			

MENTAL CHALLENGES					
#	**Description**	**Hours**	**Rate**	**Deposit**	**Withdrawal**
1					
2					
3					
4					
5					
		Total:			

PHYSICAL CHALLENGES					
#	**Description**	**Hours**	**Rate**	**Deposit**	**Withdrawal**
1					
2					
3					
4					
5					
		Total:			

SOCIAL CHALLENGES					
#	**Description**	**Hours**	**Rate**	**Deposit**	**Withdrawal**
1					
2					
3					
4					
5					
		Total:			

Prodigy Planner Workbook

SPIRITUAL CHALLENGES					
#	**Description**	**Hours**	**Rate**	**Deposit**	**Withdrawal**
1					
2					
3					
4					
5					
		Total:			

DAILY SUMMARY			
#	**Description**	**Yesterday's Balance**	**Add Today's Balance**
1	Financial		
2	Mental		
3	Physical		
4	Social		
5	Spiritual		
Total			

NOTES:____

AFFIRMATIONS:____

SIGNATURE:____________________________ DATE:________________

FINANCIAL CHALLENGES					
#	Description	Hours	Rate	Deposit	Withdrawal
1					
2					
3					
4					
5					
		Total:			

MENTAL CHALLENGES					
#	Description	Hours	Rate	Deposit	Withdrawal
1					
2					
3					
4					
5					
		Total:			

PHYSICAL CHALLENGES					
#	Description	Hours	Rate	Deposit	Withdrawal
1					
2					
3					
4					
5					
		Total:			

SOCIAL CHALLENGES					
#	Description	Hours	Rate	Deposit	Withdrawal
1					
2					
3					
4					
5					
		Total:			

Prodigy Planner Workbook

SPIRITUAL CHALLENGES					
#	Description	Hours	Rate	Deposit	Withdrawal
1					
2					
3					
4					
5					
		Total:			

DAILY SUMMARY			
#	Description	Yesterday's Balance	Add Today's Balance
1	Financial		
2	Mental		
3	Physical		
4	Social		
5	Spiritual		
Total			

NOTES:____

____

____

____

____

____

AFFIRMATIONS:____

____

____

____

____

____

____

SIGNATURE:______________________________ DATE:________________

FINANCIAL CHALLENGES					
#	Description	Hours	Rate	Deposit	Withdrawal
1					
2					
3					
4					
5					
		Total:			

MENTAL CHALLENGES					
#	Description	Hours	Rate	Deposit	Withdrawal
1					
2					
3					
4					
5					
		Total:			

PHYSICAL CHALLENGES					
#	Description	Hours	Rate	Deposit	Withdrawal
1					
2					
3					
4					
5					
		Total:			

SOCIAL CHALLENGES					
#	Description	Hours	Rate	Deposit	Withdrawal
1					
2					
3					
4					
5					
		Total:			

SPIRITUAL CHALLENGES					
#	Description	Hours	Rate	Deposit	Withdrawal
1					
2					
3					
4					
5					
		Total:			

DAILY SUMMARY			
#	Description	Yesterday's Balance	Add Today's Balance
1	Financial		
2	Mental		
3	Physical		
4	Social		
5	Spiritual		
Total			

NOTES:____

____

____

____

____

____

AFFIRMATIONS:____

____

____

____

____

____

____

SIGNATURE:______________________________ DATE:________________

FINANCIAL CHALLENGES					
#	Description	Hours	Rate	Deposit	Withdrawal
1					
2					
3					
4					
5					
		Total:			

MENTAL CHALLENGES					
#	Description	Hours	Rate	Deposit	Withdrawal
1					
2					
3					
4					
5					
		Total:			

PHYSICAL CHALLENGES					
#	Description	Hours	Rate	Deposit	Withdrawal
1					
2					
3					
4					
5					
		Total:			

SOCIAL CHALLENGES					
#	Description	Hours	Rate	Deposit	Withdrawal
1					
2					
3					
4					
5					
		Total:			

Prodigy Planner Workbook

SPIRITUAL CHALLENGES					
#	Description	Hours	Rate	Deposit	Withdrawal
1					
2					
3					
4					
5					
		Total:			

DAILY SUMMARY			
#	Description	Yesterday's Balance	Add Today's Balance
1	Financial		
2	Mental		
3	Physical		
4	Social		
5	Spiritual		
Total			

NOTES:____

____

____

____

____

____

AFFIRMATIONS:______________________________________

____

____

____

____

____

____

SIGNATURE:______________________________ DATE:________________

FINANCIAL CHALLENGES					
#	Description	Hours	Rate	Deposit	Withdrawal
1					
2					
3					
4					
5					
		Total:			

MENTAL CHALLENGES					
#	Description	Hours	Rate	Deposit	Withdrawal
1					
2					
3					
4					
5					
		Total:			

PHYSICAL CHALLENGES					
#	Description	Hours	Rate	Deposit	Withdrawal
1					
2					
3					
4					
5					
		Total:			

SOCIAL CHALLENGES					
#	Description	Hours	Rate	Deposit	Withdrawal
1					
2					
3					
4					
5					
		Total:			

Prodigy Planner Workbook

SPIRITUAL CHALLENGES					
#	**Description**	**Hours**	**Rate**	**Deposit**	**Withdrawal**
1					
2					
3					
4					
5					
		Total:			

DAILY SUMMARY			
#	**Description**	**Yesterday's Balance**	**Add Today's Balance**
1	Financial		
2	Mental		
3	Physical		
4	Social		
5	Spiritual		
	Total		

NOTES:____

____

____

____

____

____

AFFIRMATIONS:______________________________________

____

____

____

____

____

____

SIGNATURE:______________________________ DATE:________________

FINANCIAL CHALLENGES					
#	Description	Hours	Rate	Deposit	Withdrawal
1					
2					
3					
4					
5					
		Total:			

MENTAL CHALLENGES					
#	Description	Hours	Rate	Deposit	Withdrawal
1					
2					
3					
4					
5					
		Total:			

PHYSICAL CHALLENGES					
#	Description	Hours	Rate	Deposit	Withdrawal
1					
2					
3					
4					
5					
		Total:			

SOCIAL CHALLENGES					
#	Description	Hours	Rate	Deposit	Withdrawal
1					
2					
3					
4					
5					
		Total:			

SPIRITUAL CHALLENGES					
#	**Description**	**Hours**	**Rate**	**Deposit**	**Withdrawal**
1					
2					
3					
4					
5					
		Total:			

DAILY SUMMARY			
#	**Description**	**Yesterday's Balance**	**Add Today's Balance**
1	Financial		
2	Mental		
3	Physical		
4	Social		
5	Spiritual		
Total			

NOTES:______________________________

AFFIRMATIONS:______________________________

SIGNATURE:____________________ DATE:______________

FINANCIAL CHALLENGES					
#	Description	Hours	Rate	Deposit	Withdrawal
1					
2					
3					
4					
5					
		Total:			

MENTAL CHALLENGES					
#	Description	Hours	Rate	Deposit	Withdrawal
1					
2					
3					
4					
5					
		Total:			

PHYSICAL CHALLENGES					
#	Description	Hours	Rate	Deposit	Withdrawal
1					
2					
3					
4					
5					
		Total:			

SOCIAL CHALLENGES					
#	Description	Hours	Rate	Deposit	Withdrawal
1					
2					
3					
4					
5					
		Total:			

SPIRITUAL CHALLENGES					
#	Description	Hours	Rate	Deposit	Withdrawal
1					
2					
3					
4					
5					
		Total:			

DAILY SUMMARY			
#	Description	Yesterday's Balance	Add Today's Balance
1	Financial		
2	Mental		
3	Physical		
4	Social		
5	Spiritual		
Total			

NOTES:____

AFFIRMATIONS:____________________________________

SIGNATURE:__________________________ DATE:_______________

FINANCIAL CHALLENGES					
#	Description	Hours	Rate	Deposit	Withdrawal
1					
2					
3					
4					
5					
		Total:			

MENTAL CHALLENGES					
#	Description	Hours	Rate	Deposit	Withdrawal
1					
2					
3					
4					
5					
		Total:			

PHYSICAL CHALLENGES					
#	Description	Hours	Rate	Deposit	Withdrawal
1					
2					
3					
4					
5					
		Total:			

SOCIAL CHALLENGES					
#	Description	Hours	Rate	Deposit	Withdrawal
1					
2					
3					
4					
5					
		Total:			

Prodigy Planner Workbook

SPIRITUAL CHALLENGES					
#	Description	Hours	Rate	Deposit	Withdrawal
1					
2					
3					
4					
5					
		Total:			

DAILY SUMMARY			
#	Description	Yesterday's Balance	Add Today's Balance
1	Financial		
2	Mental		
3	Physical		
4	Social		
5	Spiritual		
Total			

NOTES:______________________________

AFFIRMATIONS:______________________________

SIGNATURE:____________________ DATE:____________

FINANCIAL CHALLENGES					
#	Description	Hours	Rate	Deposit	Withdrawal
1					
2					
3					
4					
5					
		Total:			

MENTAL CHALLENGES					
#	Description	Hours	Rate	Deposit	Withdrawal
1					
2					
3					
4					
5					
		Total:			

PHYSICAL CHALLENGES					
#	Description	Hours	Rate	Deposit	Withdrawal
1					
2					
3					
4					
5					
		Total:			

SOCIAL CHALLENGES					
#	Description	Hours	Rate	Deposit	Withdrawal
1					
2					
3					
4					
5					
		Total:			

SPIRITUAL CHALLENGES					
#	**Description**	**Hours**	**Rate**	**Deposit**	**Withdrawal**
1					
2					
3					
4					
5					
		Total:			

DAILY SUMMARY			
#	**Description**	**Yesterday's Balance**	**Add Today's Balance**
1	Financial		
2	Mental		
3	Physical		
4	Social		
5	Spiritual		
Total			

NOTES:______________________________

AFFIRMATIONS:______________________________

SIGNATURE:____________________ DATE:____________

WEALTH LEVEL 1 - Essentials		
#	**Description**	**Deposit**
1	Have Earned Income	
2	Have Investment Income	
3	Have Leveraged Income	
4	Have Residual Income	
5	Have More Than One Type Of Income	

WEALTH LEVEL 2 - Fundamentals		
#	**Description**	**Deposit**
1	10% Of Income Saved Upon Payment	
2	6-Month Emergency Cash Fund Reserved	
3	1-Year Emergency Electronic Fund Reserved	
4	All Monthly Bills Are Paid On Time	
5	Bills Do Not Exceed 50% Of Monthly Income	
6	No Debt – With Exception Of Mortgage	

WEALTH LEVEL 3 - Safety Net		
#	**Description**	**Deposit**
1	Life Insurance – All Dependents	
2	Medical Insurance – All Dependents	
3	Disability Insurance – If Not Retired	
4	Dental Insurance – All Dependents	
5	Optical Insurance - All Dependents	
6	Long Term Care Insurance – If Retired	
7	Umbrella Insurance	
8	Property Insurance – Homeowner/Renters	
9	Auto Insurance	
10	Filed All Bills & Receipts	

WEALTH LEVEL 4 - Look Good On Paper		
#	**Description**	**Deposit**
1	Have A Credit Score Above 760	
2	Have A Secured Credit Cards Only	
3	10% Of Income Invested Upon Payment	
4	Monitor Your Credit Report Monthly	
WEALTH LEVEL 5 - Sustainability		
#	**Description**	**Deposit**
1	Sustainable Power Supply – No Bill	
2	Sustainable Water Supply – No Bill	
3	Recycle & Eliminate Own Waste	
4	Have No Mortgage Or Rent Bill	
5	20-Year Property Tax Funds Reserved	
6	Homestead	
	Total:	

NOTES:____

AFFIRMATIONS:__________________________________

SIGNATURE:________________________ DATE:____________

FINANCIAL CHALLENGES					
#	Description	Hours	Rate	Deposit	Withdrawal
1					
2					
3					
4					
5					
		Total:			

MENTAL CHALLENGES					
#	Description	Hours	Rate	Deposit	Withdrawal
1					
2					
3					
4					
5					
		Total:			

PHYSICAL CHALLENGES					
#	Description	Hours	Rate	Deposit	Withdrawal
1					
2					
3					
4					
5					
		Total:			

SOCIAL CHALLENGES					
#	Description	Hours	Rate	Deposit	Withdrawal
1					
2					
3					
4					
5					
		Total:			

Prodigy Planner Workbook

SPIRITUAL CHALLENGES					
#	**Description**	**Hours**	**Rate**	**Deposit**	**Withdrawal**
1					
2					
3					
4					
5					
		Total:			

DAILY SUMMARY			
#	**Description**	**Yesterday's Balance**	**Add Today's Balance**
1	Financial		
2	Mental		
3	Physical		
4	Social		
5	Spiritual		
Monthly Wealth Bonus			
Total			

NOTES:______________________________

____

____

____

____

____

AFFIRMATIONS:______________________________

____

____

____

____

____

SIGNATURE:______________________ DATE:______________

FINANCIAL CHALLENGES					
#	Description	Hours	Rate	Deposit	Withdrawal
1					
2					
3					
4					
5					
		Total:			

MENTAL CHALLENGES					
#	Description	Hours	Rate	Deposit	Withdrawal
1					
2					
3					
4					
5					
		Total:			

PHYSICAL CHALLENGES					
#	Description	Hours	Rate	Deposit	Withdrawal
1					
2					
3					
4					
5					
		Total:			

SOCIAL CHALLENGES					
#	Description	Hours	Rate	Deposit	Withdrawal
1					
2					
3					
4					
5					
		Total:			

SPIRITUAL CHALLENGES					
#	Description	Hours	Rate	Deposit	Withdrawal
1					
2					
3					
4					
5					
		Total:			

DAILY SUMMARY			
#	Description	Yesterday's Balance	Add Today's Balance
1	Financial		
2	Mental		
3	Physical		
4	Social		
5	Spiritual		
Total			

NOTES:____

AFFIRMATIONS:__________________________________

SIGNATURE:________________________ DATE:____________

FINANCIAL CHALLENGES					
#	Description	Hours	Rate	Deposit	Withdrawal
1					
2					
3					
4					
5					
		Total:			

MENTAL CHALLENGES					
#	Description	Hours	Rate	Deposit	Withdrawal
1					
2					
3					
4					
5					
		Total:			

PHYSICAL CHALLENGES					
#	Description	Hours	Rate	Deposit	Withdrawal
1					
2					
3					
4					
5					
		Total:			

SOCIAL CHALLENGES					
#	Description	Hours	Rate	Deposit	Withdrawal
1					
2					
3					
4					
5					
		Total:			

Prodigy Planner Workbook

SPIRITUAL CHALLENGES					
#	**Description**	**Hours**	**Rate**	**Deposit**	**Withdrawal**
1					
2					
3					
4					
5					
		Total:			

DAILY SUMMARY			
#	**Description**	**Yesterday's Balance**	**Add Today's Balance**
1	Financial		
2	Mental		
3	Physical		
4	Social		
5	Spiritual		
Total			

NOTES:____

AFFIRMATIONS:________________________________

SIGNATURE:________________________ DATE:______________

FINANCIAL CHALLENGES					
#	Description	Hours	Rate	Deposit	Withdrawal
1					
2					
3					
4					
5					
		Total:			

MENTAL CHALLENGES					
#	Description	Hours	Rate	Deposit	Withdrawal
1					
2					
3					
4					
5					
		Total:			

PHYSICAL CHALLENGES					
#	Description	Hours	Rate	Deposit	Withdrawal
1					
2					
3					
4					
5					
		Total:			

SOCIAL CHALLENGES					
#	Description	Hours	Rate	Deposit	Withdrawal
1					
2					
3					
4					
5					
		Total:			

Prodigy Planner Workbook

SPIRITUAL CHALLENGES					
#	Description	Hours	Rate	Deposit	Withdrawal
1					
2					
3					
4					
5					
		Total:			

DAILY SUMMARY			
#	Description	Yesterday's Balance	Add Today's Balance
1	Financial		
2	Mental		
3	Physical		
4	Social		
5	Spiritual		
Total			

NOTES:______________________________

AFFIRMATIONS:______________________________

SIGNATURE:______________________ DATE:______________

FINANCIAL CHALLENGES					
#	Description	Hours	Rate	Deposit	Withdrawal
1					
2					
3					
4					
5					
		Total:			

MENTAL CHALLENGES					
#	Description	Hours	Rate	Deposit	Withdrawal
1					
2					
3					
4					
5					
		Total:			

PHYSICAL CHALLENGES					
#	Description	Hours	Rate	Deposit	Withdrawal
1					
2					
3					
4					
5					
		Total:			

SOCIAL CHALLENGES					
#	Description	Hours	Rate	Deposit	Withdrawal
1					
2					
3					
4					
5					
		Total:			

Prodigy Planner Workbook

SPIRITUAL CHALLENGES					
#	**Description**	**Hours**	**Rate**	**Deposit**	**Withdrawal**
1					
2					
3					
4					
5					
		Total:			

DAILY SUMMARY			
#	**Description**	**Yesterday's Balance**	**Add Today's Balance**
1	Financial		
2	Mental		
3	Physical		
4	Social		
5	Spiritual		
Total			

NOTES:______________________________

AFFIRMATIONS:______________________________

SIGNATURE:____________________ DATE:____________

FINANCIAL CHALLENGES					
#	Description	Hours	Rate	Deposit	Withdrawal
1					
2					
3					
4					
5					
		Total:			

MENTAL CHALLENGES					
#	Description	Hours	Rate	Deposit	Withdrawal
1					
2					
3					
4					
5					
		Total:			

PHYSICAL CHALLENGES					
#	Description	Hours	Rate	Deposit	Withdrawal
1					
2					
3					
4					
5					
		Total:			

SOCIAL CHALLENGES					
#	Description	Hours	Rate	Deposit	Withdrawal
1					
2					
3					
4					
5					
		Total:			

SPIRITUAL CHALLENGES					
#	Description	Hours	Rate	Deposit	Withdrawal
1					
2					
3					
4					
5					
		Total:			

DAILY SUMMARY			
#	Description	Yesterday's Balance	Add Today's Balance
1	Financial		
2	Mental		
3	Physical		
4	Social		
5	Spiritual		
Total			

NOTES:____

____

____

____

____

____

AFFIRMATIONS:______________________________________

____

____

____

____

____

____

SIGNATURE:____________________________ DATE:________________

FINANCIAL CHALLENGES					
#	Description	Hours	Rate	Deposit	Withdrawal
1					
2					
3					
4					
5					
		Total:			

MENTAL CHALLENGES					
#	Description	Hours	Rate	Deposit	Withdrawal
1					
2					
3					
4					
5					
		Total:			

PHYSICAL CHALLENGES					
#	Description	Hours	Rate	Deposit	Withdrawal
1					
2					
3					
4					
5					
		Total:			

SOCIAL CHALLENGES					
#	Description	Hours	Rate	Deposit	Withdrawal
1					
2					
3					
4					
5					
		Total:			

Prodigy Planner Workbook

SPIRITUAL CHALLENGES					
#	**Description**	**Hours**	**Rate**	**Deposit**	**Withdrawal**
1					
2					
3					
4					
5					
		Total:			

DAILY SUMMARY			
#	**Description**	**Yesterday's Balance**	**Add Today's Balance**
1	Financial		
2	Mental		
3	Physical		
4	Social		
5	Spiritual		
Total			

NOTES:____

AFFIRMATIONS:__________________________________

SIGNATURE:________________________ DATE:______________

FINANCIAL CHALLENGES					
#	Description	Hours	Rate	Deposit	Withdrawal
1					
2					
3					
4					
5					
		Total:			

MENTAL CHALLENGES					
#	Description	Hours	Rate	Deposit	Withdrawal
1					
2					
3					
4					
5					
		Total:			

PHYSICAL CHALLENGES					
#	Description	Hours	Rate	Deposit	Withdrawal
1					
2					
3					
4					
5					
		Total:			

SOCIAL CHALLENGES					
#	Description	Hours	Rate	Deposit	Withdrawal
1					
2					
3					
4					
5					
		Total:			

SPIRITUAL CHALLENGES					
#	**Description**	**Hours**	**Rate**	**Deposit**	**Withdrawal**
1					
2					
3					
4					
5					
		Total:			

DAILY SUMMARY			
#	**Description**	**Yesterday's Balance**	**Add Today's Balance**
1	Financial		
2	Mental		
3	Physical		
4	Social		
5	Spiritual		
Total			

NOTES:____

AFFIRMATIONS:________________________________

SIGNATURE:____________________ DATE:____________

FINANCIAL CHALLENGES					
#	Description	Hours	Rate	Deposit	Withdrawal
1					
2					
3					
4					
5					
		Total:			

MENTAL CHALLENGES					
#	Description	Hours	Rate	Deposit	Withdrawal
1					
2					
3					
4					
5					
		Total:			

PHYSICAL CHALLENGES					
#	Description	Hours	Rate	Deposit	Withdrawal
1					
2					
3					
4					
5					
		Total:			

SOCIAL CHALLENGES					
#	Description	Hours	Rate	Deposit	Withdrawal
1					
2					
3					
4					
5					
		Total:			

Prodigy Planner Workbook

SPIRITUAL CHALLENGES					
#	Description	Hours	Rate	Deposit	Withdrawal
1					
2					
3					
4					
5					
		Total:			

DAILY SUMMARY			
#	Description	Yesterday's Balance	Add Today's Balance
1	Financial		
2	Mental		
3	Physical		
4	Social		
5	Spiritual		
Total			

NOTES:____

AFFIRMATIONS:__________________________________

SIGNATURE:________________________ DATE:____________

FINANCIAL CHALLENGES					
#	Description	Hours	Rate	Deposit	Withdrawal
1					
2					
3					
4					
5					
		Total:			

MENTAL CHALLENGES					
#	Description	Hours	Rate	Deposit	Withdrawal
1					
2					
3					
4					
5					
		Total:			

PHYSICAL CHALLENGES					
#	Description	Hours	Rate	Deposit	Withdrawal
1					
2					
3					
4					
5					
		Total:			

SOCIAL CHALLENGES					
#	Description	Hours	Rate	Deposit	Withdrawal
1					
2					
3					
4					
5					
		Total:			

SPIRITUAL CHALLENGES					
#	**Description**	**Hours**	**Rate**	**Deposit**	**Withdrawal**
1					
2					
3					
4					
5					
		Total:			

DAILY SUMMARY			
#	**Description**	**Yesterday's Balance**	**Add Today's Balance**
1	Financial		
2	Mental		
3	Physical		
4	Social		
5	Spiritual		
Total			

NOTES:____

AFFIRMATIONS:__________________________________

SIGNATURE:________________________ DATE:____________

FINANCIAL CHALLENGES					
#	Description	Hours	Rate	Deposit	Withdrawal
1					
2					
3					
4					
5					
		Total:			

MENTAL CHALLENGES					
#	Description	Hours	Rate	Deposit	Withdrawal
1					
2					
3					
4					
5					
		Total:			

PHYSICAL CHALLENGES					
#	Description	Hours	Rate	Deposit	Withdrawal
1					
2					
3					
4					
5					
		Total:			

SOCIAL CHALLENGES					
#	Description	Hours	Rate	Deposit	Withdrawal
1					
2					
3					
4					
5					
		Total:			

SPIRITUAL CHALLENGES					
#	Description	Hours	Rate	Deposit	Withdrawal
1					
2					
3					
4					
5					
		Total:			

DAILY SUMMARY			
#	Description	Yesterday's Balance	Add Today's Balance
1	Financial		
2	Mental		
3	Physical		
4	Social		
5	Spiritual		
Total			

NOTES:______________________________

AFFIRMATIONS:______________________________

SIGNATURE:______________________ DATE:______________

FINANCIAL CHALLENGES					
#	Description	Hours	Rate	Deposit	Withdrawal
1					
2					
3					
4					
5					
		Total:			

MENTAL CHALLENGES					
#	Description	Hours	Rate	Deposit	Withdrawal
1					
2					
3					
4					
5					
		Total:			

PHYSICAL CHALLENGES					
#	Description	Hours	Rate	Deposit	Withdrawal
1					
2					
3					
4					
5					
		Total:			

SOCIAL CHALLENGES					
#	Description	Hours	Rate	Deposit	Withdrawal
1					
2					
3					
4					
5					
		Total:			

SPIRITUAL CHALLENGES					
#	Description	Hours	Rate	Deposit	Withdrawal
1					
2					
3					
4					
5					
		Total:			

DAILY SUMMARY			
#	Description	Yesterday's Balance	Add Today's Balance
1	Financial		
2	Mental		
3	Physical		
4	Social		
5	Spiritual		
Total			

NOTES:____

AFFIRMATIONS:_______________________________________

SIGNATURE:___________________________ DATE:______________

FINANCIAL CHALLENGES					
#	Description	Hours	Rate	Deposit	Withdrawal
1					
2					
3					
4					
5					
		Total:			

MENTAL CHALLENGES					
#	Description	Hours	Rate	Deposit	Withdrawal
1					
2					
3					
4					
5					
		Total:			

PHYSICAL CHALLENGES					
#	Description	Hours	Rate	Deposit	Withdrawal
1					
2					
3					
4					
5					
		Total:			

SOCIAL CHALLENGES					
#	Description	Hours	Rate	Deposit	Withdrawal
1					
2					
3					
4					
5					
		Total:			

Prodigy Planner Workbook

SPIRITUAL CHALLENGES					
#	**Description**	**Hours**	**Rate**	**Deposit**	**Withdrawal**
1					
2					
3					
4					
5					
		Total:			

DAILY SUMMARY			
#	**Description**	**Yesterday's Balance**	**Add Today's Balance**
1	Financial		
2	Mental		
3	Physical		
4	Social		
5	Spiritual		
Total			

NOTES:____

____

____

____

____

____

AFFIRMATIONS:____

____

____

____

____

____

____

SIGNATURE:______________________________ DATE:________________

Prodigy Planner Workbook

FINANCIAL CHALLENGES					
#	Description	Hours	Rate	Deposit	Withdrawal
1					
2					
3					
4					
5					
		Total:			

MENTAL CHALLENGES					
#	Description	Hours	Rate	Deposit	Withdrawal
1					
2					
3					
4					
5					
		Total:			

PHYSICAL CHALLENGES					
#	Description	Hours	Rate	Deposit	Withdrawal
1					
2					
3					
4					
5					
		Total:			

SOCIAL CHALLENGES					
#	Description	Hours	Rate	Deposit	Withdrawal
1					
2					
3					
4					
5					
		Total:			

Prodigy Planner Workbook

SPIRITUAL CHALLENGES					
#	Description	Hours	Rate	Deposit	Withdrawal
1					
2					
3					
4					
5					
		Total:			

DAILY SUMMARY			
#	Description	Yesterday's Balance	Add Today's Balance
1	Financial		
2	Mental		
3	Physical		
4	Social		
5	Spiritual		
Total			

NOTES:______________________________

____

____

____

____

____

AFFIRMATIONS:______________________________

____

____

____

____

____

____

SIGNATURE:______________________________ DATE:________________

FINANCIAL CHALLENGES					
#	Description	Hours	Rate	Deposit	Withdrawal
1					
2					
3					
4					
5					
		Total:			

MENTAL CHALLENGES					
#	Description	Hours	Rate	Deposit	Withdrawal
1					
2					
3					
4					
5					
		Total:			

PHYSICAL CHALLENGES					
#	Description	Hours	Rate	Deposit	Withdrawal
1					
2					
3					
4					
5					
		Total:			

SOCIAL CHALLENGES					
#	Description	Hours	Rate	Deposit	Withdrawal
1					
2					
3					
4					
5					
		Total:			

Prodigy Planner Workbook

SPIRITUAL CHALLENGES					
#	Description	Hours	Rate	Deposit	Withdrawal
1					
2					
3					
4					
5					
		Total:			

DAILY SUMMARY			
#	Description	Yesterday's Balance	Add Today's Balance
1	Financial		
2	Mental		
3	Physical		
4	Social		
5	Spiritual		
Total			

NOTES:____

____

____

____

____

____

AFFIRMATIONS:_______________________________________

____

____

____

____

____

____

SIGNATURE:______________________________ DATE:________________

FINANCIAL CHALLENGES					
#	Description	Hours	Rate	Deposit	Withdrawal
1					
2					
3					
4					
5					
		Total:			

MENTAL CHALLENGES					
#	Description	Hours	Rate	Deposit	Withdrawal
1					
2					
3					
4					
5					
		Total:			

PHYSICAL CHALLENGES					
#	Description	Hours	Rate	Deposit	Withdrawal
1					
2					
3					
4					
5					
		Total:			

SOCIAL CHALLENGES					
#	Description	Hours	Rate	Deposit	Withdrawal
1					
2					
3					
4					
5					
		Total:			

SPIRITUAL CHALLENGES					
#	**Description**	**Hours**	**Rate**	**Deposit**	**Withdrawal**
1					
2					
3					
4					
5					
		Total:			

DAILY SUMMARY			
#	**Description**	**Yesterday's Balance**	**Add Today's Balance**
1	Financial		
2	Mental		
3	Physical		
4	Social		
5	Spiritual		
Total			

NOTES:____

AFFIRMATIONS:__________________________________

SIGNATURE:____________________ DATE:____________

FINANCIAL CHALLENGES					
#	Description	Hours	Rate	Deposit	Withdrawal
1					
2					
3					
4					
5					
		Total:			

MENTAL CHALLENGES					
#	Description	Hours	Rate	Deposit	Withdrawal
1					
2					
3					
4					
5					
		Total:			

PHYSICAL CHALLENGES					
#	Description	Hours	Rate	Deposit	Withdrawal
1					
2					
3					
4					
5					
		Total:			

SOCIAL CHALLENGES					
#	Description	Hours	Rate	Deposit	Withdrawal
1					
2					
3					
4					
5					
		Total:			

SPIRITUAL CHALLENGES					
#	Description	Hours	Rate	Deposit	Withdrawal
1					
2					
3					
4					
5					
		Total:			

DAILY SUMMARY			
#	Description	Yesterday's Balance	Add Today's Balance
1	Financial		
2	Mental		
3	Physical		
4	Social		
5	Spiritual		
Total			

NOTES:____

AFFIRMATIONS:____________________________________

SIGNATURE:___________________________ DATE:_______________

FINANCIAL CHALLENGES					
#	Description	Hours	Rate	Deposit	Withdrawal
1					
2					
3					
4					
5					
		Total:			

MENTAL CHALLENGES					
#	Description	Hours	Rate	Deposit	Withdrawal
1					
2					
3					
4					
5					
		Total:			

PHYSICAL CHALLENGES					
#	Description	Hours	Rate	Deposit	Withdrawal
1					
2					
3					
4					
5					
		Total:			

SOCIAL CHALLENGES					
#	Description	Hours	Rate	Deposit	Withdrawal
1					
2					
3					
4					
5					
		Total:			

Prodigy Planner Workbook

SPIRITUAL CHALLENGES					
#	Description	Hours	Rate	Deposit	Withdrawal
1					
2					
3					
4					
5					
		Total:			

DAILY SUMMARY			
#	Description	Yesterday's Balance	Add Today's Balance
1	Financial		
2	Mental		
3	Physical		
4	Social		
5	Spiritual		
Total			

NOTES:____

AFFIRMATIONS:__________________________________

SIGNATURE:________________________ DATE:____________

FINANCIAL CHALLENGES					
#	Description	Hours	Rate	Deposit	Withdrawal
1					
2					
3					
4					
5					
		Total:			

MENTAL CHALLENGES					
#	Description	Hours	Rate	Deposit	Withdrawal
1					
2					
3					
4					
5					
		Total:			

PHYSICAL CHALLENGES					
#	Description	Hours	Rate	Deposit	Withdrawal
1					
2					
3					
4					
5					
		Total:			

SOCIAL CHALLENGES					
#	Description	Hours	Rate	Deposit	Withdrawal
1					
2					
3					
4					
5					
		Total:			

Prodigy Planner Workbook

SPIRITUAL CHALLENGES					
#	Description	Hours	Rate	Deposit	Withdrawal
1					
2					
3					
4					
5					
		Total:			

DAILY SUMMARY			
#	Description	Yesterday's Balance	Add Today's Balance
1	Financial		
2	Mental		
3	Physical		
4	Social		
5	Spiritual		
Total			

NOTES:______________________________

AFFIRMATIONS:______________________________

SIGNATURE:____________________ DATE:____________

FINANCIAL CHALLENGES					
#	Description	Hours	Rate	Deposit	Withdrawal
1					
2					
3					
4					
5					
		Total:			

MENTAL CHALLENGES					
#	Description	Hours	Rate	Deposit	Withdrawal
1					
2					
3					
4					
5					
		Total:			

PHYSICAL CHALLENGES					
#	Description	Hours	Rate	Deposit	Withdrawal
1					
2					
3					
4					
5					
		Total:			

SOCIAL CHALLENGES					
#	Description	Hours	Rate	Deposit	Withdrawal
1					
2					
3					
4					
5					
		Total:			

Prodigy Planner Workbook

SPIRITUAL CHALLENGES					
#	Description	Hours	Rate	Deposit	Withdrawal
1					
2					
3					
4					
5					
		Total:			

DAILY SUMMARY			
#	Description	Yesterday's Balance	Add Today's Balance
1	Financial		
2	Mental		
3	Physical		
4	Social		
5	Spiritual		
Total			

NOTES:____

AFFIRMATIONS:____

SIGNATURE:______________________ DATE:______________

FINANCIAL CHALLENGES					
#	Description	Hours	Rate	Deposit	Withdrawal
1					
2					
3					
4					
5					
		Total:			

MENTAL CHALLENGES					
#	Description	Hours	Rate	Deposit	Withdrawal
1					
2					
3					
4					
5					
		Total:			

PHYSICAL CHALLENGES					
#	Description	Hours	Rate	Deposit	Withdrawal
1					
2					
3					
4					
5					
		Total:			

SOCIAL CHALLENGES					
#	Description	Hours	Rate	Deposit	Withdrawal
1					
2					
3					
4					
5					
		Total:			

Prodigy Planner Workbook

SPIRITUAL CHALLENGES					
#	Description	Hours	Rate	Deposit	Withdrawal
1					
2					
3					
4					
5					
			Total:		

DAILY SUMMARY			
#	Description	Yesterday's Balance	Add Today's Balance
1	Financial		
2	Mental		
3	Physical		
4	Social		
5	Spiritual		
Total			

NOTES:____

AFFIRMATIONS:_______________________________________

SIGNATURE:____________________________ DATE:________________

FINANCIAL CHALLENGES					
#	Description	Hours	Rate	Deposit	Withdrawal
1					
2					
3					
4					
5					
		Total:			

MENTAL CHALLENGES					
#	Description	Hours	Rate	Deposit	Withdrawal
1					
2					
3					
4					
5					
		Total:			

PHYSICAL CHALLENGES					
#	Description	Hours	Rate	Deposit	Withdrawal
1					
2					
3					
4					
5					
		Total:			

SOCIAL CHALLENGES					
#	Description	Hours	Rate	Deposit	Withdrawal
1					
2					
3					
4					
5					
		Total:			

Prodigy Planner Workbook

SPIRITUAL CHALLENGES					
#	Description	Hours	Rate	Deposit	Withdrawal
1					
2					
3					
4					
5					
		Total:			

DAILY SUMMARY			
#	Description	Yesterday's Balance	Add Today's Balance
1	Financial		
2	Mental		
3	Physical		
4	Social		
5	Spiritual		
Total			

NOTES:____

AFFIRMATIONS:______________________________________

SIGNATURE:__________________________ DATE:______________

FINANCIAL CHALLENGES					
#	Description	Hours	Rate	Deposit	Withdrawal
1					
2					
3					
4					
5					
		Total:			

MENTAL CHALLENGES					
#	Description	Hours	Rate	Deposit	Withdrawal
1					
2					
3					
4					
5					
		Total:			

PHYSICAL CHALLENGES					
#	Description	Hours	Rate	Deposit	Withdrawal
1					
2					
3					
4					
5					
		Total:			

SOCIAL CHALLENGES					
#	Description	Hours	Rate	Deposit	Withdrawal
1					
2					
3					
4					
5					
		Total:			

SPIRITUAL CHALLENGES					
#	**Description**	**Hours**	**Rate**	**Deposit**	**Withdrawal**
1					
2					
3					
4					
5					
		Total:			

DAILY SUMMARY			
#	**Description**	**Yesterday's Balance**	**Add Today's Balance**
1	Financial		
2	Mental		
3	Physical		
4	Social		
5	Spiritual		
Total			

NOTES:____

____

____

____

____

____

AFFIRMATIONS:____

____

____

____

____

____

____

SIGNATURE:______________________________ DATE:________________

FINANCIAL CHALLENGES					
#	Description	Hours	Rate	Deposit	Withdrawal
1					
2					
3					
4					
5					
		Total:			

MENTAL CHALLENGES					
#	Description	Hours	Rate	Deposit	Withdrawal
1					
2					
3					
4					
5					
		Total:			

PHYSICAL CHALLENGES					
#	Description	Hours	Rate	Deposit	Withdrawal
1					
2					
3					
4					
5					
		Total:			

SOCIAL CHALLENGES					
#	Description	Hours	Rate	Deposit	Withdrawal
1					
2					
3					
4					
5					
		Total:			

Prodigy Planner Workbook

SPIRITUAL CHALLENGES					
#	Description	Hours	Rate	Deposit	Withdrawal
1					
2					
3					
4					
5					
		Total:			

DAILY SUMMARY			
#	Description	Yesterday's Balance	Add Today's Balance
1	Financial		
2	Mental		
3	Physical		
4	Social		
5	Spiritual		
Total			

NOTES:______________________________

AFFIRMATIONS:______________________________

SIGNATURE:______________________ DATE:______________

FINANCIAL CHALLENGES					
#	Description	Hours	Rate	Deposit	Withdrawal
1					
2					
3					
4					
5					
		Total:			

MENTAL CHALLENGES					
#	Description	Hours	Rate	Deposit	Withdrawal
1					
2					
3					
4					
5					
		Total:			

PHYSICAL CHALLENGES					
#	Description	Hours	Rate	Deposit	Withdrawal
1					
2					
3					
4					
5					
		Total:			

SOCIAL CHALLENGES					
#	Description	Hours	Rate	Deposit	Withdrawal
1					
2					
3					
4					
5					
		Total:			

SPIRITUAL CHALLENGES					
#	Description	Hours	Rate	Deposit	Withdrawal
1					
2					
3					
4					
5					
		Total:			

DAILY SUMMARY			
#	Description	Yesterday's Balance	Add Today's Balance
1	Financial		
2	Mental		
3	Physical		
4	Social		
5	Spiritual		
Total			

NOTES:____

____

____

____

____

____

AFFIRMATIONS:____

____

____

____

____

____

____

SIGNATURE:______________________________ DATE:________________

FINANCIAL CHALLENGES					
#	Description	Hours	Rate	Deposit	Withdrawal
1					
2					
3					
4					
5					
		Total:			

MENTAL CHALLENGES					
#	Description	Hours	Rate	Deposit	Withdrawal
1					
2					
3					
4					
5					
		Total:			

PHYSICAL CHALLENGES					
#	Description	Hours	Rate	Deposit	Withdrawal
1					
2					
3					
4					
5					
		Total:			

SOCIAL CHALLENGES					
#	Description	Hours	Rate	Deposit	Withdrawal
1					
2					
3					
4					
5					
		Total:			

SPIRITUAL CHALLENGES					
#	**Description**	**Hours**	**Rate**	**Deposit**	**Withdrawal**
1					
2					
3					
4					
5					
		Total:			

DAILY SUMMARY			
#	**Description**	**Yesterday's Balance**	**Add Today's Balance**
1	Financial		
2	Mental		
3	Physical		
4	Social		
5	Spiritual		
Total			

NOTES:____

AFFIRMATIONS:____

SIGNATURE:____________________________ DATE:________________

FINANCIAL CHALLENGES					
#	Description	Hours	Rate	Deposit	Withdrawal
1					
2					
3					
4					
5					
		Total:			

MENTAL CHALLENGES					
#	Description	Hours	Rate	Deposit	Withdrawal
1					
2					
3					
4					
5					
		Total:			

PHYSICAL CHALLENGES					
#	Description	Hours	Rate	Deposit	Withdrawal
1					
2					
3					
4					
5					
		Total:			

SOCIAL CHALLENGES					
#	Description	Hours	Rate	Deposit	Withdrawal
1					
2					
3					
4					
5					
		Total:			

SPIRITUAL CHALLENGES					
#	Description	Hours	Rate	Deposit	Withdrawal
1					
2					
3					
4					
5					
			Total:		

DAILY SUMMARY			
#	Description	Yesterday's Balance	Add Today's Balance
1	Financial		
2	Mental		
3	Physical		
4	Social		
5	Spiritual		
Total			

NOTES:____

AFFIRMATIONS:_______________________________________

SIGNATURE:________________________ DATE:______________

FINANCIAL CHALLENGES					
#	Description	Hours	Rate	Deposit	Withdrawal
1					
2					
3					
4					
5					
		Total:			

MENTAL CHALLENGES					
#	Description	Hours	Rate	Deposit	Withdrawal
1					
2					
3					
4					
5					
		Total:			

PHYSICAL CHALLENGES					
#	Description	Hours	Rate	Deposit	Withdrawal
1					
2					
3					
4					
5					
		Total:			

SOCIAL CHALLENGES					
#	Description	Hours	Rate	Deposit	Withdrawal
1					
2					
3					
4					
5					
		Total:			

SPIRITUAL CHALLENGES					
#	**Description**	**Hours**	**Rate**	**Deposit**	**Withdrawal**
1					
2					
3					
4					
5					
		Total:			

DAILY SUMMARY			
#	**Description**	**Yesterday's Balance**	**Add Today's Balance**
1	Financial		
2	Mental		
3	Physical		
4	Social		
5	Spiritual		
Total			

NOTES:____

____

____

____

____

____

AFFIRMATIONS:____

____

____

____

____

____

____

SIGNATURE:______________________________ DATE:________________

WEALTH LEVEL 1 - Essentials		
#	**Description**	**Deposit**
1	Have Earned Income	
2	Have Investment Income	
3	Have Leveraged Income	
4	Have Residual Income	
5	Have More Than One Type Of Income	
WEALTH LEVEL 2 - Fundamentals		
#	**Description**	**Deposit**
1	10% Of Income Saved Upon Payment	
2	6-Month Emergency Cash Fund Reserved	
3	1-Year Emergency Electronic Fund Reserved	
4	All Monthly Bills Are Paid On Time	
5	Bills Do Not Exceed 50% Of Monthly Income	
6	No Debt – With Exception Of Mortgage	
WEALTH LEVEL 3 - Safety Net		
#	**Description**	**Deposit**
1	Life Insurance – All Dependents	
2	Medical Insurance – All Dependents	
3	Disability Insurance – If Not Retired	
4	Dental Insurance – All Dependents	
5	Optical Insurance - All Dependents	
6	Long Term Care Insurance – If Retired	
7	Umbrella Insurance	
8	Property Insurance – Homeowner/Renters	
9	Auto Insurance	
10	Filed All Bills & Receipts	

WEALTH LEVEL 4 - Look Good On Paper		
#	**Description**	**Deposit**
1	Have A Credit Score Above 760	
2	Have A Secured Credit Cards Only	
3	10% Of Income Invested Upon Payment	
4	Monitor Your Credit Report Monthly	
WEALTH LEVEL 5 - Sustainability		
#	**Description**	**Deposit**
1	Sustainable Power Supply – No Bill	
2	Sustainable Water Supply – No Bill	
3	Recycle & Eliminate Own Waste	
4	Have No Mortgage Or Rent Bill	
5	20-Year Property Tax Funds Reserved	
6	Homestead	
	Total:	

NOTES:____

____

____

____

____

____

AFFIRMATIONS:______________________________________

____

____

____

____

____

____

SIGNATURE:______________________________ DATE:________________

FINANCIAL CHALLENGES					
#	Description	Hours	Rate	Deposit	Withdrawal
1					
2					
3					
4					
5					
		Total:			

MENTAL CHALLENGES					
#	Description	Hours	Rate	Deposit	Withdrawal
1					
2					
3					
4					
5					
		Total:			

PHYSICAL CHALLENGES					
#	Description	Hours	Rate	Deposit	Withdrawal
1					
2					
3					
4					
5					
		Total:			

SOCIAL CHALLENGES					
#	Description	Hours	Rate	Deposit	Withdrawal
1					
2					
3					
4					
5					
		Total:			

SPIRITUAL CHALLENGES					
#	**Description**	**Hours**	**Rate**	**Deposit**	**Withdrawal**
1					
2					
3					
4					
5					
		Total:			

DAILY SUMMARY			
#	**Description**	**Yesterday's Balance**	**Add Today's Balance**
1	Financial		
2	Mental		
3	Physical		
4	Social		
5	Spiritual		
Monthly Wealth Bonus			
Total			

NOTES:____

AFFIRMATIONS:____

SIGNATURE:______________________ DATE:______________

FINANCIAL CHALLENGES					
#	Description	Hours	Rate	Deposit	Withdrawal
1					
2					
3					
4					
5					
		Total:			

MENTAL CHALLENGES					
#	Description	Hours	Rate	Deposit	Withdrawal
1					
2					
3					
4					
5					
		Total:			

PHYSICAL CHALLENGES					
#	Description	Hours	Rate	Deposit	Withdrawal
1					
2					
3					
4					
5					
		Total:			

SOCIAL CHALLENGES					
#	Description	Hours	Rate	Deposit	Withdrawal
1					
2					
3					
4					
5					
		Total:			

Prodigy Planner Workbook

SPIRITUAL CHALLENGES					
#	Description	Hours	Rate	Deposit	Withdrawal
1					
2					
3					
4					
5					
		Total:			

DAILY SUMMARY			
#	Description	Yesterday's Balance	Add Today's Balance
1	Financial		
2	Mental		
3	Physical		
4	Social		
5	Spiritual		
Total			

NOTES:____

AFFIRMATIONS:____________________________________

SIGNATURE:________________________ DATE:______________

Prodigy Planner Workbook

FINANCIAL CHALLENGES					
#	**Description**	**Hours**	**Rate**	**Deposit**	**Withdrawal**
1					
2					
3					
4					
5					
		Total:			

MENTAL CHALLENGES					
#	**Description**	**Hours**	**Rate**	**Deposit**	**Withdrawal**
1					
2					
3					
4					
5					
		Total:			

PHYSICAL CHALLENGES					
#	**Description**	**Hours**	**Rate**	**Deposit**	**Withdrawal**
1					
2					
3					
4					
5					
		Total:			

SOCIAL CHALLENGES					
#	**Description**	**Hours**	**Rate**	**Deposit**	**Withdrawal**
1					
2					
3					
4					
5					
		Total:			

SPIRITUAL CHALLENGES					
#	**Description**	**Hours**	**Rate**	**Deposit**	**Withdrawal**
1					
2					
3					
4					
5					
		Total:			

DAILY SUMMARY			
#	**Description**	**Yesterday's Balance**	**Add Today's Balance**
1	Financial		
2	Mental		
3	Physical		
4	Social		
5	Spiritual		
Total			

NOTES:____

____

____

____

____

____

AFFIRMATIONS:______________________________________

____

____

____

____

____

____

SIGNATURE:____________________________ DATE:________________

FINANCIAL CHALLENGES					
#	Description	Hours	Rate	Deposit	Withdrawal
1					
2					
3					
4					
5					
		Total:			

MENTAL CHALLENGES					
#	Description	Hours	Rate	Deposit	Withdrawal
1					
2					
3					
4					
5					
		Total:			

PHYSICAL CHALLENGES					
#	Description	Hours	Rate	Deposit	Withdrawal
1					
2					
3					
4					
5					
		Total:			

SOCIAL CHALLENGES					
#	Description	Hours	Rate	Deposit	Withdrawal
1					
2					
3					
4					
5					
		Total:			

Prodigy Planner Workbook

SPIRITUAL CHALLENGES					
#	Description	Hours	Rate	Deposit	Withdrawal
1					
2					
3					
4					
5					
		Total:			

DAILY SUMMARY			
#	Description	Yesterday's Balance	Add Today's Balance
1	Financial		
2	Mental		
3	Physical		
4	Social		
5	Spiritual		
Total			

NOTES:____

____

____

____

____

____

AFFIRMATIONS:____

____

____

____

____

____

____

SIGNATURE:______________________________ DATE:________________

FINANCIAL CHALLENGES					
#	Description	Hours	Rate	Deposit	Withdrawal
1					
2					
3					
4					
5					
		Total:			

MENTAL CHALLENGES					
#	Description	Hours	Rate	Deposit	Withdrawal
1					
2					
3					
4					
5					
		Total:			

PHYSICAL CHALLENGES					
#	Description	Hours	Rate	Deposit	Withdrawal
1					
2					
3					
4					
5					
		Total:			

SOCIAL CHALLENGES					
#	Description	Hours	Rate	Deposit	Withdrawal
1					
2					
3					
4					
5					
		Total:			

SPIRITUAL CHALLENGES					
#	**Description**	**Hours**	**Rate**	**Deposit**	**Withdrawal**
1					
2					
3					
4					
5					
		Total:			

DAILY SUMMARY			
#	**Description**	**Yesterday's Balance**	**Add Today's Balance**
1	Financial		
2	Mental		
3	Physical		
4	Social		
5	Spiritual		
Total			

NOTES:____

AFFIRMATIONS:__________________________________

SIGNATURE:________________________ DATE:______________

FINANCIAL CHALLENGES					
#	Description	Hours	Rate	Deposit	Withdrawal
1					
2					
3					
4					
5					
		Total:			

MENTAL CHALLENGES					
#	Description	Hours	Rate	Deposit	Withdrawal
1					
2					
3					
4					
5					
		Total:			

PHYSICAL CHALLENGES					
#	Description	Hours	Rate	Deposit	Withdrawal
1					
2					
3					
4					
5					
		Total:			

SOCIAL CHALLENGES					
#	Description	Hours	Rate	Deposit	Withdrawal
1					
2					
3					
4					
5					
		Total:			

SPIRITUAL CHALLENGES					
#	Description	Hours	Rate	Deposit	Withdrawal
1					
2					
3					
4					
5					
		Total:			

DAILY SUMMARY			
#	Description	Yesterday's Balance	Add Today's Balance
1	Financial		
2	Mental		
3	Physical		
4	Social		
5	Spiritual		
Total			

NOTES:____

____

____

____

____

____

AFFIRMATIONS:____

____

____

____

____

____

____

SIGNATURE:______________________________ DATE:________________

FINANCIAL CHALLENGES					
#	Description	Hours	Rate	Deposit	Withdrawal
1					
2					
3					
4					
5					
		Total:			

MENTAL CHALLENGES					
#	Description	Hours	Rate	Deposit	Withdrawal
1					
2					
3					
4					
5					
		Total:			

PHYSICAL CHALLENGES					
#	Description	Hours	Rate	Deposit	Withdrawal
1					
2					
3					
4					
5					
		Total:			

SOCIAL CHALLENGES					
#	Description	Hours	Rate	Deposit	Withdrawal
1					
2					
3					
4					
5					
		Total:			

SPIRITUAL CHALLENGES					
#	Description	Hours	Rate	Deposit	Withdrawal
1					
2					
3					
4					
5					
		Total:			

DAILY SUMMARY			
#	Description	Yesterday's Balance	Add Today's Balance
1	Financial		
2	Mental		
3	Physical		
4	Social		
5	Spiritual		
	Total		

NOTES:____

AFFIRMATIONS:____

SIGNATURE:______________________ DATE:______________

FINANCIAL CHALLENGES					
#	Description	Hours	Rate	Deposit	Withdrawal
1					
2					
3					
4					
5					
		Total:			

MENTAL CHALLENGES					
#	Description	Hours	Rate	Deposit	Withdrawal
1					
2					
3					
4					
5					
		Total:			

PHYSICAL CHALLENGES					
#	Description	Hours	Rate	Deposit	Withdrawal
1					
2					
3					
4					
5					
		Total:			

SOCIAL CHALLENGES					
#	Description	Hours	Rate	Deposit	Withdrawal
1					
2					
3					
4					
5					
		Total:			

SPIRITUAL CHALLENGES					
#	Description	Hours	Rate	Deposit	Withdrawal
1					
2					
3					
4					
5					
		Total:			

DAILY SUMMARY			
#	Description	Yesterday's Balance	Add Today's Balance
1	Financial		
2	Mental		
3	Physical		
4	Social		
5	Spiritual		
Total			

NOTES:____

____

____

____

____

____

AFFIRMATIONS:______________________________________

____

____

____

____

____

____

SIGNATURE:______________________________ DATE:________________

FINANCIAL CHALLENGES					
#	Description	Hours	Rate	Deposit	Withdrawal
1					
2					
3					
4					
5					
		Total:			

MENTAL CHALLENGES					
#	Description	Hours	Rate	Deposit	Withdrawal
1					
2					
3					
4					
5					
		Total:			

PHYSICAL CHALLENGES					
#	Description	Hours	Rate	Deposit	Withdrawal
1					
2					
3					
4					
5					
		Total:			

SOCIAL CHALLENGES					
#	Description	Hours	Rate	Deposit	Withdrawal
1					
2					
3					
4					
5					
		Total:			

Prodigy Planner Workbook

SPIRITUAL CHALLENGES					
#	**Description**	**Hours**	**Rate**	**Deposit**	**Withdrawal**
1					
2					
3					
4					
5					
		Total:			

DAILY SUMMARY			
#	**Description**	**Yesterday's Balance**	**Add Today's Balance**
1	Financial		
2	Mental		
3	Physical		
4	Social		
5	Spiritual		
Total			

NOTES:____

AFFIRMATIONS:____

SIGNATURE:________________________ DATE:______________

FINANCIAL CHALLENGES					
#	Description	Hours	Rate	Deposit	Withdrawal
1					
2					
3					
4					
5					
		Total:			

MENTAL CHALLENGES					
#	Description	Hours	Rate	Deposit	Withdrawal
1					
2					
3					
4					
5					
		Total:			

PHYSICAL CHALLENGES					
#	Description	Hours	Rate	Deposit	Withdrawal
1					
2					
3					
4					
5					
		Total:			

SOCIAL CHALLENGES					
#	Description	Hours	Rate	Deposit	Withdrawal
1					
2					
3					
4					
5					
		Total:			

Prodigy Planner Workbook

SPIRITUAL CHALLENGES					
#	Description	Hours	Rate	Deposit	Withdrawal
1					
2					
3					
4					
5					
		Total:			

DAILY SUMMARY			
#	Description	Yesterday's Balance	Add Today's Balance
1	Financial		
2	Mental		
3	Physical		
4	Social		
5	Spiritual		
Total			

NOTES:____

AFFIRMATIONS:__________________________________

SIGNATURE:______________________ DATE:____________

FINANCIAL CHALLENGES					
#	Description	Hours	Rate	Deposit	Withdrawal
1					
2					
3					
4					
5					
		Total:			

MENTAL CHALLENGES					
#	Description	Hours	Rate	Deposit	Withdrawal
1					
2					
3					
4					
5					
		Total:			

PHYSICAL CHALLENGES					
#	Description	Hours	Rate	Deposit	Withdrawal
1					
2					
3					
4					
5					
		Total:			

SOCIAL CHALLENGES					
#	Description	Hours	Rate	Deposit	Withdrawal
1					
2					
3					
4					
5					
		Total:			

SPIRITUAL CHALLENGES					
#	Description	Hours	Rate	Deposit	Withdrawal
1					
2					
3					
4					
5					
		Total:			

DAILY SUMMARY			
#	Description	Yesterday's Balance	Add Today's Balance
1	Financial		
2	Mental		
3	Physical		
4	Social		
5	Spiritual		
Total			

NOTES:____

____

____

____

____

____

AFFIRMATIONS:_______________________________________

____

____

____

____

____

____

SIGNATURE:_____________________________ DATE:________________

FINANCIAL CHALLENGES					
#	Description	Hours	Rate	Deposit	Withdrawal
1					
2					
3					
4					
5					
		Total:			

MENTAL CHALLENGES					
#	Description	Hours	Rate	Deposit	Withdrawal
1					
2					
3					
4					
5					
		Total:			

PHYSICAL CHALLENGES					
#	Description	Hours	Rate	Deposit	Withdrawal
1					
2					
3					
4					
5					
		Total:			

SOCIAL CHALLENGES					
#	Description	Hours	Rate	Deposit	Withdrawal
1					
2					
3					
4					
5					
		Total:			

Prodigy Planner Workbook

SPIRITUAL CHALLENGES					
#	Description	Hours	Rate	Deposit	Withdrawal
1					
2					
3					
4					
5					
		Total:			

DAILY SUMMARY			
#	Description	Yesterday's Balance	Add Today's Balance
1	Financial		
2	Mental		
3	Physical		
4	Social		
5	Spiritual		
Total			

NOTES:____

AFFIRMATIONS:____________________________________

SIGNATURE:________________________ DATE:______________

FINANCIAL CHALLENGES					
#	Description	Hours	Rate	Deposit	Withdrawal
1					
2					
3					
4					
5					
			Total:		

MENTAL CHALLENGES					
#	Description	Hours	Rate	Deposit	Withdrawal
1					
2					
3					
4					
5					
			Total:		

PHYSICAL CHALLENGES					
#	Description	Hours	Rate	Deposit	Withdrawal
1					
2					
3					
4					
5					
			Total:		

SOCIAL CHALLENGES					
#	Description	Hours	Rate	Deposit	Withdrawal
1					
2					
3					
4					
5					
			Total:		

SPIRITUAL CHALLENGES					
#	**Description**	**Hours**	**Rate**	**Deposit**	**Withdrawal**
1					
2					
3					
4					
5					
		Total:			

DAILY SUMMARY			
#	**Description**	**Yesterday's Balance**	**Add Today's Balance**
1	Financial		
2	Mental		
3	Physical		
4	Social		
5	Spiritual		
Total			

NOTES:____

____

____

____

____

____

AFFIRMATIONS:______________________________________

____

____

____

____

____

____

SIGNATURE:_________________________ DATE:_______________

FINANCIAL CHALLENGES					
#	Description	Hours	Rate	Deposit	Withdrawal
1					
2					
3					
4					
5					
		Total:			

MENTAL CHALLENGES					
#	Description	Hours	Rate	Deposit	Withdrawal
1					
2					
3					
4					
5					
		Total:			

PHYSICAL CHALLENGES					
#	Description	Hours	Rate	Deposit	Withdrawal
1					
2					
3					
4					
5					
		Total:			

SOCIAL CHALLENGES					
#	Description	Hours	Rate	Deposit	Withdrawal
1					
2					
3					
4					
5					
		Total:			

SPIRITUAL CHALLENGES					
#	**Description**	**Hours**	**Rate**	**Deposit**	**Withdrawal**
1					
2					
3					
4					
5					
		Total:			

DAILY SUMMARY			
#	**Description**	**Yesterday's Balance**	**Add Today's Balance**
1	Financial		
2	Mental		
3	Physical		
4	Social		
5	Spiritual		
Total			

NOTES:____

____

____

____

____

____

AFFIRMATIONS:______________________________________

____

____

____

____

____

____

SIGNATURE:____________________________ DATE:________________

FINANCIAL CHALLENGES					
#	Description	Hours	Rate	Deposit	Withdrawal
1					
2					
3					
4					
5					
		Total:			

MENTAL CHALLENGES					
#	Description	Hours	Rate	Deposit	Withdrawal
1					
2					
3					
4					
5					
		Total:			

PHYSICAL CHALLENGES					
#	Description	Hours	Rate	Deposit	Withdrawal
1					
2					
3					
4					
5					
		Total:			

SOCIAL CHALLENGES					
#	Description	Hours	Rate	Deposit	Withdrawal
1					
2					
3					
4					
5					
		Total:			

SPIRITUAL CHALLENGES					
#	Description	Hours	Rate	Deposit	Withdrawal
1					
2					
3					
4					
5					
		Total:			

DAILY SUMMARY			
#	Description	Yesterday's Balance	Add Today's Balance
1	Financial		
2	Mental		
3	Physical		
4	Social		
5	Spiritual		
Total			

NOTES:____

____

____

____

____

____

AFFIRMATIONS:____

____

____

____

____

____

____

SIGNATURE:______________________________ DATE:________________

FINANCIAL CHALLENGES					
#	Description	Hours	Rate	Deposit	Withdrawal
1					
2					
3					
4					
5					
		Total:			

MENTAL CHALLENGES					
#	Description	Hours	Rate	Deposit	Withdrawal
1					
2					
3					
4					
5					
		Total:			

PHYSICAL CHALLENGES					
#	Description	Hours	Rate	Deposit	Withdrawal
1					
2					
3					
4					
5					
		Total:			

SOCIAL CHALLENGES					
#	Description	Hours	Rate	Deposit	Withdrawal
1					
2					
3					
4					
5					
		Total:			

Prodigy Planner Workbook

SPIRITUAL CHALLENGES					
#	Description	Hours	Rate	Deposit	Withdrawal
1					
2					
3					
4					
5					
		Total:			

DAILY SUMMARY			
#	Description	Yesterday's Balance	Add Today's Balance
1	Financial		
2	Mental		
3	Physical		
4	Social		
5	Spiritual		
Total			

NOTES:____

____

____

____

____

____

AFFIRMATIONS:____

____

____

____

____

____

____

SIGNATURE:______________________________ DATE:________________

FINANCIAL CHALLENGES					
#	Description	Hours	Rate	Deposit	Withdrawal
1					
2					
3					
4					
5					
		Total:			

MENTAL CHALLENGES					
#	Description	Hours	Rate	Deposit	Withdrawal
1					
2					
3					
4					
5					
		Total:			

PHYSICAL CHALLENGES					
#	Description	Hours	Rate	Deposit	Withdrawal
1					
2					
3					
4					
5					
		Total:			

SOCIAL CHALLENGES					
#	Description	Hours	Rate	Deposit	Withdrawal
1					
2					
3					
4					
5					
		Total:			

SPIRITUAL CHALLENGES					
#	Description	Hours	Rate	Deposit	Withdrawal
1					
2					
3					
4					
5					
		Total:			

DAILY SUMMARY			
#	Description	Yesterday's Balance	Add Today's Balance
1	Financial		
2	Mental		
3	Physical		
4	Social		
5	Spiritual		
Total			

NOTES:____

AFFIRMATIONS:____

SIGNATURE:______________________ DATE:______________

FINANCIAL CHALLENGES					
#	Description	Hours	Rate	Deposit	Withdrawal
1					
2					
3					
4					
5					
		Total:			

MENTAL CHALLENGES					
#	Description	Hours	Rate	Deposit	Withdrawal
1					
2					
3					
4					
5					
		Total:			

PHYSICAL CHALLENGES					
#	Description	Hours	Rate	Deposit	Withdrawal
1					
2					
3					
4					
5					
		Total:			

SOCIAL CHALLENGES					
#	Description	Hours	Rate	Deposit	Withdrawal
1					
2					
3					
4					
5					
		Total:			

SPIRITUAL CHALLENGES					
#	Description	Hours	Rate	Deposit	Withdrawal
1					
2					
3					
4					
5					
		Total:			

DAILY SUMMARY			
#	Description	Yesterday's Balance	Add Today's Balance
1	Financial		
2	Mental		
3	Physical		
4	Social		
5	Spiritual		
Total			

NOTES:____

____

____

____

____

____

AFFIRMATIONS:______________________________________

____

____

____

____

____

____

SIGNATURE:______________________________ DATE:________________

FINANCIAL CHALLENGES					
#	**Description**	**Hours**	**Rate**	**Deposit**	**Withdrawal**
1					
2					
3					
4					
5					
		Total:			

MENTAL CHALLENGES					
#	**Description**	**Hours**	**Rate**	**Deposit**	**Withdrawal**
1					
2					
3					
4					
5					
		Total:			

PHYSICAL CHALLENGES					
#	**Description**	**Hours**	**Rate**	**Deposit**	**Withdrawal**
1					
2					
3					
4					
5					
		Total:			

SOCIAL CHALLENGES					
#	**Description**	**Hours**	**Rate**	**Deposit**	**Withdrawal**
1					
2					
3					
4					
5					
		Total:			

SPIRITUAL CHALLENGES					
#	**Description**	**Hours**	**Rate**	**Deposit**	**Withdrawal**
1					
2					
3					
4					
5					
		Total:			

DAILY SUMMARY			
#	**Description**	**Yesterday's Balance**	**Add Today's Balance**
1	Financial		
2	Mental		
3	Physical		
4	Social		
5	Spiritual		
Total			

NOTES:____

AFFIRMATIONS:__________________________________

SIGNATURE:________________________ DATE:______________

FINANCIAL CHALLENGES					
#	Description	Hours	Rate	Deposit	Withdrawal
1					
2					
3					
4					
5					
		Total:			

MENTAL CHALLENGES					
#	Description	Hours	Rate	Deposit	Withdrawal
1					
2					
3					
4					
5					
		Total:			

PHYSICAL CHALLENGES					
#	Description	Hours	Rate	Deposit	Withdrawal
1					
2					
3					
4					
5					
		Total:			

SOCIAL CHALLENGES					
#	Description	Hours	Rate	Deposit	Withdrawal
1					
2					
3					
4					
5					
		Total:			

SPIRITUAL CHALLENGES					
#	**Description**	**Hours**	**Rate**	**Deposit**	**Withdrawal**
1					
2					
3					
4					
5					
		Total:			

DAILY SUMMARY			
#	**Description**	**Yesterday's Balance**	**Add Today's Balance**
1	Financial		
2	Mental		
3	Physical		
4	Social		
5	Spiritual		
Total			

NOTES:____

AFFIRMATIONS:__________________________________

SIGNATURE:____________________ DATE:____________

FINANCIAL CHALLENGES					
#	Description	Hours	Rate	Deposit	Withdrawal
1					
2					
3					
4					
5					
		Total:			

MENTAL CHALLENGES					
#	Description	Hours	Rate	Deposit	Withdrawal
1					
2					
3					
4					
5					
		Total:			

PHYSICAL CHALLENGES					
#	Description	Hours	Rate	Deposit	Withdrawal
1					
2					
3					
4					
5					
		Total:			

SOCIAL CHALLENGES					
#	Description	Hours	Rate	Deposit	Withdrawal
1					
2					
3					
4					
5					
		Total:			

SPIRITUAL CHALLENGES					
#	**Description**	**Hours**	**Rate**	**Deposit**	**Withdrawal**
1					
2					
3					
4					
5					
		Total:			

DAILY SUMMARY			
#	**Description**	**Yesterday's Balance**	**Add Today's Balance**
1	Financial		
2	Mental		
3	Physical		
4	Social		
5	Spiritual		
Total			

NOTES:____

AFFIRMATIONS:______________________________________

SIGNATURE:_________________________ DATE:______________

FINANCIAL CHALLENGES					
#	Description	Hours	Rate	Deposit	Withdrawal
1					
2					
3					
4					
5					
		Total:			

MENTAL CHALLENGES					
#	Description	Hours	Rate	Deposit	Withdrawal
1					
2					
3					
4					
5					
		Total:			

PHYSICAL CHALLENGES					
#	Description	Hours	Rate	Deposit	Withdrawal
1					
2					
3					
4					
5					
		Total:			

SOCIAL CHALLENGES					
#	Description	Hours	Rate	Deposit	Withdrawal
1					
2					
3					
4					
5					
		Total:			

Prodigy Planner Workbook

SPIRITUAL CHALLENGES					
#	Description	Hours	Rate	Deposit	Withdrawal
1					
2					
3					
4					
5					
			Total:		

DAILY SUMMARY			
#	Description	Yesterday's Balance	Add Today's Balance
1	Financial		
2	Mental		
3	Physical		
4	Social		
5	Spiritual		
Total			

NOTES:______________________________

AFFIRMATIONS:______________________________

SIGNATURE:______________________ DATE:______________

FINANCIAL CHALLENGES					
#	Description	Hours	Rate	Deposit	Withdrawal
1					
2					
3					
4					
5					
		Total:			

MENTAL CHALLENGES					
#	Description	Hours	Rate	Deposit	Withdrawal
1					
2					
3					
4					
5					
		Total:			

PHYSICAL CHALLENGES					
#	Description	Hours	Rate	Deposit	Withdrawal
1					
2					
3					
4					
5					
		Total:			

SOCIAL CHALLENGES					
#	Description	Hours	Rate	Deposit	Withdrawal
1					
2					
3					
4					
5					
		Total:			

Prodigy Planner Workbook

SPIRITUAL CHALLENGES					
#	Description	Hours	Rate	Deposit	Withdrawal
1					
2					
3					
4					
5					
		Total:			

DAILY SUMMARY			
#	Description	Yesterday's Balance	Add Today's Balance
1	Financial		
2	Mental		
3	Physical		
4	Social		
5	Spiritual		
Total			

NOTES:____

AFFIRMATIONS:________________________________

SIGNATURE:________________________ DATE:____________

FINANCIAL CHALLENGES					
#	Description	Hours	Rate	Deposit	Withdrawal
1					
2					
3					
4					
5					
		Total:			

MENTAL CHALLENGES					
#	Description	Hours	Rate	Deposit	Withdrawal
1					
2					
3					
4					
5					
		Total:			

PHYSICAL CHALLENGES					
#	Description	Hours	Rate	Deposit	Withdrawal
1					
2					
3					
4					
5					
		Total:			

SOCIAL CHALLENGES					
#	Description	Hours	Rate	Deposit	Withdrawal
1					
2					
3					
4					
5					
		Total:			

Prodigy Planner Workbook

SPIRITUAL CHALLENGES					
#	**Description**	**Hours**	**Rate**	**Deposit**	**Withdrawal**
1					
2					
3					
4					
5					
		Total:			

DAILY SUMMARY			
#	**Description**	**Yesterday's Balance**	**Add Today's Balance**
1	Financial		
2	Mental		
3	Physical		
4	Social		
5	Spiritual		
Total			

NOTES:____________________________________

AFFIRMATIONS:______________________________

SIGNATURE:____________________ DATE:____________

FINANCIAL CHALLENGES					
#	Description	Hours	Rate	Deposit	Withdrawal
1					
2					
3					
4					
5					
		Total:			

MENTAL CHALLENGES					
#	Description	Hours	Rate	Deposit	Withdrawal
1					
2					
3					
4					
5					
		Total:			

PHYSICAL CHALLENGES					
#	Description	Hours	Rate	Deposit	Withdrawal
1					
2					
3					
4					
5					
		Total:			

SOCIAL CHALLENGES					
#	Description	Hours	Rate	Deposit	Withdrawal
1					
2					
3					
4					
5					
		Total:			

SPIRITUAL CHALLENGES					
#	**Description**	**Hours**	**Rate**	**Deposit**	**Withdrawal**
1					
2					
3					
4					
5					
		Total:			

DAILY SUMMARY			
#	**Description**	**Yesterday's Balance**	**Add Today's Balance**
1	Financial		
2	Mental		
3	Physical		
4	Social		
5	Spiritual		
Total			

NOTES:____

AFFIRMATIONS:__________________________________

SIGNATURE:____________________ DATE:____________

FINANCIAL CHALLENGES					
#	Description	Hours	Rate	Deposit	Withdrawal
1					
2					
3					
4					
5					
		Total:			

MENTAL CHALLENGES					
#	Description	Hours	Rate	Deposit	Withdrawal
1					
2					
3					
4					
5					
		Total:			

PHYSICAL CHALLENGES					
#	Description	Hours	Rate	Deposit	Withdrawal
1					
2					
3					
4					
5					
		Total:			

SOCIAL CHALLENGES					
#	Description	Hours	Rate	Deposit	Withdrawal
1					
2					
3					
4					
5					
		Total:			

SPIRITUAL CHALLENGES					
#	Description	Hours	Rate	Deposit	Withdrawal
1					
2					
3					
4					
5					
			Total:		

DAILY SUMMARY			
#	Description	Yesterday's Balance	Add Today's Balance
1	Financial		
2	Mental		
3	Physical		
4	Social		
5	Spiritual		
Total			

NOTES:____

AFFIRMATIONS:__________________________________

SIGNATURE:________________________ DATE:____________

Prodigy Planner Workbook

FINANCIAL CHALLENGES					
#	**Description**	**Hours**	**Rate**	**Deposit**	**Withdrawal**
1					
2					
3					
4					
5					
		Total:			

MENTAL CHALLENGES					
#	**Description**	**Hours**	**Rate**	**Deposit**	**Withdrawal**
1					
2					
3					
4					
5					
		Total:			

PHYSICAL CHALLENGES					
#	**Description**	**Hours**	**Rate**	**Deposit**	**Withdrawal**
1					
2					
3					
4					
5					
		Total:			

SOCIAL CHALLENGES					
#	**Description**	**Hours**	**Rate**	**Deposit**	**Withdrawal**
1					
2					
3					
4					
5					
		Total:			

Prodigy Planner Workbook

SPIRITUAL CHALLENGES					
#	**Description**	**Hours**	**Rate**	**Deposit**	**Withdrawal**
1					
2					
3					
4					
5					
		Total:			

DAILY SUMMARY			
#	**Description**	**Yesterday's Balance**	**Add Today's Balance**
1	Financial		
2	Mental		
3	Physical		
4	Social		
5	Spiritual		
Total			

NOTES:____

____

____

____

____

____

AFFIRMATIONS:______________________________________

____

____

____

____

____

____

SIGNATURE:______________________ DATE:____________

FINANCIAL CHALLENGES					
#	Description	Hours	Rate	Deposit	Withdrawal
1					
2					
3					
4					
5					
		Total:			

MENTAL CHALLENGES					
#	Description	Hours	Rate	Deposit	Withdrawal
1					
2					
3					
4					
5					
		Total:			

PHYSICAL CHALLENGES					
#	Description	Hours	Rate	Deposit	Withdrawal
1					
2					
3					
4					
5					
		Total:			

SOCIAL CHALLENGES					
#	Description	Hours	Rate	Deposit	Withdrawal
1					
2					
3					
4					
5					
		Total:			

SPIRITUAL CHALLENGES					
#	Description	Hours	Rate	Deposit	Withdrawal
1					
2					
3					
4					
5					
		Total:			

DAILY SUMMARY			
#	Description	Yesterday's Balance	Add Today's Balance
1	Financial		
2	Mental		
3	Physical		
4	Social		
5	Spiritual		
Total			

NOTES:____

____

____

____

____

____

AFFIRMATIONS:____

____

____

____

____

____

____

SIGNATURE:______________________ DATE:______________

WEALTH LEVEL 1 - Essentials		
#	**Description**	**Deposit**
1	Have Earned Income	
2	Have Investment Income	
3	Have Leveraged Income	
4	Have Residual Income	
5	Have More Than One Type Of Income	

WEALTH LEVEL 2 - Fundamentals		
#	**Description**	**Deposit**
1	10% Of Income Saved Upon Payment	
2	6-Month Emergency Cash Fund Reserved	
3	1-Year Emergency Electronic Fund Reserved	
4	All Monthly Bills Are Paid On Time	
5	Bills Do Not Exceed 50% Of Monthly Income	
6	No Debt – With Exception Of Mortgage	

WEALTH LEVEL 3 - Safety Net		
#	**Description**	**Deposit**
1	Life Insurance – All Dependents	
2	Medical Insurance – All Dependents	
3	Disability Insurance – If Not Retired	
4	Dental Insurance – All Dependents	
5	Optical Insurance - All Dependents	
6	Long Term Care Insurance – If Retired	
7	Umbrella Insurance	
8	Property Insurance – Homeowner/Renters	
9	Auto Insurance	
10	Filed All Bills & Receipts	

WEALTH LEVEL 4 - Look Good On Paper		
#	**Description**	**Deposit**
1	Have A Credit Score Above 760	
2	Have A Secured Credit Cards Only	
3	10% Of Income Invested Upon Payment	
4	Monitor Your Credit Report Monthly	
WEALTH LEVEL 5 - Sustainability		
#	**Description**	**Deposit**
1	Sustainable Power Supply – No Bill	
2	Sustainable Water Supply – No Bill	
3	Recycle & Eliminate Own Waste	
4	Have No Mortgage Or Rent Bill	
5	20-Year Property Tax Funds Reserved	
6	Homestead	
	Total:	

NOTES:____

AFFIRMATIONS:____________________________________

SIGNATURE:________________________ DATE:______________

FINANCIAL CHALLENGES					
#	Description	Hours	Rate	Deposit	Withdrawal
1					
2					
3					
4					
5					
		Total:			

MENTAL CHALLENGES					
#	Description	Hours	Rate	Deposit	Withdrawal
1					
2					
3					
4					
5					
		Total:			

PHYSICAL CHALLENGES					
#	Description	Hours	Rate	Deposit	Withdrawal
1					
2					
3					
4					
5					
		Total:			

SOCIAL CHALLENGES					
#	Description	Hours	Rate	Deposit	Withdrawal
1					
2					
3					
4					
5					
		Total:			

SPIRITUAL CHALLENGES					
#	Description	Hours	Rate	Deposit	Withdrawal
1					
2					
3					
4					
5					
		Total:			

DAILY SUMMARY			
#	Description	Yesterday's Balance	Add Today's Balance
1	Financial		
2	Mental		
3	Physical		
4	Social		
5	Spiritual		
Monthly Wealth Bonus			
Total			

NOTES:____

____

____

____

____

____

AFFIRMATIONS:____

____

____

____

____

____

SIGNATURE:______________________________ DATE:________________

FINANCIAL CHALLENGES					
#	Description	Hours	Rate	Deposit	Withdrawal
1					
2					
3					
4					
5					
		Total:			

MENTAL CHALLENGES					
#	Description	Hours	Rate	Deposit	Withdrawal
1					
2					
3					
4					
5					
		Total:			

PHYSICAL CHALLENGES					
#	Description	Hours	Rate	Deposit	Withdrawal
1					
2					
3					
4					
5					
		Total:			

SOCIAL CHALLENGES					
#	Description	Hours	Rate	Deposit	Withdrawal
1					
2					
3					
4					
5					
		Total:			

SPIRITUAL CHALLENGES					
#	Description	Hours	Rate	Deposit	Withdrawal
1					
2					
3					
4					
5					
		Total:			

DAILY SUMMARY			
#	Description	Yesterday's Balance	Add Today's Balance
1	Financial		
2	Mental		
3	Physical		
4	Social		
5	Spiritual		
Total			

NOTES:____

AFFIRMATIONS:__________________________________

SIGNATURE:________________________ DATE:______________

FINANCIAL CHALLENGES					
#	Description	Hours	Rate	Deposit	Withdrawal
1					
2					
3					
4					
5					
		Total:			

MENTAL CHALLENGES					
#	Description	Hours	Rate	Deposit	Withdrawal
1					
2					
3					
4					
5					
		Total:			

PHYSICAL CHALLENGES					
#	Description	Hours	Rate	Deposit	Withdrawal
1					
2					
3					
4					
5					
		Total:			

SOCIAL CHALLENGES					
#	Description	Hours	Rate	Deposit	Withdrawal
1					
2					
3					
4					
5					
		Total:			

SPIRITUAL CHALLENGES					
#	Description	Hours	Rate	Deposit	Withdrawal
1					
2					
3					
4					
5					
		Total:			

DAILY SUMMARY			
#	Description	Yesterday's Balance	Add Today's Balance
1	Financial		
2	Mental		
3	Physical		
4	Social		
5	Spiritual		
Total			

NOTES:____

AFFIRMATIONS:__________________________________

SIGNATURE:____________________ DATE:____________

FINANCIAL CHALLENGES					
#	Description	Hours	Rate	Deposit	Withdrawal
1					
2					
3					
4					
5					
		Total:			

MENTAL CHALLENGES					
#	Description	Hours	Rate	Deposit	Withdrawal
1					
2					
3					
4					
5					
		Total:			

PHYSICAL CHALLENGES					
#	Description	Hours	Rate	Deposit	Withdrawal
1					
2					
3					
4					
5					
		Total:			

SOCIAL CHALLENGES					
#	Description	Hours	Rate	Deposit	Withdrawal
1					
2					
3					
4					
5					
		Total:			

Prodigy Planner Workbook

SPIRITUAL CHALLENGES					
#	Description	Hours	Rate	Deposit	Withdrawal
1					
2					
3					
4					
5					
		Total:			

DAILY SUMMARY			
#	Description	Yesterday's Balance	Add Today's Balance
1	Financial		
2	Mental		
3	Physical		
4	Social		
5	Spiritual		
Total			

NOTES:____

____

____

____

____

____

AFFIRMATIONS:____

____

____

____

____

____

____

SIGNATURE:______________________________ DATE:________________

FINANCIAL CHALLENGES					
#	Description	Hours	Rate	Deposit	Withdrawal
1					
2					
3					
4					
5					
		Total:			

MENTAL CHALLENGES					
#	Description	Hours	Rate	Deposit	Withdrawal
1					
2					
3					
4					
5					
		Total:			

PHYSICAL CHALLENGES					
#	Description	Hours	Rate	Deposit	Withdrawal
1					
2					
3					
4					
5					
		Total:			

SOCIAL CHALLENGES					
#	Description	Hours	Rate	Deposit	Withdrawal
1					
2					
3					
4					
5					
		Total:			

SPIRITUAL CHALLENGES					
#	**Description**	**Hours**	**Rate**	**Deposit**	**Withdrawal**
1					
2					
3					
4					
5					
		Total:			

DAILY SUMMARY			
#	**Description**	**Yesterday's Balance**	**Add Today's Balance**
1	Financial		
2	Mental		
3	Physical		
4	Social		
5	Spiritual		
Total			

NOTES:____

AFFIRMATIONS:____________________________________

SIGNATURE:________________________ DATE:______________

FINANCIAL CHALLENGES					
#	Description	Hours	Rate	Deposit	Withdrawal
1					
2					
3					
4					
5					
		Total:			

MENTAL CHALLENGES					
#	Description	Hours	Rate	Deposit	Withdrawal
1					
2					
3					
4					
5					
		Total:			

PHYSICAL CHALLENGES					
#	Description	Hours	Rate	Deposit	Withdrawal
1					
2					
3					
4					
5					
		Total:			

SOCIAL CHALLENGES					
#	Description	Hours	Rate	Deposit	Withdrawal
1					
2					
3					
4					
5					
		Total:			

Prodigy Planner Workbook

SPIRITUAL CHALLENGES					
#	Description	Hours	Rate	Deposit	Withdrawal
1					
2					
3					
4					
5					
		Total:			

DAILY SUMMARY			
#	Description	Yesterday's Balance	Add Today's Balance
1	Financial		
2	Mental		
3	Physical		
4	Social		
5	Spiritual		
Total			

NOTES:____

AFFIRMATIONS:____

SIGNATURE:__________________________ DATE:_______________

FINANCIAL CHALLENGES					
#	Description	Hours	Rate	Deposit	Withdrawal
1					
2					
3					
4					
5					
		Total:			

MENTAL CHALLENGES					
#	Description	Hours	Rate	Deposit	Withdrawal
1					
2					
3					
4					
5					
		Total:			

PHYSICAL CHALLENGES					
#	Description	Hours	Rate	Deposit	Withdrawal
1					
2					
3					
4					
5					
		Total:			

SOCIAL CHALLENGES					
#	Description	Hours	Rate	Deposit	Withdrawal
1					
2					
3					
4					
5					
		Total:			

SPIRITUAL CHALLENGES					
#	**Description**	**Hours**	**Rate**	**Deposit**	**Withdrawal**
1					
2					
3					
4					
5					
		Total:			

DAILY SUMMARY			
#	**Description**	**Yesterday's Balance**	**Add Today's Balance**
1	Financial		
2	Mental		
3	Physical		
4	Social		
5	Spiritual		
Total			

NOTES:____

AFFIRMATIONS:__________________________________

SIGNATURE:________________________ DATE:____________

Prodigy Planner Workbook

FINANCIAL CHALLENGES					
#	**Description**	**Hours**	**Rate**	**Deposit**	**Withdrawal**
1					
2					
3					
4					
5					
		Total:			

MENTAL CHALLENGES					
#	**Description**	**Hours**	**Rate**	**Deposit**	**Withdrawal**
1					
2					
3					
4					
5					
		Total:			

PHYSICAL CHALLENGES					
#	**Description**	**Hours**	**Rate**	**Deposit**	**Withdrawal**
1					
2					
3					
4					
5					
		Total:			

SOCIAL CHALLENGES					
#	**Description**	**Hours**	**Rate**	**Deposit**	**Withdrawal**
1					
2					
3					
4					
5					
		Total:			

Prodigy Planner Workbook

SPIRITUAL CHALLENGES					
#	Description	Hours	Rate	Deposit	Withdrawal
1					
2					
3					
4					
5					
		Total:			

DAILY SUMMARY			
#	Description	Yesterday's Balance	Add Today's Balance
1	Financial		
2	Mental		
3	Physical		
4	Social		
5	Spiritual		
Total			

NOTES:____

____

____

____

____

____

AFFIRMATIONS:____

____

____

____

____

____

____

SIGNATURE:______________________________ DATE:________________

Prodigy Planner Workbook

FINANCIAL CHALLENGES					
#	**Description**	**Hours**	**Rate**	**Deposit**	**Withdrawal**
1					
2					
3					
4					
5					
		Total:			

MENTAL CHALLENGES					
#	**Description**	**Hours**	**Rate**	**Deposit**	**Withdrawal**
1					
2					
3					
4					
5					
		Total:			

PHYSICAL CHALLENGES					
#	**Description**	**Hours**	**Rate**	**Deposit**	**Withdrawal**
1					
2					
3					
4					
5					
		Total:			

SOCIAL CHALLENGES					
#	**Description**	**Hours**	**Rate**	**Deposit**	**Withdrawal**
1					
2					
3					
4					
5					
		Total:			

SPIRITUAL CHALLENGES					
#	**Description**	**Hours**	**Rate**	**Deposit**	**Withdrawal**
1					
2					
3					
4					
5					
		Total:			

DAILY SUMMARY			
#	**Description**	**Yesterday's Balance**	**Add Today's Balance**
1	Financial		
2	Mental		
3	Physical		
4	Social		
5	Spiritual		
Total			

NOTES:____

____

____

____

____

____

AFFIRMATIONS:______________________________________

____

____

____

____

____

____

SIGNATURE:______________________________ DATE:________________

FINANCIAL CHALLENGES					
#	Description	Hours	Rate	Deposit	Withdrawal
1					
2					
3					
4					
5					
		Total:			

MENTAL CHALLENGES					
#	Description	Hours	Rate	Deposit	Withdrawal
1					
2					
3					
4					
5					
		Total:			

PHYSICAL CHALLENGES					
#	Description	Hours	Rate	Deposit	Withdrawal
1					
2					
3					
4					
5					
		Total:			

SOCIAL CHALLENGES					
#	Description	Hours	Rate	Deposit	Withdrawal
1					
2					
3					
4					
5					
		Total:			

SPIRITUAL CHALLENGES					
#	Description	Hours	Rate	Deposit	Withdrawal
1					
2					
3					
4					
5					
		Total:			

DAILY SUMMARY			
#	Description	Yesterday's Balance	Add Today's Balance
1	Financial		
2	Mental		
3	Physical		
4	Social		
5	Spiritual		
Total			

NOTES:____

____

____

____

____

____

AFFIRMATIONS:____

____

____

____

____

____

____

SIGNATURE:____________________________ DATE:______________

FINANCIAL CHALLENGES					
#	Description	Hours	Rate	Deposit	Withdrawal
1					
2					
3					
4					
5					
		Total:			

MENTAL CHALLENGES					
#	Description	Hours	Rate	Deposit	Withdrawal
1					
2					
3					
4					
5					
		Total:			

PHYSICAL CHALLENGES					
#	Description	Hours	Rate	Deposit	Withdrawal
1					
2					
3					
4					
5					
		Total:			

SOCIAL CHALLENGES					
#	Description	Hours	Rate	Deposit	Withdrawal
1					
2					
3					
4					
5					
		Total:			

SPIRITUAL CHALLENGES					
#	Description	Hours	Rate	Deposit	Withdrawal
1					
2					
3					
4					
5					
		Total:			

DAILY SUMMARY			
#	Description	Yesterday's Balance	Add Today's Balance
1	Financial		
2	Mental		
3	Physical		
4	Social		
5	Spiritual		
Total			

NOTES:____

AFFIRMATIONS:__________________________________

SIGNATURE:________________________ DATE:____________

FINANCIAL CHALLENGES					
#	Description	Hours	Rate	Deposit	Withdrawal
1					
2					
3					
4					
5					
		Total:			

MENTAL CHALLENGES					
#	Description	Hours	Rate	Deposit	Withdrawal
1					
2					
3					
4					
5					
		Total:			

PHYSICAL CHALLENGES					
#	Description	Hours	Rate	Deposit	Withdrawal
1					
2					
3					
4					
5					
		Total:			

SOCIAL CHALLENGES					
#	Description	Hours	Rate	Deposit	Withdrawal
1					
2					
3					
4					
5					
		Total:			

SPIRITUAL CHALLENGES					
#	Description	Hours	Rate	Deposit	Withdrawal
1					
2					
3					
4					
5					
		Total:			

DAILY SUMMARY			
#	Description	Yesterday's Balance	Add Today's Balance
1	Financial		
2	Mental		
3	Physical		
4	Social		
5	Spiritual		
Total			

NOTES:____

AFFIRMATIONS:__________________________________

SIGNATURE:______________________ DATE:____________

Prodigy Planner Workbook

FINANCIAL CHALLENGES					
#	**Description**	**Hours**	**Rate**	**Deposit**	**Withdrawal**
1					
2					
3					
4					
5					
		Total:			

MENTAL CHALLENGES					
#	**Description**	**Hours**	**Rate**	**Deposit**	**Withdrawal**
1					
2					
3					
4					
5					
		Total:			

PHYSICAL CHALLENGES					
#	**Description**	**Hours**	**Rate**	**Deposit**	**Withdrawal**
1					
2					
3					
4					
5					
		Total:			

SOCIAL CHALLENGES					
#	**Description**	**Hours**	**Rate**	**Deposit**	**Withdrawal**
1					
2					
3					
4					
5					
		Total:			

SPIRITUAL CHALLENGES					
#	Description	Hours	Rate	Deposit	Withdrawal
1					
2					
3					
4					
5					
		Total:			

DAILY SUMMARY			
#	Description	Yesterday's Balance	Add Today's Balance
1	Financial		
2	Mental		
3	Physical		
4	Social		
5	Spiritual		
Total			

NOTES:____

AFFIRMATIONS:__________________________________

SIGNATURE:______________________ DATE:____________

FINANCIAL CHALLENGES					
#	Description	Hours	Rate	Deposit	Withdrawal
1					
2					
3					
4					
5					
			Total:		

MENTAL CHALLENGES					
#	Description	Hours	Rate	Deposit	Withdrawal
1					
2					
3					
4					
5					
			Total:		

PHYSICAL CHALLENGES					
#	Description	Hours	Rate	Deposit	Withdrawal
1					
2					
3					
4					
5					
			Total:		

SOCIAL CHALLENGES					
#	Description	Hours	Rate	Deposit	Withdrawal
1					
2					
3					
4					
5					
			Total:		

SPIRITUAL CHALLENGES					
#	**Description**	**Hours**	**Rate**	**Deposit**	**Withdrawal**
1					
2					
3					
4					
5					
			Total:		

DAILY SUMMARY			
#	**Description**	**Yesterday's Balance**	**Add Today's Balance**
1	Financial		
2	Mental		
3	Physical		
4	Social		
5	Spiritual		
	Total		

NOTES:____

AFFIRMATIONS:__________________________________

SIGNATURE:________________________ DATE:____________

FINANCIAL CHALLENGES					
#	Description	Hours	Rate	Deposit	Withdrawal
1					
2					
3					
4					
5					
		Total:			

MENTAL CHALLENGES					
#	Description	Hours	Rate	Deposit	Withdrawal
1					
2					
3					
4					
5					
		Total:			

PHYSICAL CHALLENGES					
#	Description	Hours	Rate	Deposit	Withdrawal
1					
2					
3					
4					
5					
		Total:			

SOCIAL CHALLENGES					
#	Description	Hours	Rate	Deposit	Withdrawal
1					
2					
3					
4					
5					
		Total:			

SPIRITUAL CHALLENGES					
#	Description	Hours	Rate	Deposit	Withdrawal
1					
2					
3					
4					
5					
		Total:			

DAILY SUMMARY			
#	Description	Yesterday's Balance	Add Today's Balance
1	Financial		
2	Mental		
3	Physical		
4	Social		
5	Spiritual		
Total			

NOTES:____

AFFIRMATIONS:____

SIGNATURE:_________________________ DATE:______________

FINANCIAL CHALLENGES					
#	Description	Hours	Rate	Deposit	Withdrawal
1					
2					
3					
4					
5					
		Total:			

MENTAL CHALLENGES					
#	Description	Hours	Rate	Deposit	Withdrawal
1					
2					
3					
4					
5					
		Total:			

PHYSICAL CHALLENGES					
#	Description	Hours	Rate	Deposit	Withdrawal
1					
2					
3					
4					
5					
		Total:			

SOCIAL CHALLENGES					
#	Description	Hours	Rate	Deposit	Withdrawal
1					
2					
3					
4					
5					
		Total:			

SPIRITUAL CHALLENGES					
#	**Description**	**Hours**	**Rate**	**Deposit**	**Withdrawal**
1					
2					
3					
4					
5					
		Total:			

DAILY SUMMARY			
#	**Description**	**Yesterday's Balance**	**Add Today's Balance**
1	Financial		
2	Mental		
3	Physical		
4	Social		
5	Spiritual		
Total			

NOTES:____

AFFIRMATIONS:____________________________________

SIGNATURE:______________________ DATE:____________

FINANCIAL CHALLENGES					
#	Description	Hours	Rate	Deposit	Withdrawal
1					
2					
3					
4					
5					
		Total:			

MENTAL CHALLENGES					
#	Description	Hours	Rate	Deposit	Withdrawal
1					
2					
3					
4					
5					
		Total:			

PHYSICAL CHALLENGES					
#	Description	Hours	Rate	Deposit	Withdrawal
1					
2					
3					
4					
5					
		Total:			

SOCIAL CHALLENGES					
#	Description	Hours	Rate	Deposit	Withdrawal
1					
2					
3					
4					
5					
		Total:			

SPIRITUAL CHALLENGES					
#	Description	Hours	Rate	Deposit	Withdrawal
1					
2					
3					
4					
5					
		Total:			

DAILY SUMMARY			
#	Description	Yesterday's Balance	Add Today's Balance
1	Financial		
2	Mental		
3	Physical		
4	Social		
5	Spiritual		
Total			

NOTES:______________________________

AFFIRMATIONS:______________________________

SIGNATURE:____________________ DATE:____________

FINANCIAL CHALLENGES					
#	Description	Hours	Rate	Deposit	Withdrawal
1					
2					
3					
4					
5					
		Total:			

MENTAL CHALLENGES					
#	Description	Hours	Rate	Deposit	Withdrawal
1					
2					
3					
4					
5					
		Total:			

PHYSICAL CHALLENGES					
#	Description	Hours	Rate	Deposit	Withdrawal
1					
2					
3					
4					
5					
		Total:			

SOCIAL CHALLENGES					
#	Description	Hours	Rate	Deposit	Withdrawal
1					
2					
3					
4					
5					
		Total:			

Prodigy Planner Workbook

SPIRITUAL CHALLENGES					
#	Description	Hours	Rate	Deposit	Withdrawal
1					
2					
3					
4					
5					
		Total:			

DAILY SUMMARY			
#	Description	Yesterday's Balance	Add Today's Balance
1	Financial		
2	Mental		
3	Physical		
4	Social		
5	Spiritual		
Total			

NOTES:____

____

____

____

____

____

AFFIRMATIONS:______________________________________

____

____

____

____

____

____

SIGNATURE:______________________________ DATE:________________

FINANCIAL CHALLENGES					
#	Description	Hours	Rate	Deposit	Withdrawal
1					
2					
3					
4					
5					
		Total:			

MENTAL CHALLENGES					
#	Description	Hours	Rate	Deposit	Withdrawal
1					
2					
3					
4					
5					
		Total:			

PHYSICAL CHALLENGES					
#	Description	Hours	Rate	Deposit	Withdrawal
1					
2					
3					
4					
5					
		Total:			

SOCIAL CHALLENGES					
#	Description	Hours	Rate	Deposit	Withdrawal
1					
2					
3					
4					
5					
		Total:			

SPIRITUAL CHALLENGES					
#	Description	Hours	Rate	Deposit	Withdrawal
1					
2					
3					
4					
5					
		Total:			

DAILY SUMMARY			
#	Description	Yesterday's Balance	Add Today's Balance
1	Financial		
2	Mental		
3	Physical		
4	Social		
5	Spiritual		
Total			

NOTES:____

AFFIRMATIONS:____________________________________

SIGNATURE:________________________ DATE:______________

FINANCIAL CHALLENGES					
#	Description	Hours	Rate	Deposit	Withdrawal
1					
2					
3					
4					
5					
		Total:			

MENTAL CHALLENGES					
#	Description	Hours	Rate	Deposit	Withdrawal
1					
2					
3					
4					
5					
		Total:			

PHYSICAL CHALLENGES					
#	Description	Hours	Rate	Deposit	Withdrawal
1					
2					
3					
4					
5					
		Total:			

SOCIAL CHALLENGES					
#	Description	Hours	Rate	Deposit	Withdrawal
1					
2					
3					
4					
5					
		Total:			

Prodigy Planner Workbook

SPIRITUAL CHALLENGES					
#	**Description**	**Hours**	**Rate**	**Deposit**	**Withdrawal**
1					
2					
3					
4					
5					
		Total:			

DAILY SUMMARY			
#	**Description**	**Yesterday's Balance**	**Add Today's Balance**
1	Financial		
2	Mental		
3	Physical		
4	Social		
5	Spiritual		
Total			

NOTES:____

____

____

____

____

____

AFFIRMATIONS:______________________________________

____

____

____

____

____

____

SIGNATURE:_____________________________ DATE:______________

FINANCIAL CHALLENGES					
#	Description	Hours	Rate	Deposit	Withdrawal
1					
2					
3					
4					
5					
		Total:			

MENTAL CHALLENGES					
#	Description	Hours	Rate	Deposit	Withdrawal
1					
2					
3					
4					
5					
		Total:			

PHYSICAL CHALLENGES					
#	Description	Hours	Rate	Deposit	Withdrawal
1					
2					
3					
4					
5					
		Total:			

SOCIAL CHALLENGES					
#	Description	Hours	Rate	Deposit	Withdrawal
1					
2					
3					
4					
5					
		Total:			

SPIRITUAL CHALLENGES					
#	Description	Hours	Rate	Deposit	Withdrawal
1					
2					
3					
4					
5					
		Total:			

DAILY SUMMARY			
#	Description	Yesterday's Balance	Add Today's Balance
1	Financial		
2	Mental		
3	Physical		
4	Social		
5	Spiritual		
Total			

NOTES:____

AFFIRMATIONS:_______________________________________

SIGNATURE:____________________ DATE:______________

FINANCIAL CHALLENGES					
#	Description	Hours	Rate	Deposit	Withdrawal
1					
2					
3					
4					
5					
		Total:			

MENTAL CHALLENGES					
#	Description	Hours	Rate	Deposit	Withdrawal
1					
2					
3					
4					
5					
		Total:			

PHYSICAL CHALLENGES					
#	Description	Hours	Rate	Deposit	Withdrawal
1					
2					
3					
4					
5					
		Total:			

SOCIAL CHALLENGES					
#	Description	Hours	Rate	Deposit	Withdrawal
1					
2					
3					
4					
5					
		Total:			

Prodigy Planner Workbook

SPIRITUAL CHALLENGES					
#	Description	Hours	Rate	Deposit	Withdrawal
1					
2					
3					
4					
5					
		Total:			

DAILY SUMMARY			
#	Description	Yesterday's Balance	Add Today's Balance
1	Financial		
2	Mental		
3	Physical		
4	Social		
5	Spiritual		
Total			

NOTES:____

AFFIRMATIONS:________________________________

SIGNATURE:____________________ DATE:____________

FINANCIAL CHALLENGES					
#	Description	Hours	Rate	Deposit	Withdrawal
1					
2					
3					
4					
5					
		Total:			

MENTAL CHALLENGES					
#	Description	Hours	Rate	Deposit	Withdrawal
1					
2					
3					
4					
5					
		Total:			

PHYSICAL CHALLENGES					
#	Description	Hours	Rate	Deposit	Withdrawal
1					
2					
3					
4					
5					
		Total:			

SOCIAL CHALLENGES					
#	Description	Hours	Rate	Deposit	Withdrawal
1					
2					
3					
4					
5					
		Total:			

SPIRITUAL CHALLENGES					
#	Description	Hours	Rate	Deposit	Withdrawal
1					
2					
3					
4					
5					
		Total:			

DAILY SUMMARY			
#	Description	Yesterday's Balance	Add Today's Balance
1	Financial		
2	Mental		
3	Physical		
4	Social		
5	Spiritual		
Total			

NOTES:____

____

____

____

____

____

AFFIRMATIONS:______________________________________

____

____

____

____

____

____

SIGNATURE:_________________________ DATE:______________

FINANCIAL CHALLENGES					
#	Description	Hours	Rate	Deposit	Withdrawal
1					
2					
3					
4					
5					
		Total:			

MENTAL CHALLENGES					
#	Description	Hours	Rate	Deposit	Withdrawal
1					
2					
3					
4					
5					
		Total:			

PHYSICAL CHALLENGES					
#	Description	Hours	Rate	Deposit	Withdrawal
1					
2					
3					
4					
5					
		Total:			

SOCIAL CHALLENGES					
#	Description	Hours	Rate	Deposit	Withdrawal
1					
2					
3					
4					
5					
		Total:			

SPIRITUAL CHALLENGES					
#	Description	Hours	Rate	Deposit	Withdrawal
1					
2					
3					
4					
5					
		Total:			

DAILY SUMMARY			
#	Description	Yesterday's Balance	Add Today's Balance
1	Financial		
2	Mental		
3	Physical		
4	Social		
5	Spiritual		
Total			

NOTES:______________________________

AFFIRMATIONS:______________________________

SIGNATURE:____________________ DATE:______________

FINANCIAL CHALLENGES					
#	Description	Hours	Rate	Deposit	Withdrawal
1					
2					
3					
4					
5					
		Total:			

MENTAL CHALLENGES					
#	Description	Hours	Rate	Deposit	Withdrawal
1					
2					
3					
4					
5					
		Total:			

PHYSICAL CHALLENGES					
#	Description	Hours	Rate	Deposit	Withdrawal
1					
2					
3					
4					
5					
		Total:			

SOCIAL CHALLENGES					
#	Description	Hours	Rate	Deposit	Withdrawal
1					
2					
3					
4					
5					
		Total:			

SPIRITUAL CHALLENGES					
#	Description	Hours	Rate	Deposit	Withdrawal
1					
2					
3					
4					
5					
		Total:			

DAILY SUMMARY			
#	Description	Yesterday's Balance	Add Today's Balance
1	Financial		
2	Mental		
3	Physical		
4	Social		
5	Spiritual		
Total			

NOTES:______________________________

AFFIRMATIONS:______________________________

SIGNATURE:____________________ DATE:______________

FINANCIAL CHALLENGES					
#	Description	Hours	Rate	Deposit	Withdrawal
1					
2					
3					
4					
5					
		Total:			

MENTAL CHALLENGES					
#	Description	Hours	Rate	Deposit	Withdrawal
1					
2					
3					
4					
5					
		Total:			

PHYSICAL CHALLENGES					
#	Description	Hours	Rate	Deposit	Withdrawal
1					
2					
3					
4					
5					
		Total:			

SOCIAL CHALLENGES					
#	Description	Hours	Rate	Deposit	Withdrawal
1					
2					
3					
4					
5					
		Total:			

Prodigy Planner Workbook

SPIRITUAL CHALLENGES					
#	Description	Hours	Rate	Deposit	Withdrawal
1					
2					
3					
4					
5					
		Total:			

DAILY SUMMARY			
#	Description	Yesterday's Balance	Add Today's Balance
1	Financial		
2	Mental		
3	Physical		
4	Social		
5	Spiritual		
Total			

NOTES:____

AFFIRMATIONS:____________________________________

SIGNATURE:____________________________ DATE:________________

FINANCIAL CHALLENGES					
#	Description	Hours	Rate	Deposit	Withdrawal
1					
2					
3					
4					
5					
		Total:			

MENTAL CHALLENGES					
#	Description	Hours	Rate	Deposit	Withdrawal
1					
2					
3					
4					
5					
		Total:			

PHYSICAL CHALLENGES					
#	Description	Hours	Rate	Deposit	Withdrawal
1					
2					
3					
4					
5					
		Total:			

SOCIAL CHALLENGES					
#	Description	Hours	Rate	Deposit	Withdrawal
1					
2					
3					
4					
5					
		Total:			

SPIRITUAL CHALLENGES					
#	Description	Hours	Rate	Deposit	Withdrawal
1					
2					
3					
4					
5					
		Total:			

DAILY SUMMARY			
#	Description	Yesterday's Balance	Add Today's Balance
1	Financial		
2	Mental		
3	Physical		
4	Social		
5	Spiritual		
Total			

NOTES:____

AFFIRMATIONS:__________________________________

SIGNATURE:________________________ DATE:______________

FINANCIAL CHALLENGES					
#	Description	Hours	Rate	Deposit	Withdrawal
1					
2					
3					
4					
5					
		Total:			

MENTAL CHALLENGES					
#	Description	Hours	Rate	Deposit	Withdrawal
1					
2					
3					
4					
5					
		Total:			

PHYSICAL CHALLENGES					
#	Description	Hours	Rate	Deposit	Withdrawal
1					
2					
3					
4					
5					
		Total:			

SOCIAL CHALLENGES					
#	Description	Hours	Rate	Deposit	Withdrawal
1					
2					
3					
4					
5					
		Total:			

Prodigy Planner Workbook

SPIRITUAL CHALLENGES					
#	**Description**	**Hours**	**Rate**	**Deposit**	**Withdrawal**
1					
2					
3					
4					
5					
		Total:			

DAILY SUMMARY			
#	**Description**	**Yesterday's Balance**	**Add Today's Balance**
1	Financial		
2	Mental		
3	Physical		
4	Social		
5	Spiritual		
Total			

NOTES:____

____

____

____

____

____

AFFIRMATIONS:____

____

____

____

____

____

____

SIGNATURE:______________________________ DATE:________________

WEALTH LEVEL 1 - Essentials		
#	**Description**	**Deposit**
1	Have Earned Income	
2	Have Investment Income	
3	Have Leveraged Income	
4	Have Residual Income	
5	Have More Than One Type Of Income	

WEALTH LEVEL 2 - Fundamentals		
#	**Description**	**Deposit**
1	10% Of Income Saved Upon Payment	
2	6-Month Emergency Cash Fund Reserved	
3	1-Year Emergency Electronic Fund Reserved	
4	All Monthly Bills Are Paid On Time	
5	Bills Do Not Exceed 50% Of Monthly Income	
6	No Debt – With Exception Of Mortgage	

WEALTH LEVEL 3 - Safety Net		
#	**Description**	**Deposit**
1	Life Insurance – All Dependents	
2	Medical Insurance – All Dependents	
3	Disability Insurance – If Not Retired	
4	Dental Insurance – All Dependents	
5	Optical Insurance - All Dependents	
6	Long Term Care Insurance – If Retired	
7	Umbrella Insurance	
8	Property Insurance – Homeowner/Renters	
9	Auto Insurance	
10	Filed All Bills & Receipts	

WEALTH LEVEL 4 - Look Good On Paper		
#	**Description**	**Deposit**
1	Have A Credit Score Above 760	
2	Have A Secured Credit Cards Only	
3	10% Of Income Invested Upon Payment	
4	Monitor Your Credit Report Monthly	
WEALTH LEVEL 5 - Sustainability		
#	**Description**	**Deposit**
1	Sustainable Power Supply – No Bill	
2	Sustainable Water Supply – No Bill	
3	Recycle & Eliminate Own Waste	
4	Have No Mortgage Or Rent Bill	
5	20-Year Property Tax Funds Reserved	
6	Homestead	
	Total:	

NOTES:____

____

____

____

____

____

AFFIRMATIONS:_______________________________________

____

____

____

____

____

____

SIGNATURE:____________________________ DATE:________________

Prodigy Planner Workbook

FINANCIAL CHALLENGES					
#	**Description**	**Hours**	**Rate**	**Deposit**	**Withdrawal**
1					
2					
3					
4					
5					
		Total:			

MENTAL CHALLENGES					
#	**Description**	**Hours**	**Rate**	**Deposit**	**Withdrawal**
1					
2					
3					
4					
5					
		Total:			

PHYSICAL CHALLENGES					
#	**Description**	**Hours**	**Rate**	**Deposit**	**Withdrawal**
1					
2					
3					
4					
5					
		Total:			

SOCIAL CHALLENGES					
#	**Description**	**Hours**	**Rate**	**Deposit**	**Withdrawal**
1					
2					
3					
4					
5					
		Total:			

SPIRITUAL CHALLENGES					
#	Description	Hours	Rate	Deposit	Withdrawal
1					
2					
3					
4					
5					
		Total:			

DAILY SUMMARY			
#	Description	Yesterday's Balance	Add Today's Balance
1	Financial		
2	Mental		
3	Physical		
4	Social		
5	Spiritual		
Monthly Wealth Bonus			
Total			

NOTES:______________________________

AFFIRMATIONS:______________________________

SIGNATURE:____________________ DATE:____________

FINANCIAL CHALLENGES					
#	Description	Hours	Rate	Deposit	Withdrawal
1					
2					
3					
4					
5					
		Total:			

MENTAL CHALLENGES					
#	Description	Hours	Rate	Deposit	Withdrawal
1					
2					
3					
4					
5					
		Total:			

PHYSICAL CHALLENGES					
#	Description	Hours	Rate	Deposit	Withdrawal
1					
2					
3					
4					
5					
		Total:			

SOCIAL CHALLENGES					
#	Description	Hours	Rate	Deposit	Withdrawal
1					
2					
3					
4					
5					
		Total:			

SPIRITUAL CHALLENGES					
#	Description	Hours	Rate	Deposit	Withdrawal
1					
2					
3					
4					
5					
		Total:			

DAILY SUMMARY			
#	Description	Yesterday's Balance	Add Today's Balance
1	Financial		
2	Mental		
3	Physical		
4	Social		
5	Spiritual		
Total			

NOTES:____

AFFIRMATIONS:____

SIGNATURE:__________________________ DATE:______________

FINANCIAL CHALLENGES					
#	**Description**	**Hours**	**Rate**	**Deposit**	**Withdrawal**
1					
2					
3					
4					
5					
		Total:			

MENTAL CHALLENGES					
#	**Description**	**Hours**	**Rate**	**Deposit**	**Withdrawal**
1					
2					
3					
4					
5					
		Total:			

PHYSICAL CHALLENGES					
#	**Description**	**Hours**	**Rate**	**Deposit**	**Withdrawal**
1					
2					
3					
4					
5					
		Total:			

SOCIAL CHALLENGES					
#	**Description**	**Hours**	**Rate**	**Deposit**	**Withdrawal**
1					
2					
3					
4					
5					
		Total:			

SPIRITUAL CHALLENGES					
#	Description	Hours	Rate	Deposit	Withdrawal
1					
2					
3					
4					
5					
		Total:			

DAILY SUMMARY			
#	Description	Yesterday's Balance	Add Today's Balance
1	Financial		
2	Mental		
3	Physical		
4	Social		
5	Spiritual		
Total			

NOTES:____

AFFIRMATIONS:__________________________________

SIGNATURE:________________________ DATE:____________

FINANCIAL CHALLENGES					
#	Description	Hours	Rate	Deposit	Withdrawal
1					
2					
3					
4					
5					
		Total:			

MENTAL CHALLENGES					
#	Description	Hours	Rate	Deposit	Withdrawal
1					
2					
3					
4					
5					
		Total:			

PHYSICAL CHALLENGES					
#	Description	Hours	Rate	Deposit	Withdrawal
1					
2					
3					
4					
5					
		Total:			

SOCIAL CHALLENGES					
#	Description	Hours	Rate	Deposit	Withdrawal
1					
2					
3					
4					
5					
		Total:			

SPIRITUAL CHALLENGES					
#	**Description**	**Hours**	**Rate**	**Deposit**	**Withdrawal**
1					
2					
3					
4					
5					
		Total:			

DAILY SUMMARY			
#	**Description**	**Yesterday's Balance**	**Add Today's Balance**
1	Financial		
2	Mental		
3	Physical		
4	Social		
5	Spiritual		
Total			

NOTES:____

AFFIRMATIONS:____

SIGNATURE:____________________________ DATE:________________

FINANCIAL CHALLENGES					
#	Description	Hours	Rate	Deposit	Withdrawal
1					
2					
3					
4					
5					
		Total:			

MENTAL CHALLENGES					
#	Description	Hours	Rate	Deposit	Withdrawal
1					
2					
3					
4					
5					
		Total:			

PHYSICAL CHALLENGES					
#	Description	Hours	Rate	Deposit	Withdrawal
1					
2					
3					
4					
5					
		Total:			

SOCIAL CHALLENGES					
#	Description	Hours	Rate	Deposit	Withdrawal
1					
2					
3					
4					
5					
		Total:			

Prodigy Planner Workbook

SPIRITUAL CHALLENGES					
#	Description	Hours	Rate	Deposit	Withdrawal
1					
2					
3					
4					
5					
		Total:			

DAILY SUMMARY			
#	Description	Yesterday's Balance	Add Today's Balance
1	Financial		
2	Mental		
3	Physical		
4	Social		
5	Spiritual		
Total			

NOTES:____

AFFIRMATIONS:____________________________________

SIGNATURE:________________________ DATE:________________

FINANCIAL CHALLENGES					
#	Description	Hours	Rate	Deposit	Withdrawal
1					
2					
3					
4					
5					
		Total:			

MENTAL CHALLENGES					
#	Description	Hours	Rate	Deposit	Withdrawal
1					
2					
3					
4					
5					
		Total:			

PHYSICAL CHALLENGES					
#	Description	Hours	Rate	Deposit	Withdrawal
1					
2					
3					
4					
5					
		Total:			

SOCIAL CHALLENGES					
#	Description	Hours	Rate	Deposit	Withdrawal
1					
2					
3					
4					
5					
		Total:			

SPIRITUAL CHALLENGES					
#	Description	Hours	Rate	Deposit	Withdrawal
1					
2					
3					
4					
5					
		Total:			

DAILY SUMMARY			
#	Description	Yesterday's Balance	Add Today's Balance
1	Financial		
2	Mental		
3	Physical		
4	Social		
5	Spiritual		
Total			

NOTES:____

AFFIRMATIONS:____

SIGNATURE:______________________ DATE:______________

FINANCIAL CHALLENGES					
#	Description	Hours	Rate	Deposit	Withdrawal
1					
2					
3					
4					
5					
		Total:			

MENTAL CHALLENGES					
#	Description	Hours	Rate	Deposit	Withdrawal
1					
2					
3					
4					
5					
		Total:			

PHYSICAL CHALLENGES					
#	Description	Hours	Rate	Deposit	Withdrawal
1					
2					
3					
4					
5					
		Total:			

SOCIAL CHALLENGES					
#	Description	Hours	Rate	Deposit	Withdrawal
1					
2					
3					
4					
5					
		Total:			

Prodigy Planner Workbook

SPIRITUAL CHALLENGES					
#	**Description**	**Hours**	**Rate**	**Deposit**	**Withdrawal**
1					
2					
3					
4					
5					
		Total:			

DAILY SUMMARY			
#	**Description**	**Yesterday's Balance**	**Add Today's Balance**
1	Financial		
2	Mental		
3	Physical		
4	Social		
5	Spiritual		
Total			

NOTES:____

AFFIRMATIONS:______________________________________

SIGNATURE:______________________ DATE:____________

Prodigy Planner Workbook

FINANCIAL CHALLENGES					
#	**Description**	**Hours**	**Rate**	**Deposit**	**Withdrawal**
1					
2					
3					
4					
5					
		Total:			

MENTAL CHALLENGES					
#	**Description**	**Hours**	**Rate**	**Deposit**	**Withdrawal**
1					
2					
3					
4					
5					
		Total:			

PHYSICAL CHALLENGES					
#	**Description**	**Hours**	**Rate**	**Deposit**	**Withdrawal**
1					
2					
3					
4					
5					
		Total:			

SOCIAL CHALLENGES					
#	**Description**	**Hours**	**Rate**	**Deposit**	**Withdrawal**
1					
2					
3					
4					
5					
		Total:			

Prodigy Planner Workbook

SPIRITUAL CHALLENGES					
#	Description	Hours	Rate	Deposit	Withdrawal
1					
2					
3					
4					
5					
		Total:			

DAILY SUMMARY			
#	Description	Yesterday's Balance	Add Today's Balance
1	Financial		
2	Mental		
3	Physical		
4	Social		
5	Spiritual		
Total			

NOTES:____

____

____

____

____

____

AFFIRMATIONS:____

____

____

____

____

____

____

SIGNATURE:_______________________________ DATE:_________________

FINANCIAL CHALLENGES					
#	Description	Hours	Rate	Deposit	Withdrawal
1					
2					
3					
4					
5					
		Total:			

MENTAL CHALLENGES					
#	Description	Hours	Rate	Deposit	Withdrawal
1					
2					
3					
4					
5					
		Total:			

PHYSICAL CHALLENGES					
#	Description	Hours	Rate	Deposit	Withdrawal
1					
2					
3					
4					
5					
		Total:			

SOCIAL CHALLENGES					
#	Description	Hours	Rate	Deposit	Withdrawal
1					
2					
3					
4					
5					
		Total:			

SPIRITUAL CHALLENGES					
#	**Description**	**Hours**	**Rate**	**Deposit**	**Withdrawal**
1					
2					
3					
4					
5					
		Total:			

DAILY SUMMARY			
#	**Description**	**Yesterday's Balance**	**Add Today's Balance**
1	Financial		
2	Mental		
3	Physical		
4	Social		
5	Spiritual		
Total			

NOTES:____

AFFIRMATIONS:_______________________________________

SIGNATURE:____________________________ DATE:________________

FINANCIAL CHALLENGES					
#	Description	Hours	Rate	Deposit	Withdrawal
1					
2					
3					
4					
5					
		Total:			

MENTAL CHALLENGES					
#	Description	Hours	Rate	Deposit	Withdrawal
1					
2					
3					
4					
5					
		Total:			

PHYSICAL CHALLENGES					
#	Description	Hours	Rate	Deposit	Withdrawal
1					
2					
3					
4					
5					
		Total:			

SOCIAL CHALLENGES					
#	Description	Hours	Rate	Deposit	Withdrawal
1					
2					
3					
4					
5					
		Total:			

SPIRITUAL CHALLENGES					
#	**Description**	**Hours**	**Rate**	**Deposit**	**Withdrawal**
1					
2					
3					
4					
5					
		Total:			

DAILY SUMMARY			
#	**Description**	**Yesterday's Balance**	**Add Today's Balance**
1	Financial		
2	Mental		
3	Physical		
4	Social		
5	Spiritual		
Total			

NOTES:____

AFFIRMATIONS:____________________________________

SIGNATURE:_________________________ DATE:_______________

FINANCIAL CHALLENGES					
#	Description	Hours	Rate	Deposit	Withdrawal
1					
2					
3					
4					
5					
		Total:			

MENTAL CHALLENGES					
#	Description	Hours	Rate	Deposit	Withdrawal
1					
2					
3					
4					
5					
		Total:			

PHYSICAL CHALLENGES					
#	Description	Hours	Rate	Deposit	Withdrawal
1					
2					
3					
4					
5					
		Total:			

SOCIAL CHALLENGES					
#	Description	Hours	Rate	Deposit	Withdrawal
1					
2					
3					
4					
5					
		Total:			

Prodigy Planner Workbook

SPIRITUAL CHALLENGES					
#	Description	Hours	Rate	Deposit	Withdrawal
1					
2					
3					
4					
5					
		Total:			

DAILY SUMMARY			
#	Description	Yesterday's Balance	Add Today's Balance
1	Financial		
2	Mental		
3	Physical		
4	Social		
5	Spiritual		
Total			

NOTES:______________________________

AFFIRMATIONS:______________________________

SIGNATURE:______________________ DATE:______________

Prodigy Planner Workbook

FINANCIAL CHALLENGES					
#	**Description**	**Hours**	**Rate**	**Deposit**	**Withdrawal**
1					
2					
3					
4					
5					
		Total:			

MENTAL CHALLENGES					
#	**Description**	**Hours**	**Rate**	**Deposit**	**Withdrawal**
1					
2					
3					
4					
5					
		Total:			

PHYSICAL CHALLENGES					
#	**Description**	**Hours**	**Rate**	**Deposit**	**Withdrawal**
1					
2					
3					
4					
5					
		Total:			

SOCIAL CHALLENGES					
#	**Description**	**Hours**	**Rate**	**Deposit**	**Withdrawal**
1					
2					
3					
4					
5					
		Total:			

SPIRITUAL CHALLENGES					
#	Description	Hours	Rate	Deposit	Withdrawal
1					
2					
3					
4					
5					
		Total:			

DAILY SUMMARY			
#	Description	Yesterday's Balance	Add Today's Balance
1	Financial		
2	Mental		
3	Physical		
4	Social		
5	Spiritual		
Total			

NOTES:______________________________

AFFIRMATIONS:______________________________

SIGNATURE:____________________ DATE:______________

FINANCIAL CHALLENGES					
#	Description	Hours	Rate	Deposit	Withdrawal
1					
2					
3					
4					
5					
		Total:			

MENTAL CHALLENGES					
#	Description	Hours	Rate	Deposit	Withdrawal
1					
2					
3					
4					
5					
		Total:			

PHYSICAL CHALLENGES					
#	Description	Hours	Rate	Deposit	Withdrawal
1					
2					
3					
4					
5					
		Total:			

SOCIAL CHALLENGES					
#	Description	Hours	Rate	Deposit	Withdrawal
1					
2					
3					
4					
5					
		Total:			

SPIRITUAL CHALLENGES					
#	**Description**	**Hours**	**Rate**	**Deposit**	**Withdrawal**
1					
2					
3					
4					
5					
		Total:			

DAILY SUMMARY			
#	**Description**	**Yesterday's Balance**	**Add Today's Balance**
1	Financial		
2	Mental		
3	Physical		
4	Social		
5	Spiritual		
Total			

NOTES:____

____

____

____

____

____

AFFIRMATIONS:______________________________________

____

____

____

____

____

____

SIGNATURE:____________________________ DATE:________________

FINANCIAL CHALLENGES					
#	Description	Hours	Rate	Deposit	Withdrawal
1					
2					
3					
4					
5					
		Total:			

MENTAL CHALLENGES					
#	Description	Hours	Rate	Deposit	Withdrawal
1					
2					
3					
4					
5					
		Total:			

PHYSICAL CHALLENGES					
#	Description	Hours	Rate	Deposit	Withdrawal
1					
2					
3					
4					
5					
		Total:			

SOCIAL CHALLENGES					
#	Description	Hours	Rate	Deposit	Withdrawal
1					
2					
3					
4					
5					
		Total:			

SPIRITUAL CHALLENGES					
#	**Description**	**Hours**	**Rate**	**Deposit**	**Withdrawal**
1					
2					
3					
4					
5					
		Total:			

DAILY SUMMARY			
#	**Description**	**Yesterday's Balance**	**Add Today's Balance**
1	Financial		
2	Mental		
3	Physical		
4	Social		
5	Spiritual		
Total			

NOTES:____

____

____

____

____

____

AFFIRMATIONS:______________________________________

____

____

____

____

____

____

SIGNATURE:______________________________ DATE:________________

FINANCIAL CHALLENGES					
#	Description	Hours	Rate	Deposit	Withdrawal
1					
2					
3					
4					
5					
		Total:			

MENTAL CHALLENGES					
#	Description	Hours	Rate	Deposit	Withdrawal
1					
2					
3					
4					
5					
		Total:			

PHYSICAL CHALLENGES					
#	Description	Hours	Rate	Deposit	Withdrawal
1					
2					
3					
4					
5					
		Total:			

SOCIAL CHALLENGES					
#	Description	Hours	Rate	Deposit	Withdrawal
1					
2					
3					
4					
5					
		Total:			

Prodigy Planner Workbook

SPIRITUAL CHALLENGES					
#	Description	Hours	Rate	Deposit	Withdrawal
1					
2					
3					
4					
5					
		Total:			

DAILY SUMMARY			
#	Description	Yesterday's Balance	Add Today's Balance
1	Financial		
2	Mental		
3	Physical		
4	Social		
5	Spiritual		
Total			

NOTES:____

AFFIRMATIONS:__________________________________

SIGNATURE:____________________ DATE:____________

FINANCIAL CHALLENGES					
#	Description	Hours	Rate	Deposit	Withdrawal
1					
2					
3					
4					
5					
		Total:			

MENTAL CHALLENGES					
#	Description	Hours	Rate	Deposit	Withdrawal
1					
2					
3					
4					
5					
		Total:			

PHYSICAL CHALLENGES					
#	Description	Hours	Rate	Deposit	Withdrawal
1					
2					
3					
4					
5					
		Total:			

SOCIAL CHALLENGES					
#	Description	Hours	Rate	Deposit	Withdrawal
1					
2					
3					
4					
5					
		Total:			

SPIRITUAL CHALLENGES					
#	Description	Hours	Rate	Deposit	Withdrawal
1					
2					
3					
4					
5					
		Total:			

DAILY SUMMARY			
#	Description	Yesterday's Balance	Add Today's Balance
1	Financial		
2	Mental		
3	Physical		
4	Social		
5	Spiritual		
Total			

NOTES:____

____

____

____

____

____

AFFIRMATIONS:_________________________________

____

____

____

____

____

____

SIGNATURE:____________________ DATE:____________

FINANCIAL CHALLENGES					
#	Description	Hours	Rate	Deposit	Withdrawal
1					
2					
3					
4					
5					
		Total:			

MENTAL CHALLENGES					
#	Description	Hours	Rate	Deposit	Withdrawal
1					
2					
3					
4					
5					
		Total:			

PHYSICAL CHALLENGES					
#	Description	Hours	Rate	Deposit	Withdrawal
1					
2					
3					
4					
5					
		Total:			

SOCIAL CHALLENGES					
#	Description	Hours	Rate	Deposit	Withdrawal
1					
2					
3					
4					
5					
		Total:			

Prodigy Planner Workbook

SPIRITUAL CHALLENGES					
#	**Description**	**Hours**	**Rate**	**Deposit**	**Withdrawal**
1					
2					
3					
4					
5					
		Total:			

DAILY SUMMARY			
#	**Description**	**Yesterday's Balance**	**Add Today's Balance**
1	Financial		
2	Mental		
3	Physical		
4	Social		
5	Spiritual		
Total			

NOTES:

AFFIRMATIONS:

SIGNATURE:________________________ DATE:______________

FINANCIAL CHALLENGES					
#	Description	Hours	Rate	Deposit	Withdrawal
1					
2					
3					
4					
5					
		Total:			

MENTAL CHALLENGES					
#	Description	Hours	Rate	Deposit	Withdrawal
1					
2					
3					
4					
5					
		Total:			

PHYSICAL CHALLENGES					
#	Description	Hours	Rate	Deposit	Withdrawal
1					
2					
3					
4					
5					
		Total:			

SOCIAL CHALLENGES					
#	Description	Hours	Rate	Deposit	Withdrawal
1					
2					
3					
4					
5					
		Total:			

SPIRITUAL CHALLENGES					
#	Description	Hours	Rate	Deposit	Withdrawal
1					
2					
3					
4					
5					
		Total:			

DAILY SUMMARY			
#	Description	Yesterday's Balance	Add Today's Balance
1	Financial		
2	Mental		
3	Physical		
4	Social		
5	Spiritual		
Total			

NOTES:____

____

____

____

____

____

AFFIRMATIONS:______________________________________

____

____

____

____

____

____

SIGNATURE:____________________________ DATE:______________

FINANCIAL CHALLENGES					
#	Description	Hours	Rate	Deposit	Withdrawal
1					
2					
3					
4					
5					
		Total:			

MENTAL CHALLENGES					
#	Description	Hours	Rate	Deposit	Withdrawal
1					
2					
3					
4					
5					
		Total:			

PHYSICAL CHALLENGES					
#	Description	Hours	Rate	Deposit	Withdrawal
1					
2					
3					
4					
5					
		Total:			

SOCIAL CHALLENGES					
#	Description	Hours	Rate	Deposit	Withdrawal
1					
2					
3					
4					
5					
		Total:			

SPIRITUAL CHALLENGES					
#	Description	Hours	Rate	Deposit	Withdrawal
1					
2					
3					
4					
5					
		Total:			

DAILY SUMMARY			
#	Description	Yesterday's Balance	Add Today's Balance
1	Financial		
2	Mental		
3	Physical		
4	Social		
5	Spiritual		
Total			

NOTES:____

____

____

____

____

____

AFFIRMATIONS:____

____

____

____

____

____

____

SIGNATURE:______________________________ DATE:________________

FINANCIAL CHALLENGES					
#	Description	Hours	Rate	Deposit	Withdrawal
1					
2					
3					
4					
5					
		Total:			

MENTAL CHALLENGES					
#	Description	Hours	Rate	Deposit	Withdrawal
1					
2					
3					
4					
5					
		Total:			

PHYSICAL CHALLENGES					
#	Description	Hours	Rate	Deposit	Withdrawal
1					
2					
3					
4					
5					
		Total:			

SOCIAL CHALLENGES					
#	Description	Hours	Rate	Deposit	Withdrawal
1					
2					
3					
4					
5					
		Total:			

SPIRITUAL CHALLENGES					
#	Description	Hours	Rate	Deposit	Withdrawal
1					
2					
3					
4					
5					
		Total:			

DAILY SUMMARY			
#	Description	Yesterday's Balance	Add Today's Balance
1	Financial		
2	Mental		
3	Physical		
4	Social		
5	Spiritual		
Total			

NOTES:______________________________

AFFIRMATIONS:______________________________

SIGNATURE:____________________ DATE:____________

FINANCIAL CHALLENGES					
#	Description	Hours	Rate	Deposit	Withdrawal
1					
2					
3					
4					
5					
		Total:			

MENTAL CHALLENGES					
#	Description	Hours	Rate	Deposit	Withdrawal
1					
2					
3					
4					
5					
		Total:			

PHYSICAL CHALLENGES					
#	Description	Hours	Rate	Deposit	Withdrawal
1					
2					
3					
4					
5					
		Total:			

SOCIAL CHALLENGES					
#	Description	Hours	Rate	Deposit	Withdrawal
1					
2					
3					
4					
5					
		Total:			

SPIRITUAL CHALLENGES					
#	**Description**	**Hours**	**Rate**	**Deposit**	**Withdrawal**
1					
2					
3					
4					
5					
		Total:			

DAILY SUMMARY			
#	**Description**	**Yesterday's Balance**	**Add Today's Balance**
1	Financial		
2	Mental		
3	Physical		
4	Social		
5	Spiritual		
	Total		

NOTES:____

AFFIRMATIONS:____

SIGNATURE:______________________ DATE:______________

FINANCIAL CHALLENGES					
#	Description	Hours	Rate	Deposit	Withdrawal
1					
2					
3					
4					
5					
		Total:			

MENTAL CHALLENGES					
#	Description	Hours	Rate	Deposit	Withdrawal
1					
2					
3					
4					
5					
		Total:			

PHYSICAL CHALLENGES					
#	Description	Hours	Rate	Deposit	Withdrawal
1					
2					
3					
4					
5					
		Total:			

SOCIAL CHALLENGES					
#	Description	Hours	Rate	Deposit	Withdrawal
1					
2					
3					
4					
5					
		Total:			

SPIRITUAL CHALLENGES					
#	Description	Hours	Rate	Deposit	Withdrawal
1					
2					
3					
4					
5					
		Total:			

DAILY SUMMARY			
#	Description	Yesterday's Balance	Add Today's Balance
1	Financial		
2	Mental		
3	Physical		
4	Social		
5	Spiritual		
Total			

NOTES:____

AFFIRMATIONS:__________________________________

SIGNATURE:____________________ DATE:__________

Prodigy Planner Workbook

FINANCIAL CHALLENGES					
#	Description	Hours	Rate	Deposit	Withdrawal
1					
2					
3					
4					
5					
		Total:			

MENTAL CHALLENGES					
#	Description	Hours	Rate	Deposit	Withdrawal
1					
2					
3					
4					
5					
		Total:			

PHYSICAL CHALLENGES					
#	Description	Hours	Rate	Deposit	Withdrawal
1					
2					
3					
4					
5					
		Total:			

SOCIAL CHALLENGES					
#	Description	Hours	Rate	Deposit	Withdrawal
1					
2					
3					
4					
5					
		Total:			

SPIRITUAL CHALLENGES					
#	**Description**	**Hours**	**Rate**	**Deposit**	**Withdrawal**
1					
2					
3					
4					
5					
		Total:			

DAILY SUMMARY			
#	**Description**	**Yesterday's Balance**	**Add Today's Balance**
1	Financial		
2	Mental		
3	Physical		
4	Social		
5	Spiritual		
Total			

NOTES:____

AFFIRMATIONS:__________________________________

SIGNATURE:________________________ DATE:____________

FINANCIAL CHALLENGES					
#	Description	Hours	Rate	Deposit	Withdrawal
1					
2					
3					
4					
5					
		Total:			

MENTAL CHALLENGES					
#	Description	Hours	Rate	Deposit	Withdrawal
1					
2					
3					
4					
5					
		Total:			

PHYSICAL CHALLENGES					
#	Description	Hours	Rate	Deposit	Withdrawal
1					
2					
3					
4					
5					
		Total:			

SOCIAL CHALLENGES					
#	Description	Hours	Rate	Deposit	Withdrawal
1					
2					
3					
4					
5					
		Total:			

SPIRITUAL CHALLENGES					
#	Description	Hours	Rate	Deposit	Withdrawal
1					
2					
3					
4					
5					
		Total:			

DAILY SUMMARY			
#	Description	Yesterday's Balance	Add Today's Balance
1	Financial		
2	Mental		
3	Physical		
4	Social		
5	Spiritual		
Total			

NOTES: ____

____

____

____

____

____

AFFIRMATIONS: ____

____

____

____

____

____

____

SIGNATURE: ______________________ DATE: ______________

Prodigy Planner Workbook

FINANCIAL CHALLENGES					
#	**Description**	**Hours**	**Rate**	**Deposit**	**Withdrawal**
1					
2					
3					
4					
5					
		Total:			

MENTAL CHALLENGES					
#	**Description**	**Hours**	**Rate**	**Deposit**	**Withdrawal**
1					
2					
3					
4					
5					
		Total:			

PHYSICAL CHALLENGES					
#	**Description**	**Hours**	**Rate**	**Deposit**	**Withdrawal**
1					
2					
3					
4					
5					
		Total:			

SOCIAL CHALLENGES					
#	**Description**	**Hours**	**Rate**	**Deposit**	**Withdrawal**
1					
2					
3					
4					
5					
		Total:			

SPIRITUAL CHALLENGES					
#	Description	Hours	Rate	Deposit	Withdrawal
1					
2					
3					
4					
5					
		Total:			

DAILY SUMMARY			
#	Description	Yesterday's Balance	Add Today's Balance
1	Financial		
2	Mental		
3	Physical		
4	Social		
5	Spiritual		
Total			

NOTES:____

AFFIRMATIONS:______________________________________

SIGNATURE:____________________________ DATE:________________

FINANCIAL CHALLENGES					
#	Description	Hours	Rate	Deposit	Withdrawal
1					
2					
3					
4					
5					
			Total:		

MENTAL CHALLENGES					
#	Description	Hours	Rate	Deposit	Withdrawal
1					
2					
3					
4					
5					
			Total:		

PHYSICAL CHALLENGES					
#	Description	Hours	Rate	Deposit	Withdrawal
1					
2					
3					
4					
5					
			Total:		

SOCIAL CHALLENGES					
#	Description	Hours	Rate	Deposit	Withdrawal
1					
2					
3					
4					
5					
			Total:		

Prodigy Planner Workbook

SPIRITUAL CHALLENGES					
#	Description	Hours	Rate	Deposit	Withdrawal
1					
2					
3					
4					
5					
		Total:			

DAILY SUMMARY			
#	Description	Yesterday's Balance	Add Today's Balance
1	Financial		
2	Mental		
3	Physical		
4	Social		
5	Spiritual		
Total			

NOTES:______________________________

AFFIRMATIONS:______________________________

SIGNATURE:____________________ DATE:____________

FINANCIAL CHALLENGES					
#	Description	Hours	Rate	Deposit	Withdrawal
1					
2					
3					
4					
5					
		Total:			

MENTAL CHALLENGES					
#	Description	Hours	Rate	Deposit	Withdrawal
1					
2					
3					
4					
5					
		Total:			

PHYSICAL CHALLENGES					
#	Description	Hours	Rate	Deposit	Withdrawal
1					
2					
3					
4					
5					
		Total:			

SOCIAL CHALLENGES					
#	Description	Hours	Rate	Deposit	Withdrawal
1					
2					
3					
4					
5					
		Total:			

Prodigy Planner Workbook

SPIRITUAL CHALLENGES					
#	Description	Hours	Rate	Deposit	Withdrawal
1					
2					
3					
4					
5					
		Total:			

DAILY SUMMARY			
#	Description	Yesterday's Balance	Add Today's Balance
1	Financial		
2	Mental		
3	Physical		
4	Social		
5	Spiritual		
Total			

NOTES:____

AFFIRMATIONS:_______________________________________

SIGNATURE:____________________________ DATE:_______________

FINANCIAL CHALLENGES					
#	Description	Hours	Rate	Deposit	Withdrawal
1					
2					
3					
4					
5					
		Total:			

MENTAL CHALLENGES					
#	Description	Hours	Rate	Deposit	Withdrawal
1					
2					
3					
4					
5					
		Total:			

PHYSICAL CHALLENGES					
#	Description	Hours	Rate	Deposit	Withdrawal
1					
2					
3					
4					
5					
		Total:			

SOCIAL CHALLENGES					
#	Description	Hours	Rate	Deposit	Withdrawal
1					
2					
3					
4					
5					
		Total:			

SPIRITUAL CHALLENGES					
#	Description	Hours	Rate	Deposit	Withdrawal
1					
2					
3					
4					
5					
		Total:			

DAILY SUMMARY			
#	Description	Yesterday's Balance	Add Today's Balance
1	Financial		
2	Mental		
3	Physical		
4	Social		
5	Spiritual		
Total			

NOTES:____

____

____

____

____

____

AFFIRMATIONS:______________________________________

____

____

____

____

____

____

SIGNATURE:______________________________ DATE:______________

WEALTH LEVEL 1 - Essentials		
#	**Description**	**Deposit**
1	Have Earned Income	
2	Have Investment Income	
3	Have Leveraged Income	
4	Have Residual Income	
5	Have More Than One Type Of Income	

WEALTH LEVEL 2 - Fundamentals		
#	**Description**	**Deposit**
1	10% Of Income Saved Upon Payment	
2	6-Month Emergency Cash Fund Reserved	
3	1-Year Emergency Electronic Fund Reserved	
4	All Monthly Bills Are Paid On Time	
5	Bills Do Not Exceed 50% Of Monthly Income	
6	No Debt – With Exception Of Mortgage	

WEALTH LEVEL 3 - Safety Net		
#	**Description**	**Deposit**
1	Life Insurance – All Dependents	
2	Medical Insurance – All Dependents	
3	Disability Insurance – If Not Retired	
4	Dental Insurance – All Dependents	
5	Optical Insurance - All Dependents	
6	Long Term Care Insurance – If Retired	
7	Umbrella Insurance	
8	Property Insurance – Homeowner/Renters	
9	Auto Insurance	
10	Filed All Bills & Receipts	

WEALTH LEVEL 4 - Look Good On Paper		
#	**Description**	**Deposit**
1	Have A Credit Score Above 760	
2	Have A Secured Credit Cards Only	
3	10% Of Income Invested Upon Payment	
4	Monitor Your Credit Report Monthly	
WEALTH LEVEL 5 - Sustainability		
#	**Description**	**Deposit**
1	Sustainable Power Supply – No Bill	
2	Sustainable Water Supply – No Bill	
3	Recycle & Eliminate Own Waste	
4	Have No Mortgage Or Rent Bill	
5	20-Year Property Tax Funds Reserved	
6	Homestead	
	Total:	

NOTES:____________________________________

AFFIRMATIONS:______________________________

SIGNATURE:____________________ DATE:____________

FINANCIAL CHALLENGES					
#	Description	Hours	Rate	Deposit	Withdrawal
1					
2					
3					
4					
5					
		Total:			

MENTAL CHALLENGES					
#	Description	Hours	Rate	Deposit	Withdrawal
1					
2					
3					
4					
5					
		Total:			

PHYSICAL CHALLENGES					
#	Description	Hours	Rate	Deposit	Withdrawal
1					
2					
3					
4					
5					
		Total:			

SOCIAL CHALLENGES					
#	Description	Hours	Rate	Deposit	Withdrawal
1					
2					
3					
4					
5					
		Total:			

Prodigy Planner Workbook

SPIRITUAL CHALLENGES					
#	Description	Hours	Rate	Deposit	Withdrawal
1					
2					
3					
4					
5					
		Total:			

DAILY SUMMARY			
#	Description	Yesterday's Balance	Add Today's Balance
1	Financial		
2	Mental		
3	Physical		
4	Social		
5	Spiritual		
Monthly Wealth Bonus			
Total			

NOTES:____

____

____

____

____

____

AFFIRMATIONS:____

____

____

____

____

____

SIGNATURE:______________________________ DATE:________________

Prodigy Planner Workbook

FINANCIAL CHALLENGES					
#	**Description**	**Hours**	**Rate**	**Deposit**	**Withdrawal**
1					
2					
3					
4					
5					
		Total:			

MENTAL CHALLENGES					
#	**Description**	**Hours**	**Rate**	**Deposit**	**Withdrawal**
1					
2					
3					
4					
5					
		Total:			

PHYSICAL CHALLENGES					
#	**Description**	**Hours**	**Rate**	**Deposit**	**Withdrawal**
1					
2					
3					
4					
5					
		Total:			

SOCIAL CHALLENGES					
#	**Description**	**Hours**	**Rate**	**Deposit**	**Withdrawal**
1					
2					
3					
4					
5					
		Total:			

Prodigy Planner Workbook

SPIRITUAL CHALLENGES					
#	Description	Hours	Rate	Deposit	Withdrawal
1					
2					
3					
4					
5					
		Total:			

DAILY SUMMARY			
#	Description	Yesterday's Balance	Add Today's Balance
1	Financial		
2	Mental		
3	Physical		
4	Social		
5	Spiritual		
Total			

NOTES:____

____

____

____

____

____

AFFIRMATIONS:____

____

____

____

____

____

____

SIGNATURE:______________________________ DATE:________________

FINANCIAL CHALLENGES					
#	Description	Hours	Rate	Deposit	Withdrawal
1					
2					
3					
4					
5					
		Total:			

MENTAL CHALLENGES					
#	Description	Hours	Rate	Deposit	Withdrawal
1					
2					
3					
4					
5					
		Total:			

PHYSICAL CHALLENGES					
#	Description	Hours	Rate	Deposit	Withdrawal
1					
2					
3					
4					
5					
		Total:			

SOCIAL CHALLENGES					
#	Description	Hours	Rate	Deposit	Withdrawal
1					
2					
3					
4					
5					
		Total:			

Prodigy Planner Workbook

SPIRITUAL CHALLENGES					
#	Description	Hours	Rate	Deposit	Withdrawal
1					
2					
3					
4					
5					
		Total:			

DAILY SUMMARY			
#	Description	Yesterday's Balance	Add Today's Balance
1	Financial		
2	Mental		
3	Physical		
4	Social		
5	Spiritual		
Total			

NOTES:____

AFFIRMATIONS:____

SIGNATURE:____________________________ DATE:________________

FINANCIAL CHALLENGES					
#	Description	Hours	Rate	Deposit	Withdrawal
1					
2					
3					
4					
5					
		Total:			

MENTAL CHALLENGES					
#	Description	Hours	Rate	Deposit	Withdrawal
1					
2					
3					
4					
5					
		Total:			

PHYSICAL CHALLENGES					
#	Description	Hours	Rate	Deposit	Withdrawal
1					
2					
3					
4					
5					
		Total:			

SOCIAL CHALLENGES					
#	Description	Hours	Rate	Deposit	Withdrawal
1					
2					
3					
4					
5					
		Total:			

Prodigy Planner Workbook

SPIRITUAL CHALLENGES					
#	Description	Hours	Rate	Deposit	Withdrawal
1					
2					
3					
4					
5					
		Total:			

DAILY SUMMARY			
#	Description	Yesterday's Balance	Add Today's Balance
1	Financial		
2	Mental		
3	Physical		
4	Social		
5	Spiritual		
Total			

NOTES:____

AFFIRMATIONS:____________________________________

SIGNATURE:__________________________ DATE:______________

FINANCIAL CHALLENGES					
#	Description	Hours	Rate	Deposit	Withdrawal
1					
2					
3					
4					
5					
		Total:			

MENTAL CHALLENGES					
#	Description	Hours	Rate	Deposit	Withdrawal
1					
2					
3					
4					
5					
		Total:			

PHYSICAL CHALLENGES					
#	Description	Hours	Rate	Deposit	Withdrawal
1					
2					
3					
4					
5					
		Total:			

SOCIAL CHALLENGES					
#	Description	Hours	Rate	Deposit	Withdrawal
1					
2					
3					
4					
5					
		Total:			

SPIRITUAL CHALLENGES					
#	Description	Hours	Rate	Deposit	Withdrawal
1					
2					
3					
4					
5					
		Total:			

DAILY SUMMARY			
#	Description	Yesterday's Balance	Add Today's Balance
1	Financial		
2	Mental		
3	Physical		
4	Social		
5	Spiritual		
Total			

NOTES:____

____

____

____

____

____

AFFIRMATIONS:______________________________________

____

____

____

____

____

____

SIGNATURE:______________________________ DATE:________________

Prodigy Planner Workbook

FINANCIAL CHALLENGES					
#	**Description**	**Hours**	**Rate**	**Deposit**	**Withdrawal**
1					
2					
3					
4					
5					
		Total:			

MENTAL CHALLENGES					
#	**Description**	**Hours**	**Rate**	**Deposit**	**Withdrawal**
1					
2					
3					
4					
5					
		Total:			

PHYSICAL CHALLENGES					
#	**Description**	**Hours**	**Rate**	**Deposit**	**Withdrawal**
1					
2					
3					
4					
5					
		Total:			

SOCIAL CHALLENGES					
#	**Description**	**Hours**	**Rate**	**Deposit**	**Withdrawal**
1					
2					
3					
4					
5					
		Total:			

Prodigy Planner Workbook

SPIRITUAL CHALLENGES					
#	Description	Hours	Rate	Deposit	Withdrawal
1					
2					
3					
4					
5					
		Total:			

DAILY SUMMARY			
#	Description	Yesterday's Balance	Add Today's Balance
1	Financial		
2	Mental		
3	Physical		
4	Social		
5	Spiritual		
Total			

NOTES:____

____

____

____

____

____

AFFIRMATIONS:____

____

____

____

____

____

____

SIGNATURE:____________________________ DATE:________________

FINANCIAL CHALLENGES					
#	Description	Hours	Rate	Deposit	Withdrawal
1					
2					
3					
4					
5					
		Total:			

MENTAL CHALLENGES					
#	Description	Hours	Rate	Deposit	Withdrawal
1					
2					
3					
4					
5					
		Total:			

PHYSICAL CHALLENGES					
#	Description	Hours	Rate	Deposit	Withdrawal
1					
2					
3					
4					
5					
		Total:			

SOCIAL CHALLENGES					
#	Description	Hours	Rate	Deposit	Withdrawal
1					
2					
3					
4					
5					
		Total:			

Prodigy Planner Workbook

SPIRITUAL CHALLENGES					
#	Description	Hours	Rate	Deposit	Withdrawal
1					
2					
3					
4					
5					
		Total:			

DAILY SUMMARY			
#	Description	Yesterday's Balance	Add Today's Balance
1	Financial		
2	Mental		
3	Physical		
4	Social		
5	Spiritual		
Total			

NOTES:____

AFFIRMATIONS:____________________________________

SIGNATURE:________________________ DATE:______________

FINANCIAL CHALLENGES					
#	Description	Hours	Rate	Deposit	Withdrawal
1					
2					
3					
4					
5					
		Total:			

MENTAL CHALLENGES					
#	Description	Hours	Rate	Deposit	Withdrawal
1					
2					
3					
4					
5					
		Total:			

PHYSICAL CHALLENGES					
#	Description	Hours	Rate	Deposit	Withdrawal
1					
2					
3					
4					
5					
		Total:			

SOCIAL CHALLENGES					
#	Description	Hours	Rate	Deposit	Withdrawal
1					
2					
3					
4					
5					
		Total:			

Prodigy Planner Workbook

SPIRITUAL CHALLENGES					
#	Description	Hours	Rate	Deposit	Withdrawal
1					
2					
3					
4					
5					
		Total:			

DAILY SUMMARY			
#	Description	Yesterday's Balance	Add Today's Balance
1	Financial		
2	Mental		
3	Physical		
4	Social		
5	Spiritual		
Total			

NOTES:____

____

____

____

____

____

AFFIRMATIONS:____

____

____

____

____

____

____

SIGNATURE:____________________________ DATE:______________

FINANCIAL CHALLENGES					
#	Description	Hours	Rate	Deposit	Withdrawal
1					
2					
3					
4					
5					
		Total:			

MENTAL CHALLENGES					
#	Description	Hours	Rate	Deposit	Withdrawal
1					
2					
3					
4					
5					
		Total:			

PHYSICAL CHALLENGES					
#	Description	Hours	Rate	Deposit	Withdrawal
1					
2					
3					
4					
5					
		Total:			

SOCIAL CHALLENGES					
#	Description	Hours	Rate	Deposit	Withdrawal
1					
2					
3					
4					
5					
		Total:			

SPIRITUAL CHALLENGES					
#	Description	Hours	Rate	Deposit	Withdrawal
1					
2					
3					
4					
5					
		Total:			

DAILY SUMMARY			
#	Description	Yesterday's Balance	Add Today's Balance
1	Financial		
2	Mental		
3	Physical		
4	Social		
5	Spiritual		
Total			

NOTES:____

____

____

____

____

____

AFFIRMATIONS:____

____

____

____

____

____

____

SIGNATURE:____________________________ DATE:________________

Prodigy Planner Workbook

FINANCIAL CHALLENGES					
#	**Description**	**Hours**	**Rate**	**Deposit**	**Withdrawal**
1					
2					
3					
4					
5					
		Total:			

MENTAL CHALLENGES					
#	**Description**	**Hours**	**Rate**	**Deposit**	**Withdrawal**
1					
2					
3					
4					
5					
		Total:			

PHYSICAL CHALLENGES					
#	**Description**	**Hours**	**Rate**	**Deposit**	**Withdrawal**
1					
2					
3					
4					
5					
		Total:			

SOCIAL CHALLENGES					
#	**Description**	**Hours**	**Rate**	**Deposit**	**Withdrawal**
1					
2					
3					
4					
5					
		Total:			

SPIRITUAL CHALLENGES					
#	Description	Hours	Rate	Deposit	Withdrawal
1					
2					
3					
4					
5					
		Total:			

DAILY SUMMARY			
#	Description	Yesterday's Balance	Add Today's Balance
1	Financial		
2	Mental		
3	Physical		
4	Social		
5	Spiritual		
Total			

NOTES:____

____

____

____

____

____

AFFIRMATIONS:______________________________________

____

____

____

____

____

____

SIGNATURE:______________________________ DATE:________________

FINANCIAL CHALLENGES					
#	Description	Hours	Rate	Deposit	Withdrawal
1					
2					
3					
4					
5					
		Total:			

MENTAL CHALLENGES					
#	Description	Hours	Rate	Deposit	Withdrawal
1					
2					
3					
4					
5					
		Total:			

PHYSICAL CHALLENGES					
#	Description	Hours	Rate	Deposit	Withdrawal
1					
2					
3					
4					
5					
		Total:			

SOCIAL CHALLENGES					
#	Description	Hours	Rate	Deposit	Withdrawal
1					
2					
3					
4					
5					
		Total:			

Prodigy Planner Workbook

SPIRITUAL CHALLENGES					
#	Description	Hours	Rate	Deposit	Withdrawal
1					
2					
3					
4					
5					
		Total:			

DAILY SUMMARY			
#	Description	Yesterday's Balance	Add Today's Balance
1	Financial		
2	Mental		
3	Physical		
4	Social		
5	Spiritual		
Total			

NOTES:____

AFFIRMATIONS:_______________________________________

SIGNATURE:______________________ DATE:______________

FINANCIAL CHALLENGES					
#	**Description**	**Hours**	**Rate**	**Deposit**	**Withdrawal**
1					
2					
3					
4					
5					
		Total:			

MENTAL CHALLENGES					
#	**Description**	**Hours**	**Rate**	**Deposit**	**Withdrawal**
1					
2					
3					
4					
5					
		Total:			

PHYSICAL CHALLENGES					
#	**Description**	**Hours**	**Rate**	**Deposit**	**Withdrawal**
1					
2					
3					
4					
5					
		Total:			

SOCIAL CHALLENGES					
#	**Description**	**Hours**	**Rate**	**Deposit**	**Withdrawal**
1					
2					
3					
4					
5					
		Total:			

Prodigy Planner Workbook

SPIRITUAL CHALLENGES					
#	Description	Hours	Rate	Deposit	Withdrawal
1					
2					
3					
4					
5					
		Total:			

DAILY SUMMARY			
#	Description	Yesterday's Balance	Add Today's Balance
1	Financial		
2	Mental		
3	Physical		
4	Social		
5	Spiritual		
Total			

NOTES:____

AFFIRMATIONS:__________________________________

SIGNATURE:____________________ DATE:____________

FINANCIAL CHALLENGES					
#	Description	Hours	Rate	Deposit	Withdrawal
1					
2					
3					
4					
5					
		Total:			

MENTAL CHALLENGES					
#	Description	Hours	Rate	Deposit	Withdrawal
1					
2					
3					
4					
5					
		Total:			

PHYSICAL CHALLENGES					
#	Description	Hours	Rate	Deposit	Withdrawal
1					
2					
3					
4					
5					
		Total:			

SOCIAL CHALLENGES					
#	Description	Hours	Rate	Deposit	Withdrawal
1					
2					
3					
4					
5					
		Total:			

Prodigy Planner Workbook

SPIRITUAL CHALLENGES					
#	**Description**	**Hours**	**Rate**	**Deposit**	**Withdrawal**
1					
2					
3					
4					
5					
		Total:			

DAILY SUMMARY			
#	**Description**	**Yesterday's Balance**	**Add Today's Balance**
1	Financial		
2	Mental		
3	Physical		
4	Social		
5	Spiritual		
Total			

NOTES:____

AFFIRMATIONS:____

SIGNATURE:__________________________ DATE:______________

Prodigy Planner Workbook

FINANCIAL CHALLENGES					
#	**Description**	**Hours**	**Rate**	**Deposit**	**Withdrawal**
1					
2					
3					
4					
5					
		Total:			

MENTAL CHALLENGES					
#	**Description**	**Hours**	**Rate**	**Deposit**	**Withdrawal**
1					
2					
3					
4					
5					
		Total:			

PHYSICAL CHALLENGES					
#	**Description**	**Hours**	**Rate**	**Deposit**	**Withdrawal**
1					
2					
3					
4					
5					
		Total:			

SOCIAL CHALLENGES					
#	**Description**	**Hours**	**Rate**	**Deposit**	**Withdrawal**
1					
2					
3					
4					
5					
		Total:			

SPIRITUAL CHALLENGES					
#	Description	Hours	Rate	Deposit	Withdrawal
1					
2					
3					
4					
5					
		Total:			

DAILY SUMMARY			
#	Description	Yesterday's Balance	Add Today's Balance
1	Financial		
2	Mental		
3	Physical		
4	Social		
5	Spiritual		
Total			

NOTES:____

____

____

____

____

____

AFFIRMATIONS:_______________________________________

____

____

____

____

____

____

SIGNATURE:_____________________________ DATE:________________

FINANCIAL CHALLENGES					
#	Description	Hours	Rate	Deposit	Withdrawal
1					
2					
3					
4					
5					
		Total:			

MENTAL CHALLENGES					
#	Description	Hours	Rate	Deposit	Withdrawal
1					
2					
3					
4					
5					
		Total:			

PHYSICAL CHALLENGES					
#	Description	Hours	Rate	Deposit	Withdrawal
1					
2					
3					
4					
5					
		Total:			

SOCIAL CHALLENGES					
#	Description	Hours	Rate	Deposit	Withdrawal
1					
2					
3					
4					
5					
		Total:			

SPIRITUAL CHALLENGES					
#	**Description**	**Hours**	**Rate**	**Deposit**	**Withdrawal**
1					
2					
3					
4					
5					
			Total:		

DAILY SUMMARY			
#	**Description**	**Yesterday's Balance**	**Add Today's Balance**
1	Financial		
2	Mental		
3	Physical		
4	Social		
5	Spiritual		
Total			

NOTES:____

____

____

____

____

____

AFFIRMATIONS:____

____

____

____

____

____

____

SIGNATURE:______________________________ DATE:________________

FINANCIAL CHALLENGES					
#	Description	Hours	Rate	Deposit	Withdrawal
1					
2					
3					
4					
5					
		Total:			

MENTAL CHALLENGES					
#	Description	Hours	Rate	Deposit	Withdrawal
1					
2					
3					
4					
5					
		Total:			

PHYSICAL CHALLENGES					
#	Description	Hours	Rate	Deposit	Withdrawal
1					
2					
3					
4					
5					
		Total:			

SOCIAL CHALLENGES					
#	Description	Hours	Rate	Deposit	Withdrawal
1					
2					
3					
4					
5					
		Total:			

Prodigy Planner Workbook

SPIRITUAL CHALLENGES					
#	Description	Hours	Rate	Deposit	Withdrawal
1					
2					
3					
4					
5					
		Total:			

DAILY SUMMARY			
#	Description	Yesterday's Balance	Add Today's Balance
1	Financial		
2	Mental		
3	Physical		
4	Social		
5	Spiritual		
Total			

NOTES:____

AFFIRMATIONS:________________________________

SIGNATURE:________________________ DATE:______________

FINANCIAL CHALLENGES					
#	Description	Hours	Rate	Deposit	Withdrawal
1					
2					
3					
4					
5					
		Total:			

MENTAL CHALLENGES					
#	Description	Hours	Rate	Deposit	Withdrawal
1					
2					
3					
4					
5					
		Total:			

PHYSICAL CHALLENGES					
#	Description	Hours	Rate	Deposit	Withdrawal
1					
2					
3					
4					
5					
		Total:			

SOCIAL CHALLENGES					
#	Description	Hours	Rate	Deposit	Withdrawal
1					
2					
3					
4					
5					
		Total:			

SPIRITUAL CHALLENGES					
#	Description	Hours	Rate	Deposit	Withdrawal
1					
2					
3					
4					
5					
		Total:			

DAILY SUMMARY			
#	Description	Yesterday's Balance	Add Today's Balance
1	Financial		
2	Mental		
3	Physical		
4	Social		
5	Spiritual		
Total			

NOTES:____

____

____

____

____

____

AFFIRMATIONS:_______________________________________

____

____

____

____

____

____

SIGNATURE:______________________________ DATE:________________

FINANCIAL CHALLENGES					
#	Description	Hours	Rate	Deposit	Withdrawal
1					
2					
3					
4					
5					
		Total:			

MENTAL CHALLENGES					
#	Description	Hours	Rate	Deposit	Withdrawal
1					
2					
3					
4					
5					
		Total:			

PHYSICAL CHALLENGES					
#	Description	Hours	Rate	Deposit	Withdrawal
1					
2					
3					
4					
5					
		Total:			

SOCIAL CHALLENGES					
#	Description	Hours	Rate	Deposit	Withdrawal
1					
2					
3					
4					
5					
		Total:			

Prodigy Planner Workbook

SPIRITUAL CHALLENGES					
#	Description	Hours	Rate	Deposit	Withdrawal
1					
2					
3					
4					
5					
		Total:			

DAILY SUMMARY			
#	Description	Yesterday's Balance	Add Today's Balance
1	Financial		
2	Mental		
3	Physical		
4	Social		
5	Spiritual		
Total			

NOTES:____

____

____

____

____

____

AFFIRMATIONS:______________________________________

____

____

____

____

____

____

SIGNATURE:______________________________ DATE:______________

FINANCIAL CHALLENGES					
#	Description	Hours	Rate	Deposit	Withdrawal
1					
2					
3					
4					
5					
		Total:			

MENTAL CHALLENGES					
#	Description	Hours	Rate	Deposit	Withdrawal
1					
2					
3					
4					
5					
		Total:			

PHYSICAL CHALLENGES					
#	Description	Hours	Rate	Deposit	Withdrawal
1					
2					
3					
4					
5					
		Total:			

SOCIAL CHALLENGES					
#	Description	Hours	Rate	Deposit	Withdrawal
1					
2					
3					
4					
5					
		Total:			

Prodigy Planner Workbook

SPIRITUAL CHALLENGES					
#	**Description**	**Hours**	**Rate**	**Deposit**	**Withdrawal**
1					
2					
3					
4					
5					
		Total:			

DAILY SUMMARY			
#	**Description**	**Yesterday's Balance**	**Add Today's Balance**
1	Financial		
2	Mental		
3	Physical		
4	Social		
5	Spiritual		
Total			

NOTES:____

AFFIRMATIONS:____

SIGNATURE:______________________________ DATE:________________

Prodigy Planner Workbook

FINANCIAL CHALLENGES					
#	Description	Hours	Rate	Deposit	Withdrawal
1					
2					
3					
4					
5					
		Total:			

MENTAL CHALLENGES					
#	Description	Hours	Rate	Deposit	Withdrawal
1					
2					
3					
4					
5					
		Total:			

PHYSICAL CHALLENGES					
#	Description	Hours	Rate	Deposit	Withdrawal
1					
2					
3					
4					
5					
		Total:			

SOCIAL CHALLENGES					
#	Description	Hours	Rate	Deposit	Withdrawal
1					
2					
3					
4					
5					
		Total:			

SPIRITUAL CHALLENGES					
#	Description	Hours	Rate	Deposit	Withdrawal
1					
2					
3					
4					
5					
		Total:			

DAILY SUMMARY			
#	Description	Yesterday's Balance	Add Today's Balance
1	Financial		
2	Mental		
3	Physical		
4	Social		
5	Spiritual		
Total			

NOTES:____

AFFIRMATIONS:__________________________________

SIGNATURE:____________________ DATE:____________

FINANCIAL CHALLENGES					
#	Description	Hours	Rate	Deposit	Withdrawal
1					
2					
3					
4					
5					
		Total:			

MENTAL CHALLENGES					
#	Description	Hours	Rate	Deposit	Withdrawal
1					
2					
3					
4					
5					
		Total:			

PHYSICAL CHALLENGES					
#	Description	Hours	Rate	Deposit	Withdrawal
1					
2					
3					
4					
5					
		Total:			

SOCIAL CHALLENGES					
#	Description	Hours	Rate	Deposit	Withdrawal
1					
2					
3					
4					
5					
		Total:			

SPIRITUAL CHALLENGES					
#	**Description**	**Hours**	**Rate**	**Deposit**	**Withdrawal**
1					
2					
3					
4					
5					
			Total:		

DAILY SUMMARY			
#	**Description**	**Yesterday's Balance**	**Add Today's Balance**
1	Financial		
2	Mental		
3	Physical		
4	Social		
5	Spiritual		
	Total		

NOTES:____

____

____

____

____

____

AFFIRMATIONS:______________________________________

____

____

____

____

____

____

SIGNATURE:____________________________ DATE:______________

Prodigy Planner Workbook

FINANCIAL CHALLENGES					
#	**Description**	**Hours**	**Rate**	**Deposit**	**Withdrawal**
1					
2					
3					
4					
5					
		Total:			

MENTAL CHALLENGES					
#	**Description**	**Hours**	**Rate**	**Deposit**	**Withdrawal**
1					
2					
3					
4					
5					
		Total:			

PHYSICAL CHALLENGES					
#	**Description**	**Hours**	**Rate**	**Deposit**	**Withdrawal**
1					
2					
3					
4					
5					
		Total:			

SOCIAL CHALLENGES					
#	**Description**	**Hours**	**Rate**	**Deposit**	**Withdrawal**
1					
2					
3					
4					
5					
		Total:			

SPIRITUAL CHALLENGES					
#	Description	Hours	Rate	Deposit	Withdrawal
1					
2					
3					
4					
5					
		Total:			

DAILY SUMMARY			
#	Description	Yesterday's Balance	Add Today's Balance
1	Financial		
2	Mental		
3	Physical		
4	Social		
5	Spiritual		
Total			

NOTES:______________________________________

AFFIRMATIONS:________________________________

SIGNATURE:____________________ DATE:____________

FINANCIAL CHALLENGES					
#	Description	Hours	Rate	Deposit	Withdrawal
1					
2					
3					
4					
5					
			Total:		

MENTAL CHALLENGES					
#	Description	Hours	Rate	Deposit	Withdrawal
1					
2					
3					
4					
5					
			Total:		

PHYSICAL CHALLENGES					
#	Description	Hours	Rate	Deposit	Withdrawal
1					
2					
3					
4					
5					
			Total:		

SOCIAL CHALLENGES					
#	Description	Hours	Rate	Deposit	Withdrawal
1					
2					
3					
4					
5					
			Total:		

SPIRITUAL CHALLENGES					
#	Description	Hours	Rate	Deposit	Withdrawal
1					
2					
3					
4					
5					
		Total:			

DAILY SUMMARY			
#	Description	Yesterday's Balance	Add Today's Balance
1	Financial		
2	Mental		
3	Physical		
4	Social		
5	Spiritual		
Total			

NOTES:____

AFFIRMATIONS:____

SIGNATURE:________________________ DATE:______________

Prodigy Planner Workbook

FINANCIAL CHALLENGES					
#	**Description**	**Hours**	**Rate**	**Deposit**	**Withdrawal**
1					
2					
3					
4					
5					
		Total:			

MENTAL CHALLENGES					
#	**Description**	**Hours**	**Rate**	**Deposit**	**Withdrawal**
1					
2					
3					
4					
5					
		Total:			

PHYSICAL CHALLENGES					
#	**Description**	**Hours**	**Rate**	**Deposit**	**Withdrawal**
1					
2					
3					
4					
5					
		Total:			

SOCIAL CHALLENGES					
#	**Description**	**Hours**	**Rate**	**Deposit**	**Withdrawal**
1					
2					
3					
4					
5					
		Total:			

SPIRITUAL CHALLENGES					
#	Description	Hours	Rate	Deposit	Withdrawal
1					
2					
3					
4					
5					
		Total:			

DAILY SUMMARY			
#	Description	Yesterday's Balance	Add Today's Balance
1	Financial		
2	Mental		
3	Physical		
4	Social		
5	Spiritual		
Total			

NOTES:____

____

____

____

____

____

AFFIRMATIONS:____

____

____

____

____

____

____

SIGNATURE:______________________________ DATE:________________

FINANCIAL CHALLENGES					
#	Description	Hours	Rate	Deposit	Withdrawal
1					
2					
3					
4					
5					
		Total:			

MENTAL CHALLENGES					
#	Description	Hours	Rate	Deposit	Withdrawal
1					
2					
3					
4					
5					
		Total:			

PHYSICAL CHALLENGES					
#	Description	Hours	Rate	Deposit	Withdrawal
1					
2					
3					
4					
5					
		Total:			

SOCIAL CHALLENGES					
#	Description	Hours	Rate	Deposit	Withdrawal
1					
2					
3					
4					
5					
		Total:			

SPIRITUAL CHALLENGES					
#	**Description**	**Hours**	**Rate**	**Deposit**	**Withdrawal**
1					
2					
3					
4					
5					
		Total:			

DAILY SUMMARY			
#	**Description**	**Yesterday's Balance**	**Add Today's Balance**
1	Financial		
2	Mental		
3	Physical		
4	Social		
5	Spiritual		
Total			

NOTES:____

AFFIRMATIONS:____

SIGNATURE:____________________________ DATE:________________

FINANCIAL CHALLENGES					
#	Description	Hours	Rate	Deposit	Withdrawal
1					
2					
3					
4					
5					
		Total:			

MENTAL CHALLENGES					
#	Description	Hours	Rate	Deposit	Withdrawal
1					
2					
3					
4					
5					
		Total:			

PHYSICAL CHALLENGES					
#	Description	Hours	Rate	Deposit	Withdrawal
1					
2					
3					
4					
5					
		Total:			

SOCIAL CHALLENGES					
#	Description	Hours	Rate	Deposit	Withdrawal
1					
2					
3					
4					
5					
		Total:			

Prodigy Planner Workbook

SPIRITUAL CHALLENGES					
#	Description	Hours	Rate	Deposit	Withdrawal
1					
2					
3					
4					
5					
			Total:		

DAILY SUMMARY			
#	Description	Yesterday's Balance	Add Today's Balance
1	Financial		
2	Mental		
3	Physical		
4	Social		
5	Spiritual		
	Total		

NOTES:____

____

____

____

____

____

AFFIRMATIONS:______________________________________

____

____

____

____

____

____

SIGNATURE:______________________ DATE:______________

FINANCIAL CHALLENGES					
#	Description	Hours	Rate	Deposit	Withdrawal
1					
2					
3					
4					
5					
		Total:			

MENTAL CHALLENGES					
#	Description	Hours	Rate	Deposit	Withdrawal
1					
2					
3					
4					
5					
		Total:			

PHYSICAL CHALLENGES					
#	Description	Hours	Rate	Deposit	Withdrawal
1					
2					
3					
4					
5					
		Total:			

SOCIAL CHALLENGES					
#	Description	Hours	Rate	Deposit	Withdrawal
1					
2					
3					
4					
5					
		Total:			

SPIRITUAL CHALLENGES					
#	Description	Hours	Rate	Deposit	Withdrawal
1					
2					
3					
4					
5					
		Total:			

DAILY SUMMARY			
#	Description	Yesterday's Balance	Add Today's Balance
1	Financial		
2	Mental		
3	Physical		
4	Social		
5	Spiritual		
Total			

NOTES:____

AFFIRMATIONS:______________________________________

SIGNATURE:____________________ DATE:______________

FINANCIAL CHALLENGES					
#	Description	Hours	Rate	Deposit	Withdrawal
1					
2					
3					
4					
5					
		Total:			

MENTAL CHALLENGES					
#	Description	Hours	Rate	Deposit	Withdrawal
1					
2					
3					
4					
5					
		Total:			

PHYSICAL CHALLENGES					
#	Description	Hours	Rate	Deposit	Withdrawal
1					
2					
3					
4					
5					
		Total:			

SOCIAL CHALLENGES					
#	Description	Hours	Rate	Deposit	Withdrawal
1					
2					
3					
4					
5					
		Total:			

Prodigy Planner Workbook

SPIRITUAL CHALLENGES					
#	**Description**	**Hours**	**Rate**	**Deposit**	**Withdrawal**
1					
2					
3					
4					
5					
		Total:			

DAILY SUMMARY			
#	**Description**	**Yesterday's Balance**	**Add Today's Balance**
1	Financial		
2	Mental		
3	Physical		
4	Social		
5	Spiritual		
Total			

NOTES:____

____

____

____

____

____

AFFIRMATIONS:____

____

____

____

____

____

____

SIGNATURE:______________________________ DATE:______________

WEALTH LEVEL 1 - Essentials		
#	**Description**	**Deposit**
1	Have Earned Income	
2	Have Investment Income	
3	Have Leveraged Income	
4	Have Residual Income	
5	Have More Than One Type Of Income	

WEALTH LEVEL 2 - Fundamentals		
#	**Description**	**Deposit**
1	10% Of Income Saved Upon Payment	
2	6-Month Emergency Cash Fund Reserved	
3	1-Year Emergency Electronic Fund Reserved	
4	All Monthly Bills Are Paid On Time	
5	Bills Do Not Exceed 50% Of Monthly Income	
6	No Debt – With Exception Of Mortgage	

WEALTH LEVEL 3 - Safety Net		
#	**Description**	**Deposit**
1	Life Insurance – All Dependents	
2	Medical Insurance – All Dependents	
3	Disability Insurance – If Not Retired	
4	Dental Insurance – All Dependents	
5	Optical Insurance - All Dependents	
6	Long Term Care Insurance – If Retired	
7	Umbrella Insurance	
8	Property Insurance – Homeowner/Renters	
9	Auto Insurance	
10	Filed All Bills & Receipts	

WEALTH LEVEL 4 - Look Good On Paper		
#	**Description**	**Deposit**
1	Have A Credit Score Above 760	
2	Have A Secured Credit Cards Only	
3	10% Of Income Invested Upon Payment	
4	Monitor Your Credit Report Monthly	
WEALTH LEVEL 5 - Sustainability		
#	**Description**	**Deposit**
1	Sustainable Power Supply – No Bill	
2	Sustainable Water Supply – No Bill	
3	Recycle & Eliminate Own Waste	
4	Have No Mortgage Or Rent Bill	
5	20-Year Property Tax Funds Reserved	
6	Homestead	
	Total:	

NOTES:____

____

____

____

____

____

AFFIRMATIONS:_______________________________________

____

____

____

____

____

____

SIGNATURE:______________________________ DATE:________________

FINANCIAL CHALLENGES					
#	Description	Hours	Rate	Deposit	Withdrawal
1					
2					
3					
4					
5					
		Total:			

MENTAL CHALLENGES					
#	Description	Hours	Rate	Deposit	Withdrawal
1					
2					
3					
4					
5					
		Total:			

PHYSICAL CHALLENGES					
#	Description	Hours	Rate	Deposit	Withdrawal
1					
2					
3					
4					
5					
		Total:			

SOCIAL CHALLENGES					
#	Description	Hours	Rate	Deposit	Withdrawal
1					
2					
3					
4					
5					
		Total:			

Prodigy Planner Workbook

SPIRITUAL CHALLENGES					
#	**Description**	**Hours**	**Rate**	**Deposit**	**Withdrawal**
1					
2					
3					
4					
5					
		Total:			

DAILY SUMMARY			
#	**Description**	**Yesterday's Balance**	**Add Today's Balance**
1	Financial		
2	Mental		
3	Physical		
4	Social		
5	Spiritual		
Monthly Wealth Bonus			
Total			

NOTES:____

____

____

____

____

____

AFFIRMATIONS:____

____

____

____

____

____

SIGNATURE:_______________________________ DATE:________________

FINANCIAL CHALLENGES					
#	Description	Hours	Rate	Deposit	Withdrawal
1					
2					
3					
4					
5					
		Total:			

MENTAL CHALLENGES					
#	Description	Hours	Rate	Deposit	Withdrawal
1					
2					
3					
4					
5					
		Total:			

PHYSICAL CHALLENGES					
#	Description	Hours	Rate	Deposit	Withdrawal
1					
2					
3					
4					
5					
		Total:			

SOCIAL CHALLENGES					
#	Description	Hours	Rate	Deposit	Withdrawal
1					
2					
3					
4					
5					
		Total:			

SPIRITUAL CHALLENGES					
#	Description	Hours	Rate	Deposit	Withdrawal
1					
2					
3					
4					
5					
			Total:		

DAILY SUMMARY			
#	Description	Yesterday's Balance	Add Today's Balance
1	Financial		
2	Mental		
3	Physical		
4	Social		
5	Spiritual		
	Total		

NOTES:____

____

____

____

____

____

AFFIRMATIONS:____

____

____

____

____

____

____

SIGNATURE:______________________________ DATE:________________

FINANCIAL CHALLENGES					
#	Description	Hours	Rate	Deposit	Withdrawal
1					
2					
3					
4					
5					
		Total:			

MENTAL CHALLENGES					
#	Description	Hours	Rate	Deposit	Withdrawal
1					
2					
3					
4					
5					
		Total:			

PHYSICAL CHALLENGES					
#	Description	Hours	Rate	Deposit	Withdrawal
1					
2					
3					
4					
5					
		Total:			

SOCIAL CHALLENGES					
#	Description	Hours	Rate	Deposit	Withdrawal
1					
2					
3					
4					
5					
		Total:			

Prodigy Planner Workbook

SPIRITUAL CHALLENGES					
#	**Description**	**Hours**	**Rate**	**Deposit**	**Withdrawal**
1					
2					
3					
4					
5					
		Total:			

DAILY SUMMARY			
#	**Description**	**Yesterday's Balance**	**Add Today's Balance**
1	Financial		
2	Mental		
3	Physical		
4	Social		
5	Spiritual		
Total			

NOTES:____

____

____

____

____

____

AFFIRMATIONS:______________________________________

____

____

____

____

____

____

SIGNATURE:____________________________ DATE:________________

FINANCIAL CHALLENGES					
#	Description	Hours	Rate	Deposit	Withdrawal
1					
2					
3					
4					
5					
		Total:			

MENTAL CHALLENGES					
#	Description	Hours	Rate	Deposit	Withdrawal
1					
2					
3					
4					
5					
		Total:			

PHYSICAL CHALLENGES					
#	Description	Hours	Rate	Deposit	Withdrawal
1					
2					
3					
4					
5					
		Total:			

SOCIAL CHALLENGES					
#	Description	Hours	Rate	Deposit	Withdrawal
1					
2					
3					
4					
5					
		Total:			

Prodigy Planner Workbook

SPIRITUAL CHALLENGES					
#	Description	Hours	Rate	Deposit	Withdrawal
1					
2					
3					
4					
5					
		Total:			

DAILY SUMMARY			
#	Description	Yesterday's Balance	Add Today's Balance
1	Financial		
2	Mental		
3	Physical		
4	Social		
5	Spiritual		
Total			

NOTES:____

____

____

____

____

____

AFFIRMATIONS:____

____

____

____

____

____

____

SIGNATURE:______________________________ DATE:________________

FINANCIAL CHALLENGES					
#	Description	Hours	Rate	Deposit	Withdrawal
1					
2					
3					
4					
5					
		Total:			

MENTAL CHALLENGES					
#	Description	Hours	Rate	Deposit	Withdrawal
1					
2					
3					
4					
5					
		Total:			

PHYSICAL CHALLENGES					
#	Description	Hours	Rate	Deposit	Withdrawal
1					
2					
3					
4					
5					
		Total:			

SOCIAL CHALLENGES					
#	Description	Hours	Rate	Deposit	Withdrawal
1					
2					
3					
4					
5					
		Total:			

Prodigy Planner Workbook

SPIRITUAL CHALLENGES					
#	Description	Hours	Rate	Deposit	Withdrawal
1					
2					
3					
4					
5					
		Total:			

DAILY SUMMARY			
#	Description	Yesterday's Balance	Add Today's Balance
1	Financial		
2	Mental		
3	Physical		
4	Social		
5	Spiritual		
Total			

NOTES:____

____

____

____

____

____

AFFIRMATIONS:____

____

____

____

____

____

____

SIGNATURE:______________________ DATE:______________

FINANCIAL CHALLENGES					
#	Description	Hours	Rate	Deposit	Withdrawal
1					
2					
3					
4					
5					
		Total:			

MENTAL CHALLENGES					
#	Description	Hours	Rate	Deposit	Withdrawal
1					
2					
3					
4					
5					
		Total:			

PHYSICAL CHALLENGES					
#	Description	Hours	Rate	Deposit	Withdrawal
1					
2					
3					
4					
5					
		Total:			

SOCIAL CHALLENGES					
#	Description	Hours	Rate	Deposit	Withdrawal
1					
2					
3					
4					
5					
		Total:			

Prodigy Planner Workbook

SPIRITUAL CHALLENGES					
#	Description	Hours	Rate	Deposit	Withdrawal
1					
2					
3					
4					
5					
		Total:			

DAILY SUMMARY			
#	Description	Yesterday's Balance	Add Today's Balance
1	Financial		
2	Mental		
3	Physical		
4	Social		
5	Spiritual		
Total			

NOTES:____________________________________

AFFIRMATIONS:______________________________

SIGNATURE:____________________ DATE:____________

FINANCIAL CHALLENGES					
#	Description	Hours	Rate	Deposit	Withdrawal
1					
2					
3					
4					
5					
		Total:			

MENTAL CHALLENGES					
#	Description	Hours	Rate	Deposit	Withdrawal
1					
2					
3					
4					
5					
		Total:			

PHYSICAL CHALLENGES					
#	Description	Hours	Rate	Deposit	Withdrawal
1					
2					
3					
4					
5					
		Total:			

SOCIAL CHALLENGES					
#	Description	Hours	Rate	Deposit	Withdrawal
1					
2					
3					
4					
5					
		Total:			

Prodigy Planner Workbook

SPIRITUAL CHALLENGES					
#	Description	Hours	Rate	Deposit	Withdrawal
1					
2					
3					
4					
5					
		Total:			

DAILY SUMMARY			
#	Description	Yesterday's Balance	Add Today's Balance
1	Financial		
2	Mental		
3	Physical		
4	Social		
5	Spiritual		
Total			

NOTES:____

____

____

____

____

____

AFFIRMATIONS:______________________________________

____

____

____

____

____

____

SIGNATURE:____________________________ DATE:_______________

FINANCIAL CHALLENGES					
#	Description	Hours	Rate	Deposit	Withdrawal
1					
2					
3					
4					
5					
			Total:		

MENTAL CHALLENGES					
#	Description	Hours	Rate	Deposit	Withdrawal
1					
2					
3					
4					
5					
			Total:		

PHYSICAL CHALLENGES					
#	Description	Hours	Rate	Deposit	Withdrawal
1					
2					
3					
4					
5					
			Total:		

SOCIAL CHALLENGES					
#	Description	Hours	Rate	Deposit	Withdrawal
1					
2					
3					
4					
5					
			Total:		

SPIRITUAL CHALLENGES					
#	Description	Hours	Rate	Deposit	Withdrawal
1					
2					
3					
4					
5					
		Total:			

DAILY SUMMARY			
#	Description	Yesterday's Balance	Add Today's Balance
1	Financial		
2	Mental		
3	Physical		
4	Social		
5	Spiritual		
Total			

NOTES:____

AFFIRMATIONS:__________________________________

SIGNATURE:________________________ DATE:____________

Prodigy Planner Workbook

FINANCIAL CHALLENGES					
#	Description	Hours	Rate	Deposit	Withdrawal
1					
2					
3					
4					
5					
		Total:			

MENTAL CHALLENGES					
#	Description	Hours	Rate	Deposit	Withdrawal
1					
2					
3					
4					
5					
		Total:			

PHYSICAL CHALLENGES					
#	Description	Hours	Rate	Deposit	Withdrawal
1					
2					
3					
4					
5					
		Total:			

SOCIAL CHALLENGES					
#	Description	Hours	Rate	Deposit	Withdrawal
1					
2					
3					
4					
5					
		Total:			

Prodigy Planner Workbook

SPIRITUAL CHALLENGES					
#	Description	Hours	Rate	Deposit	Withdrawal
1					
2					
3					
4					
5					
		Total:			

DAILY SUMMARY			
#	Description	Yesterday's Balance	Add Today's Balance
1	Financial		
2	Mental		
3	Physical		
4	Social		
5	Spiritual		
Total			

NOTES:____

AFFIRMATIONS:________________________________

SIGNATURE:______________________ DATE:____________

FINANCIAL CHALLENGES					
#	Description	Hours	Rate	Deposit	Withdrawal
1					
2					
3					
4					
5					
		Total:			

MENTAL CHALLENGES					
#	Description	Hours	Rate	Deposit	Withdrawal
1					
2					
3					
4					
5					
		Total:			

PHYSICAL CHALLENGES					
#	Description	Hours	Rate	Deposit	Withdrawal
1					
2					
3					
4					
5					
		Total:			

SOCIAL CHALLENGES					
#	Description	Hours	Rate	Deposit	Withdrawal
1					
2					
3					
4					
5					
		Total:			

Prodigy Planner Workbook

SPIRITUAL CHALLENGES					
#	Description	Hours	Rate	Deposit	Withdrawal
1					
2					
3					
4					
5					
			Total:		

DAILY SUMMARY			
#	Description	Yesterday's Balance	Add Today's Balance
1	Financial		
2	Mental		
3	Physical		
4	Social		
5	Spiritual		
Total			

NOTES:____

AFFIRMATIONS:____

SIGNATURE:______________________ DATE:______________

FINANCIAL CHALLENGES					
#	Description	Hours	Rate	Deposit	Withdrawal
1					
2					
3					
4					
5					
		Total:			

MENTAL CHALLENGES					
#	Description	Hours	Rate	Deposit	Withdrawal
1					
2					
3					
4					
5					
		Total:			

PHYSICAL CHALLENGES					
#	Description	Hours	Rate	Deposit	Withdrawal
1					
2					
3					
4					
5					
		Total:			

SOCIAL CHALLENGES					
#	Description	Hours	Rate	Deposit	Withdrawal
1					
2					
3					
4					
5					
		Total:			

SPIRITUAL CHALLENGES					
#	Description	Hours	Rate	Deposit	Withdrawal
1					
2					
3					
4					
5					
		Total:			

DAILY SUMMARY			
#	Description	Yesterday's Balance	Add Today's Balance
1	Financial		
2	Mental		
3	Physical		
4	Social		
5	Spiritual		
Total			

NOTES:______________________________

AFFIRMATIONS:______________________________

SIGNATURE:____________________ DATE:____________

FINANCIAL CHALLENGES					
#	Description	Hours	Rate	Deposit	Withdrawal
1					
2					
3					
4					
5					
		Total:			

MENTAL CHALLENGES					
#	Description	Hours	Rate	Deposit	Withdrawal
1					
2					
3					
4					
5					
		Total:			

PHYSICAL CHALLENGES					
#	Description	Hours	Rate	Deposit	Withdrawal
1					
2					
3					
4					
5					
		Total:			

SOCIAL CHALLENGES					
#	Description	Hours	Rate	Deposit	Withdrawal
1					
2					
3					
4					
5					
		Total:			

Prodigy Planner Workbook

SPIRITUAL CHALLENGES					
#	Description	Hours	Rate	Deposit	Withdrawal
1					
2					
3					
4					
5					
		Total:			

DAILY SUMMARY			
#	Description	Yesterday's Balance	Add Today's Balance
1	Financial		
2	Mental		
3	Physical		
4	Social		
5	Spiritual		
Total			

NOTES:____

AFFIRMATIONS:__________________________________

SIGNATURE:____________________ DATE:____________

FINANCIAL CHALLENGES					
#	Description	Hours	Rate	Deposit	Withdrawal
1					
2					
3					
4					
5					
		Total:			

MENTAL CHALLENGES					
#	Description	Hours	Rate	Deposit	Withdrawal
1					
2					
3					
4					
5					
		Total:			

PHYSICAL CHALLENGES					
#	Description	Hours	Rate	Deposit	Withdrawal
1					
2					
3					
4					
5					
		Total:			

SOCIAL CHALLENGES					
#	Description	Hours	Rate	Deposit	Withdrawal
1					
2					
3					
4					
5					
		Total:			

Prodigy Planner Workbook

SPIRITUAL CHALLENGES					
#	Description	Hours	Rate	Deposit	Withdrawal
1					
2					
3					
4					
5					
		Total:			

DAILY SUMMARY			
#	Description	Yesterday's Balance	Add Today's Balance
1	Financial		
2	Mental		
3	Physical		
4	Social		
5	Spiritual		
Total			

NOTES:____

____

____

____

____

____

AFFIRMATIONS:______________________________________

____

____

____

____

____

____

SIGNATURE:_____________________________ DATE:_______________

FINANCIAL CHALLENGES					
#	Description	Hours	Rate	Deposit	Withdrawal
1					
2					
3					
4					
5					
		Total:			

MENTAL CHALLENGES					
#	Description	Hours	Rate	Deposit	Withdrawal
1					
2					
3					
4					
5					
		Total:			

PHYSICAL CHALLENGES					
#	Description	Hours	Rate	Deposit	Withdrawal
1					
2					
3					
4					
5					
		Total:			

SOCIAL CHALLENGES					
#	Description	Hours	Rate	Deposit	Withdrawal
1					
2					
3					
4					
5					
		Total:			

SPIRITUAL CHALLENGES					
#	Description	Hours	Rate	Deposit	Withdrawal
1					
2					
3					
4					
5					
			Total:		

DAILY SUMMARY			
#	Description	Yesterday's Balance	Add Today's Balance
1	Financial		
2	Mental		
3	Physical		
4	Social		
5	Spiritual		
Total			

NOTES:____

____

____

____

____

____

AFFIRMATIONS:____

____

____

____

____

____

____

SIGNATURE:______________________________ DATE:________________

FINANCIAL CHALLENGES					
#	Description	Hours	Rate	Deposit	Withdrawal
1					
2					
3					
4					
5					
		Total:			

MENTAL CHALLENGES					
#	Description	Hours	Rate	Deposit	Withdrawal
1					
2					
3					
4					
5					
		Total:			

PHYSICAL CHALLENGES					
#	Description	Hours	Rate	Deposit	Withdrawal
1					
2					
3					
4					
5					
		Total:			

SOCIAL CHALLENGES					
#	Description	Hours	Rate	Deposit	Withdrawal
1					
2					
3					
4					
5					
		Total:			

Prodigy Planner Workbook

SPIRITUAL CHALLENGES					
#	**Description**	**Hours**	**Rate**	**Deposit**	**Withdrawal**
1					
2					
3					
4					
5					
		Total:			

DAILY SUMMARY			
#	**Description**	**Yesterday's Balance**	**Add Today's Balance**
1	Financial		
2	Mental		
3	Physical		
4	Social		
5	Spiritual		
Total			

NOTES:____

____

____

____

____

____

AFFIRMATIONS:____

____

____

____

____

____

____

SIGNATURE:______________________________ DATE:________________

FINANCIAL CHALLENGES					
#	Description	Hours	Rate	Deposit	Withdrawal
1					
2					
3					
4					
5					
		Total:			

MENTAL CHALLENGES					
#	Description	Hours	Rate	Deposit	Withdrawal
1					
2					
3					
4					
5					
		Total:			

PHYSICAL CHALLENGES					
#	Description	Hours	Rate	Deposit	Withdrawal
1					
2					
3					
4					
5					
		Total:			

SOCIAL CHALLENGES					
#	Description	Hours	Rate	Deposit	Withdrawal
1					
2					
3					
4					
5					
		Total:			

SPIRITUAL CHALLENGES					
#	Description	Hours	Rate	Deposit	Withdrawal
1					
2					
3					
4					
5					
		Total:			

DAILY SUMMARY			
#	Description	Yesterday's Balance	Add Today's Balance
1	Financial		
2	Mental		
3	Physical		
4	Social		
5	Spiritual		
Total			

NOTES:____

AFFIRMATIONS:__________________________________

SIGNATURE:____________________ DATE:____________

FINANCIAL CHALLENGES					
#	Description	Hours	Rate	Deposit	Withdrawal
1					
2					
3					
4					
5					
		Total:			

MENTAL CHALLENGES					
#	Description	Hours	Rate	Deposit	Withdrawal
1					
2					
3					
4					
5					
		Total:			

PHYSICAL CHALLENGES					
#	Description	Hours	Rate	Deposit	Withdrawal
1					
2					
3					
4					
5					
		Total:			

SOCIAL CHALLENGES					
#	Description	Hours	Rate	Deposit	Withdrawal
1					
2					
3					
4					
5					
		Total:			

Prodigy Planner Workbook

SPIRITUAL CHALLENGES					
#	Description	Hours	Rate	Deposit	Withdrawal
1					
2					
3					
4					
5					
		Total:			

DAILY SUMMARY			
#	Description	Yesterday's Balance	Add Today's Balance
1	Financial		
2	Mental		
3	Physical		
4	Social		
5	Spiritual		
Total			

NOTES:____

AFFIRMATIONS:__________________________________

SIGNATURE:________________________ DATE:______________

FINANCIAL CHALLENGES					
#	Description	Hours	Rate	Deposit	Withdrawal
1					
2					
3					
4					
5					
		Total:			

MENTAL CHALLENGES					
#	Description	Hours	Rate	Deposit	Withdrawal
1					
2					
3					
4					
5					
		Total:			

PHYSICAL CHALLENGES					
#	Description	Hours	Rate	Deposit	Withdrawal
1					
2					
3					
4					
5					
		Total:			

SOCIAL CHALLENGES					
#	Description	Hours	Rate	Deposit	Withdrawal
1					
2					
3					
4					
5					
		Total:			

SPIRITUAL CHALLENGES					
#	Description	Hours	Rate	Deposit	Withdrawal
1					
2					
3					
4					
5					
		Total:			

DAILY SUMMARY			
#	Description	Yesterday's Balance	Add Today's Balance
1	Financial		
2	Mental		
3	Physical		
4	Social		
5	Spiritual		
Total			

NOTES:____

AFFIRMATIONS:____

SIGNATURE:______________________ DATE:______________

FINANCIAL CHALLENGES					
#	Description	Hours	Rate	Deposit	Withdrawal
1					
2					
3					
4					
5					
		Total:			

MENTAL CHALLENGES					
#	Description	Hours	Rate	Deposit	Withdrawal
1					
2					
3					
4					
5					
		Total:			

PHYSICAL CHALLENGES					
#	Description	Hours	Rate	Deposit	Withdrawal
1					
2					
3					
4					
5					
		Total:			

SOCIAL CHALLENGES					
#	Description	Hours	Rate	Deposit	Withdrawal
1					
2					
3					
4					
5					
		Total:			

Prodigy Planner Workbook

SPIRITUAL CHALLENGES					
#	Description	Hours	Rate	Deposit	Withdrawal
1					
2					
3					
4					
5					
		Total:			

DAILY SUMMARY			
#	Description	Yesterday's Balance	Add Today's Balance
1	Financial		
2	Mental		
3	Physical		
4	Social		
5	Spiritual		
	Total		

NOTES:____

____

____

____

____

____

AFFIRMATIONS:____

____

____

____

____

____

____

SIGNATURE:______________________________ DATE:________________

FINANCIAL CHALLENGES					
#	Description	Hours	Rate	Deposit	Withdrawal
1					
2					
3					
4					
5					
		Total:			

MENTAL CHALLENGES					
#	Description	Hours	Rate	Deposit	Withdrawal
1					
2					
3					
4					
5					
		Total:			

PHYSICAL CHALLENGES					
#	Description	Hours	Rate	Deposit	Withdrawal
1					
2					
3					
4					
5					
		Total:			

SOCIAL CHALLENGES					
#	Description	Hours	Rate	Deposit	Withdrawal
1					
2					
3					
4					
5					
		Total:			

Prodigy Planner Workbook

SPIRITUAL CHALLENGES					
#	**Description**	**Hours**	**Rate**	**Deposit**	**Withdrawal**
1					
2					
3					
4					
5					
		Total:			

DAILY SUMMARY			
#	**Description**	**Yesterday's Balance**	**Add Today's Balance**
1	Financial		
2	Mental		
3	Physical		
4	Social		
5	Spiritual		
Total			

NOTES:____

AFFIRMATIONS:__________________________________

SIGNATURE:____________________ DATE:____________

Prodigy Planner Workbook

FINANCIAL CHALLENGES					
#	Description	Hours	Rate	Deposit	Withdrawal
1					
2					
3					
4					
5					
		Total:			

MENTAL CHALLENGES					
#	Description	Hours	Rate	Deposit	Withdrawal
1					
2					
3					
4					
5					
		Total:			

PHYSICAL CHALLENGES					
#	Description	Hours	Rate	Deposit	Withdrawal
1					
2					
3					
4					
5					
		Total:			

SOCIAL CHALLENGES					
#	Description	Hours	Rate	Deposit	Withdrawal
1					
2					
3					
4					
5					
		Total:			

Prodigy Planner Workbook

SPIRITUAL CHALLENGES					
#	**Description**	**Hours**	**Rate**	**Deposit**	**Withdrawal**
1					
2					
3					
4					
5					
		Total:			

DAILY SUMMARY			
#	**Description**	**Yesterday's Balance**	**Add Today's Balance**
1	Financial		
2	Mental		
3	Physical		
4	Social		
5	Spiritual		
Total			

NOTES:______________________________________

AFFIRMATIONS:______________________________________

SIGNATURE:______________________ DATE:______________

FINANCIAL CHALLENGES					
#	Description	Hours	Rate	Deposit	Withdrawal
1					
2					
3					
4					
5					
		Total:			

MENTAL CHALLENGES					
#	Description	Hours	Rate	Deposit	Withdrawal
1					
2					
3					
4					
5					
		Total:			

PHYSICAL CHALLENGES					
#	Description	Hours	Rate	Deposit	Withdrawal
1					
2					
3					
4					
5					
		Total:			

SOCIAL CHALLENGES					
#	Description	Hours	Rate	Deposit	Withdrawal
1					
2					
3					
4					
5					
		Total:			

Prodigy Planner Workbook

SPIRITUAL CHALLENGES					
#	Description	Hours	Rate	Deposit	Withdrawal
1					
2					
3					
4					
5					
		Total:			

DAILY SUMMARY			
#	Description	Yesterday's Balance	Add Today's Balance
1	Financial		
2	Mental		
3	Physical		
4	Social		
5	Spiritual		
Total			

NOTES:______________________________

____

____

____

____

____

AFFIRMATIONS:______________________________

____

____

____

____

____

____

SIGNATURE:______________________ DATE:______________

FINANCIAL CHALLENGES					
#	Description	Hours	Rate	Deposit	Withdrawal
1					
2					
3					
4					
5					
		Total:			

MENTAL CHALLENGES					
#	Description	Hours	Rate	Deposit	Withdrawal
1					
2					
3					
4					
5					
		Total:			

PHYSICAL CHALLENGES					
#	Description	Hours	Rate	Deposit	Withdrawal
1					
2					
3					
4					
5					
		Total:			

SOCIAL CHALLENGES					
#	Description	Hours	Rate	Deposit	Withdrawal
1					
2					
3					
4					
5					
		Total:			

SPIRITUAL CHALLENGES					
#	**Description**	**Hours**	**Rate**	**Deposit**	**Withdrawal**
1					
2					
3					
4					
5					
		Total:			

DAILY SUMMARY			
#	**Description**	**Yesterday's Balance**	**Add Today's Balance**
1	Financial		
2	Mental		
3	Physical		
4	Social		
5	Spiritual		
Total			

NOTES:____

____

____

____

____

____

AFFIRMATIONS:____

____

____

____

____

____

____

SIGNATURE:______________________________ DATE:________________

FINANCIAL CHALLENGES					
#	Description	Hours	Rate	Deposit	Withdrawal
1					
2					
3					
4					
5					
		Total:			

MENTAL CHALLENGES					
#	Description	Hours	Rate	Deposit	Withdrawal
1					
2					
3					
4					
5					
		Total:			

PHYSICAL CHALLENGES					
#	Description	Hours	Rate	Deposit	Withdrawal
1					
2					
3					
4					
5					
		Total:			

SOCIAL CHALLENGES					
#	Description	Hours	Rate	Deposit	Withdrawal
1					
2					
3					
4					
5					
		Total:			

SPIRITUAL CHALLENGES					
#	Description	Hours	Rate	Deposit	Withdrawal
1					
2					
3					
4					
5					
		Total:			

DAILY SUMMARY			
#	Description	Yesterday's Balance	Add Today's Balance
1	Financial		
2	Mental		
3	Physical		
4	Social		
5	Spiritual		
Total			

NOTES:____

AFFIRMATIONS:____

SIGNATURE:______________________ DATE:______________

FINANCIAL CHALLENGES					
#	Description	Hours	Rate	Deposit	Withdrawal
1					
2					
3					
4					
5					
		Total:			

MENTAL CHALLENGES					
#	Description	Hours	Rate	Deposit	Withdrawal
1					
2					
3					
4					
5					
		Total:			

PHYSICAL CHALLENGES					
#	Description	Hours	Rate	Deposit	Withdrawal
1					
2					
3					
4					
5					
		Total:			

SOCIAL CHALLENGES					
#	Description	Hours	Rate	Deposit	Withdrawal
1					
2					
3					
4					
5					
		Total:			

Prodigy Planner Workbook

SPIRITUAL CHALLENGES					
#	Description	Hours	Rate	Deposit	Withdrawal
1					
2					
3					
4					
5					
		Total:			

DAILY SUMMARY			
#	Description	Yesterday's Balance	Add Today's Balance
1	Financial		
2	Mental		
3	Physical		
4	Social		
5	Spiritual		
Total			

NOTES:____

____

____

____

____

____

AFFIRMATIONS:_______________________________________

____

____

____

____

____

____

SIGNATURE:____________________________ DATE:________________

FINANCIAL CHALLENGES					
#	Description	Hours	Rate	Deposit	Withdrawal
1					
2					
3					
4					
5					
			Total:		

MENTAL CHALLENGES					
#	Description	Hours	Rate	Deposit	Withdrawal
1					
2					
3					
4					
5					
			Total:		

PHYSICAL CHALLENGES					
#	Description	Hours	Rate	Deposit	Withdrawal
1					
2					
3					
4					
5					
			Total:		

SOCIAL CHALLENGES					
#	Description	Hours	Rate	Deposit	Withdrawal
1					
2					
3					
4					
5					
			Total:		

SPIRITUAL CHALLENGES					
#	Description	Hours	Rate	Deposit	Withdrawal
1					
2					
3					
4					
5					
		Total:			

DAILY SUMMARY			
#	Description	Yesterday's Balance	Add Today's Balance
1	Financial		
2	Mental		
3	Physical		
4	Social		
5	Spiritual		
Total			

NOTES:____

AFFIRMATIONS:____________________________________

SIGNATURE:________________________ DATE:______________

Prodigy Planner Workbook

FINANCIAL CHALLENGES					
#	Description	Hours	Rate	Deposit	Withdrawal
1					
2					
3					
4					
5					
		Total:			

MENTAL CHALLENGES					
#	Description	Hours	Rate	Deposit	Withdrawal
1					
2					
3					
4					
5					
		Total:			

PHYSICAL CHALLENGES					
#	Description	Hours	Rate	Deposit	Withdrawal
1					
2					
3					
4					
5					
		Total:			

SOCIAL CHALLENGES					
#	Description	Hours	Rate	Deposit	Withdrawal
1					
2					
3					
4					
5					
		Total:			

Prodigy Planner Workbook

SPIRITUAL CHALLENGES					
#	**Description**	**Hours**	**Rate**	**Deposit**	**Withdrawal**
1					
2					
3					
4					
5					
		Total:			

DAILY SUMMARY			
#	**Description**	**Yesterday's Balance**	**Add Today's Balance**
1	Financial		
2	Mental		
3	Physical		
4	Social		
5	Spiritual		
Total			

NOTES:____

____

____

____

____

____

AFFIRMATIONS:______________________________________

____

____

____

____

____

____

SIGNATURE:_____________________________ DATE:_______________

FINANCIAL CHALLENGES					
#	Description	Hours	Rate	Deposit	Withdrawal
1					
2					
3					
4					
5					
		Total:			

MENTAL CHALLENGES					
#	Description	Hours	Rate	Deposit	Withdrawal
1					
2					
3					
4					
5					
		Total:			

PHYSICAL CHALLENGES					
#	Description	Hours	Rate	Deposit	Withdrawal
1					
2					
3					
4					
5					
		Total:			

SOCIAL CHALLENGES					
#	Description	Hours	Rate	Deposit	Withdrawal
1					
2					
3					
4					
5					
		Total:			

SPIRITUAL CHALLENGES					
#	**Description**	**Hours**	**Rate**	**Deposit**	**Withdrawal**
1					
2					
3					
4					
5					
		Total:			

DAILY SUMMARY			
#	**Description**	**Yesterday's Balance**	**Add Today's Balance**
1	Financial		
2	Mental		
3	Physical		
4	Social		
5	Spiritual		
Total			

NOTES:____

____

____

____

____

____

AFFIRMATIONS:____

____

____

____

____

____

____

SIGNATURE:______________________________ DATE:________________

WEALTH LEVEL 1 - Essentials		
#	**Description**	**Deposit**
1	Have Earned Income	
2	Have Investment Income	
3	Have Leveraged Income	
4	Have Residual Income	
5	Have More Than One Type Of Income	

WEALTH LEVEL 2 - Fundamentals		
#	**Description**	**Deposit**
1	10% Of Income Saved Upon Payment	
2	6-Month Emergency Cash Fund Reserved	
3	1-Year Emergency Electronic Fund Reserved	
4	All Monthly Bills Are Paid On Time	
5	Bills Do Not Exceed 50% Of Monthly Income	
6	No Debt – With Exception Of Mortgage	

WEALTH LEVEL 3 - Safety Net		
#	**Description**	**Deposit**
1	Life Insurance – All Dependents	
2	Medical Insurance – All Dependents	
3	Disability Insurance – If Not Retired	
4	Dental Insurance – All Dependents	
5	Optical Insurance - All Dependents	
6	Long Term Care Insurance – If Retired	
7	Umbrella Insurance	
8	Property Insurance – Homeowner/Renters	
9	Auto Insurance	
10	Filed All Bills & Receipts	

WEALTH LEVEL 4 - Look Good On Paper		
#	**Description**	**Deposit**
1	Have A Credit Score Above 760	
2	Have A Secured Credit Cards Only	
3	10% Of Income Invested Upon Payment	
4	Monitor Your Credit Report Monthly	
WEALTH LEVEL 5 - Sustainability		
#	**Description**	**Deposit**
1	Sustainable Power Supply – No Bill	
2	Sustainable Water Supply – No Bill	
3	Recycle & Eliminate Own Waste	
4	Have No Mortgage Or Rent Bill	
5	20-Year Property Tax Funds Reserved	
6	Homestead	
	Total:	

NOTES:____

AFFIRMATIONS:__________________________________

SIGNATURE:________________________ DATE:_______________

FINANCIAL CHALLENGES					
#	Description	Hours	Rate	Deposit	Withdrawal
1					
2					
3					
4					
5					
		Total:			

MENTAL CHALLENGES					
#	Description	Hours	Rate	Deposit	Withdrawal
1					
2					
3					
4					
5					
		Total:			

PHYSICAL CHALLENGES					
#	Description	Hours	Rate	Deposit	Withdrawal
1					
2					
3					
4					
5					
		Total:			

SOCIAL CHALLENGES					
#	Description	Hours	Rate	Deposit	Withdrawal
1					
2					
3					
4					
5					
		Total:			

SPIRITUAL CHALLENGES					
#	**Description**	**Hours**	**Rate**	**Deposit**	**Withdrawal**
1					
2					
3					
4					
5					
		Total:			

DAILY SUMMARY			
#	**Description**	**Yesterday's Balance**	**Add Today's Balance**
1	Financial		
2	Mental		
3	Physical		
4	Social		
5	Spiritual		
Monthly Wealth Bonus			
Total			

NOTES:____

____

____

____

____

____

AFFIRMATIONS:____

____

____

____

____

____

SIGNATURE:______________________________ DATE:________________

FINANCIAL CHALLENGES					
#	Description	Hours	Rate	Deposit	Withdrawal
1					
2					
3					
4					
5					
		Total:			

MENTAL CHALLENGES					
#	Description	Hours	Rate	Deposit	Withdrawal
1					
2					
3					
4					
5					
		Total:			

PHYSICAL CHALLENGES					
#	Description	Hours	Rate	Deposit	Withdrawal
1					
2					
3					
4					
5					
		Total:			

SOCIAL CHALLENGES					
#	Description	Hours	Rate	Deposit	Withdrawal
1					
2					
3					
4					
5					
		Total:			

Prodigy Planner Workbook

SPIRITUAL CHALLENGES					
#	**Description**	**Hours**	**Rate**	**Deposit**	**Withdrawal**
1					
2					
3					
4					
5					
		Total:			

DAILY SUMMARY			
#	**Description**	**Yesterday's Balance**	**Add Today's Balance**
1	Financial		
2	Mental		
3	Physical		
4	Social		
5	Spiritual		
Total			

NOTES:

AFFIRMATIONS:

SIGNATURE: DATE:

FINANCIAL CHALLENGES					
#	Description	Hours	Rate	Deposit	Withdrawal
1					
2					
3					
4					
5					
		Total:			

MENTAL CHALLENGES					
#	Description	Hours	Rate	Deposit	Withdrawal
1					
2					
3					
4					
5					
		Total:			

PHYSICAL CHALLENGES					
#	Description	Hours	Rate	Deposit	Withdrawal
1					
2					
3					
4					
5					
		Total:			

SOCIAL CHALLENGES					
#	Description	Hours	Rate	Deposit	Withdrawal
1					
2					
3					
4					
5					
		Total:			

SPIRITUAL CHALLENGES					
#	**Description**	**Hours**	**Rate**	**Deposit**	**Withdrawal**
1					
2					
3					
4					
5					
			Total:		

DAILY SUMMARY			
#	**Description**	**Yesterday's Balance**	**Add Today's Balance**
1	Financial		
2	Mental		
3	Physical		
4	Social		
5	Spiritual		
Total			

NOTES:____

AFFIRMATIONS:______________________________________

SIGNATURE:_____________________________ DATE:________________

Prodigy Planner Workbook

FINANCIAL CHALLENGES					
#	Description	Hours	Rate	Deposit	Withdrawal
1					
2					
3					
4					
5					
		Total:			

MENTAL CHALLENGES					
#	Description	Hours	Rate	Deposit	Withdrawal
1					
2					
3					
4					
5					
		Total:			

PHYSICAL CHALLENGES					
#	Description	Hours	Rate	Deposit	Withdrawal
1					
2					
3					
4					
5					
		Total:			

SOCIAL CHALLENGES					
#	Description	Hours	Rate	Deposit	Withdrawal
1					
2					
3					
4					
5					
		Total:			

Prodigy Planner Workbook

SPIRITUAL CHALLENGES					
#	Description	Hours	Rate	Deposit	Withdrawal
1					
2					
3					
4					
5					
		Total:			

DAILY SUMMARY			
#	Description	Yesterday's Balance	Add Today's Balance
1	Financial		
2	Mental		
3	Physical		
4	Social		
5	Spiritual		
Total			

NOTES:____

AFFIRMATIONS:__________________________________

SIGNATURE:____________________ DATE:____________

FINANCIAL CHALLENGES					
#	Description	Hours	Rate	Deposit	Withdrawal
1					
2					
3					
4					
5					
		Total:			

MENTAL CHALLENGES					
#	Description	Hours	Rate	Deposit	Withdrawal
1					
2					
3					
4					
5					
		Total:			

PHYSICAL CHALLENGES					
#	Description	Hours	Rate	Deposit	Withdrawal
1					
2					
3					
4					
5					
		Total:			

SOCIAL CHALLENGES					
#	Description	Hours	Rate	Deposit	Withdrawal
1					
2					
3					
4					
5					
		Total:			

SPIRITUAL CHALLENGES					
#	Description	Hours	Rate	Deposit	Withdrawal
1					
2					
3					
4					
5					
		Total:			

DAILY SUMMARY			
#	Description	Yesterday's Balance	Add Today's Balance
1	Financial		
2	Mental		
3	Physical		
4	Social		
5	Spiritual		
Total			

NOTES:____

AFFIRMATIONS:___________________________________

SIGNATURE:____________________ DATE:____________

FINANCIAL CHALLENGES					
#	Description	Hours	Rate	Deposit	Withdrawal
1					
2					
3					
4					
5					
		Total:			

MENTAL CHALLENGES					
#	Description	Hours	Rate	Deposit	Withdrawal
1					
2					
3					
4					
5					
		Total:			

PHYSICAL CHALLENGES					
#	Description	Hours	Rate	Deposit	Withdrawal
1					
2					
3					
4					
5					
		Total:			

SOCIAL CHALLENGES					
#	Description	Hours	Rate	Deposit	Withdrawal
1					
2					
3					
4					
5					
		Total:			

SPIRITUAL CHALLENGES					
#	Description	Hours	Rate	Deposit	Withdrawal
1					
2					
3					
4					
5					
		Total:			

DAILY SUMMARY			
#	Description	Yesterday's Balance	Add Today's Balance
1	Financial		
2	Mental		
3	Physical		
4	Social		
5	Spiritual		
	Total		

NOTES:____

____

____

____

____

____

AFFIRMATIONS:____

____

____

____

____

____

____

SIGNATURE:______________________________ DATE:________________

FINANCIAL CHALLENGES					
#	Description	Hours	Rate	Deposit	Withdrawal
1					
2					
3					
4					
5					
		Total:			

MENTAL CHALLENGES					
#	Description	Hours	Rate	Deposit	Withdrawal
1					
2					
3					
4					
5					
		Total:			

PHYSICAL CHALLENGES					
#	Description	Hours	Rate	Deposit	Withdrawal
1					
2					
3					
4					
5					
		Total:			

SOCIAL CHALLENGES					
#	Description	Hours	Rate	Deposit	Withdrawal
1					
2					
3					
4					
5					
		Total:			

Prodigy Planner Workbook

SPIRITUAL CHALLENGES					
#	Description	Hours	Rate	Deposit	Withdrawal
1					
2					
3					
4					
5					
			Total:		

DAILY SUMMARY			
#	Description	Yesterday's Balance	Add Today's Balance
1	Financial		
2	Mental		
3	Physical		
4	Social		
5	Spiritual		
Total			

NOTES:____

AFFIRMATIONS:____________________________________

SIGNATURE:_________________________ DATE:_______________

FINANCIAL CHALLENGES					
#	Description	Hours	Rate	Deposit	Withdrawal
1					
2					
3					
4					
5					
		Total:			

MENTAL CHALLENGES					
#	Description	Hours	Rate	Deposit	Withdrawal
1					
2					
3					
4					
5					
		Total:			

PHYSICAL CHALLENGES					
#	Description	Hours	Rate	Deposit	Withdrawal
1					
2					
3					
4					
5					
		Total:			

SOCIAL CHALLENGES					
#	Description	Hours	Rate	Deposit	Withdrawal
1					
2					
3					
4					
5					
		Total:			

Prodigy Planner Workbook

SPIRITUAL CHALLENGES					
#	Description	Hours	Rate	Deposit	Withdrawal
1					
2					
3					
4					
5					
		Total:			

DAILY SUMMARY			
#	Description	Yesterday's Balance	Add Today's Balance
1	Financial		
2	Mental		
3	Physical		
4	Social		
5	Spiritual		
Total			

NOTES:____

____

____

____

____

____

AFFIRMATIONS:______________________________________

____

____

____

____

____

____

SIGNATURE:____________________________ DATE:________________

FINANCIAL CHALLENGES					
#	Description	Hours	Rate	Deposit	Withdrawal
1					
2					
3					
4					
5					
		Total:			

MENTAL CHALLENGES					
#	Description	Hours	Rate	Deposit	Withdrawal
1					
2					
3					
4					
5					
		Total:			

PHYSICAL CHALLENGES					
#	Description	Hours	Rate	Deposit	Withdrawal
1					
2					
3					
4					
5					
		Total:			

SOCIAL CHALLENGES					
#	Description	Hours	Rate	Deposit	Withdrawal
1					
2					
3					
4					
5					
		Total:			

SPIRITUAL CHALLENGES					
#	Description	Hours	Rate	Deposit	Withdrawal
1					
2					
3					
4					
5					
			Total:		

DAILY SUMMARY			
#	Description	Yesterday's Balance	Add Today's Balance
1	Financial		
2	Mental		
3	Physical		
4	Social		
5	Spiritual		
		Total	

NOTES:____

____

____

____

____

____

AFFIRMATIONS:____

____

____

____

____

____

____

SIGNATURE:______________________________ DATE:________________

FINANCIAL CHALLENGES					
#	Description	Hours	Rate	Deposit	Withdrawal
1					
2					
3					
4					
5					
		Total:			

MENTAL CHALLENGES					
#	Description	Hours	Rate	Deposit	Withdrawal
1					
2					
3					
4					
5					
		Total:			

PHYSICAL CHALLENGES					
#	Description	Hours	Rate	Deposit	Withdrawal
1					
2					
3					
4					
5					
		Total:			

SOCIAL CHALLENGES					
#	Description	Hours	Rate	Deposit	Withdrawal
1					
2					
3					
4					
5					
		Total:			

SPIRITUAL CHALLENGES					
#	**Description**	**Hours**	**Rate**	**Deposit**	**Withdrawal**
1					
2					
3					
4					
5					
		Total:			

DAILY SUMMARY			
#	**Description**	**Yesterday's Balance**	**Add Today's Balance**
1	Financial		
2	Mental		
3	Physical		
4	Social		
5	Spiritual		
Total			

NOTES:____

____

____

____

____

____

AFFIRMATIONS:____

____

____

____

____

____

____

SIGNATURE:______________________ DATE:______________

FINANCIAL CHALLENGES					
#	Description	Hours	Rate	Deposit	Withdrawal
1					
2					
3					
4					
5					
		Total:			

MENTAL CHALLENGES					
#	Description	Hours	Rate	Deposit	Withdrawal
1					
2					
3					
4					
5					
		Total:			

PHYSICAL CHALLENGES					
#	Description	Hours	Rate	Deposit	Withdrawal
1					
2					
3					
4					
5					
		Total:			

SOCIAL CHALLENGES					
#	Description	Hours	Rate	Deposit	Withdrawal
1					
2					
3					
4					
5					
		Total:			

Prodigy Planner Workbook

SPIRITUAL CHALLENGES					
#	Description	Hours	Rate	Deposit	Withdrawal
1					
2					
3					
4					
5					
		Total:			

DAILY SUMMARY			
#	Description	Yesterday's Balance	Add Today's Balance
1	Financial		
2	Mental		
3	Physical		
4	Social		
5	Spiritual		
Total			

NOTES:____

____

____

____

____

____

AFFIRMATIONS:____

____

____

____

____

____

____

SIGNATURE:______________________________ DATE:________________

Prodigy Planner Workbook

FINANCIAL CHALLENGES					
#	**Description**	**Hours**	**Rate**	**Deposit**	**Withdrawal**
1					
2					
3					
4					
5					
		Total:			

MENTAL CHALLENGES					
#	**Description**	**Hours**	**Rate**	**Deposit**	**Withdrawal**
1					
2					
3					
4					
5					
		Total:			

PHYSICAL CHALLENGES					
#	**Description**	**Hours**	**Rate**	**Deposit**	**Withdrawal**
1					
2					
3					
4					
5					
		Total:			

SOCIAL CHALLENGES					
#	**Description**	**Hours**	**Rate**	**Deposit**	**Withdrawal**
1					
2					
3					
4					
5					
		Total:			

Prodigy Planner Workbook

SPIRITUAL CHALLENGES					
#	Description	Hours	Rate	Deposit	Withdrawal
1					
2					
3					
4					
5					
			Total:		

DAILY SUMMARY			
#	Description	Yesterday's Balance	Add Today's Balance
1	Financial		
2	Mental		
3	Physical		
4	Social		
5	Spiritual		
	Total		

NOTES:______________________________

AFFIRMATIONS:______________________________

SIGNATURE:______________________ DATE:______________

FINANCIAL CHALLENGES					
#	Description	Hours	Rate	Deposit	Withdrawal
1					
2					
3					
4					
5					
		Total:			

MENTAL CHALLENGES					
#	Description	Hours	Rate	Deposit	Withdrawal
1					
2					
3					
4					
5					
		Total:			

PHYSICAL CHALLENGES					
#	Description	Hours	Rate	Deposit	Withdrawal
1					
2					
3					
4					
5					
		Total:			

SOCIAL CHALLENGES					
#	Description	Hours	Rate	Deposit	Withdrawal
1					
2					
3					
4					
5					
		Total:			

Prodigy Planner Workbook

SPIRITUAL CHALLENGES					
#	Description	Hours	Rate	Deposit	Withdrawal
1					
2					
3					
4					
5					
		Total:			

DAILY SUMMARY			
#	Description	Yesterday's Balance	Add Today's Balance
1	Financial		
2	Mental		
3	Physical		
4	Social		
5	Spiritual		
Total			

NOTES:____

AFFIRMATIONS:________________________________

SIGNATURE:________________________ DATE:______________

FINANCIAL CHALLENGES					
#	Description	Hours	Rate	Deposit	Withdrawal
1					
2					
3					
4					
5					
		Total:			

MENTAL CHALLENGES					
#	Description	Hours	Rate	Deposit	Withdrawal
1					
2					
3					
4					
5					
		Total:			

PHYSICAL CHALLENGES					
#	Description	Hours	Rate	Deposit	Withdrawal
1					
2					
3					
4					
5					
		Total:			

SOCIAL CHALLENGES					
#	Description	Hours	Rate	Deposit	Withdrawal
1					
2					
3					
4					
5					
		Total:			

Prodigy Planner Workbook

SPIRITUAL CHALLENGES					
#	**Description**	**Hours**	**Rate**	**Deposit**	**Withdrawal**
1					
2					
3					
4					
5					
		Total:			

DAILY SUMMARY			
#	**Description**	**Yesterday's Balance**	**Add Today's Balance**
1	Financial		
2	Mental		
3	Physical		
4	Social		
5	Spiritual		
Total			

NOTES:____

____

____

____

____

____

AFFIRMATIONS:____

____

____

____

____

____

____

SIGNATURE:______________________________ DATE:________________

FINANCIAL CHALLENGES					
#	Description	Hours	Rate	Deposit	Withdrawal
1					
2					
3					
4					
5					
		Total:			

MENTAL CHALLENGES					
#	Description	Hours	Rate	Deposit	Withdrawal
1					
2					
3					
4					
5					
		Total:			

PHYSICAL CHALLENGES					
#	Description	Hours	Rate	Deposit	Withdrawal
1					
2					
3					
4					
5					
		Total:			

SOCIAL CHALLENGES					
#	Description	Hours	Rate	Deposit	Withdrawal
1					
2					
3					
4					
5					
		Total:			

SPIRITUAL CHALLENGES					
#	Description	Hours	Rate	Deposit	Withdrawal
1					
2					
3					
4					
5					
		Total:			

DAILY SUMMARY			
#	Description	Yesterday's Balance	Add Today's Balance
1	Financial		
2	Mental		
3	Physical		
4	Social		
5	Spiritual		
Total			

NOTES:____

AFFIRMATIONS:__________________________________

SIGNATURE:____________________ DATE:____________

FINANCIAL CHALLENGES					
#	Description	Hours	Rate	Deposit	Withdrawal
1					
2					
3					
4					
5					
		Total:			

MENTAL CHALLENGES					
#	Description	Hours	Rate	Deposit	Withdrawal
1					
2					
3					
4					
5					
		Total:			

PHYSICAL CHALLENGES					
#	Description	Hours	Rate	Deposit	Withdrawal
1					
2					
3					
4					
5					
		Total:			

SOCIAL CHALLENGES					
#	Description	Hours	Rate	Deposit	Withdrawal
1					
2					
3					
4					
5					
		Total:			

Prodigy Planner Workbook

SPIRITUAL CHALLENGES					
#	Description	Hours	Rate	Deposit	Withdrawal
1					
2					
3					
4					
5					
		Total:			

DAILY SUMMARY			
#	Description	Yesterday's Balance	Add Today's Balance
1	Financial		
2	Mental		
3	Physical		
4	Social		
5	Spiritual		
Total			

NOTES:____

____

____

____

____

____

AFFIRMATIONS:_______________________________________

____

____

____

____

____

____

SIGNATURE:_____________________________ DATE:________________

FINANCIAL CHALLENGES					
#	Description	Hours	Rate	Deposit	Withdrawal
1					
2					
3					
4					
5					
		Total:			

MENTAL CHALLENGES					
#	Description	Hours	Rate	Deposit	Withdrawal
1					
2					
3					
4					
5					
		Total:			

PHYSICAL CHALLENGES					
#	Description	Hours	Rate	Deposit	Withdrawal
1					
2					
3					
4					
5					
		Total:			

SOCIAL CHALLENGES					
#	Description	Hours	Rate	Deposit	Withdrawal
1					
2					
3					
4					
5					
		Total:			

Prodigy Planner Workbook

SPIRITUAL CHALLENGES					
#	Description	Hours	Rate	Deposit	Withdrawal
1					
2					
3					
4					
5					
		Total:			

DAILY SUMMARY			
#	Description	Yesterday's Balance	Add Today's Balance
1	Financial		
2	Mental		
3	Physical		
4	Social		
5	Spiritual		
Total			

NOTES:______________________________

____

____

____

____

____

AFFIRMATIONS:______________________________

____

____

____

____

____

____

SIGNATURE:____________________ DATE:____________

FINANCIAL CHALLENGES					
#	Description	Hours	Rate	Deposit	Withdrawal
1					
2					
3					
4					
5					
		Total:			

MENTAL CHALLENGES					
#	Description	Hours	Rate	Deposit	Withdrawal
1					
2					
3					
4					
5					
		Total:			

PHYSICAL CHALLENGES					
#	Description	Hours	Rate	Deposit	Withdrawal
1					
2					
3					
4					
5					
		Total:			

SOCIAL CHALLENGES					
#	Description	Hours	Rate	Deposit	Withdrawal
1					
2					
3					
4					
5					
		Total:			

SPIRITUAL CHALLENGES					
#	**Description**	**Hours**	**Rate**	**Deposit**	**Withdrawal**
1					
2					
3					
4					
5					
		Total:			

DAILY SUMMARY			
#	**Description**	**Yesterday's Balance**	**Add Today's Balance**
1	Financial		
2	Mental		
3	Physical		
4	Social		
5	Spiritual		
Total			

NOTES:____

AFFIRMATIONS:________________________________

SIGNATURE:____________________ DATE:____________

FINANCIAL CHALLENGES					
#	Description	Hours	Rate	Deposit	Withdrawal
1					
2					
3					
4					
5					
		Total:			

MENTAL CHALLENGES					
#	Description	Hours	Rate	Deposit	Withdrawal
1					
2					
3					
4					
5					
		Total:			

PHYSICAL CHALLENGES					
#	Description	Hours	Rate	Deposit	Withdrawal
1					
2					
3					
4					
5					
		Total:			

SOCIAL CHALLENGES					
#	Description	Hours	Rate	Deposit	Withdrawal
1					
2					
3					
4					
5					
		Total:			

SPIRITUAL CHALLENGES					
#	Description	Hours	Rate	Deposit	Withdrawal
1					
2					
3					
4					
5					
		Total:			

DAILY SUMMARY			
#	Description	Yesterday's Balance	Add Today's Balance
1	Financial		
2	Mental		
3	Physical		
4	Social		
5	Spiritual		
Total			

NOTES:______________________________

AFFIRMATIONS:______________________________

SIGNATURE:____________________ DATE:____________

Prodigy Planner Workbook

FINANCIAL CHALLENGES					
#	Description	Hours	Rate	Deposit	Withdrawal
1					
2					
3					
4					
5					
		Total:			

MENTAL CHALLENGES					
#	Description	Hours	Rate	Deposit	Withdrawal
1					
2					
3					
4					
5					
		Total:			

PHYSICAL CHALLENGES					
#	Description	Hours	Rate	Deposit	Withdrawal
1					
2					
3					
4					
5					
		Total:			

SOCIAL CHALLENGES					
#	Description	Hours	Rate	Deposit	Withdrawal
1					
2					
3					
4					
5					
		Total:			

SPIRITUAL CHALLENGES					
#	**Description**	**Hours**	**Rate**	**Deposit**	**Withdrawal**
1					
2					
3					
4					
5					
		Total:			

DAILY SUMMARY			
#	**Description**	**Yesterday's Balance**	**Add Today's Balance**
1	Financial		
2	Mental		
3	Physical		
4	Social		
5	Spiritual		
Total			

NOTES:____

____

____

____

____

____

AFFIRMATIONS:____

____

____

____

____

____

____

SIGNATURE:______________________________ DATE:________________

Prodigy Planner Workbook

FINANCIAL CHALLENGES					
#	**Description**	**Hours**	**Rate**	**Deposit**	**Withdrawal**
1					
2					
3					
4					
5					
		Total:			

MENTAL CHALLENGES					
#	**Description**	**Hours**	**Rate**	**Deposit**	**Withdrawal**
1					
2					
3					
4					
5					
		Total:			

PHYSICAL CHALLENGES					
#	**Description**	**Hours**	**Rate**	**Deposit**	**Withdrawal**
1					
2					
3					
4					
5					
		Total:			

SOCIAL CHALLENGES					
#	**Description**	**Hours**	**Rate**	**Deposit**	**Withdrawal**
1					
2					
3					
4					
5					
		Total:			

Prodigy Planner Workbook

SPIRITUAL CHALLENGES					
#	Description	Hours	Rate	Deposit	Withdrawal
1					
2					
3					
4					
5					
		Total:			

DAILY SUMMARY			
#	Description	Yesterday's Balance	Add Today's Balance
1	Financial		
2	Mental		
3	Physical		
4	Social		
5	Spiritual		
Total			

NOTES:______________________________

____

____

____

____

____

AFFIRMATIONS:______________________________

____

____

____

____

____

____

SIGNATURE:______________________ DATE:______________

Prodigy Planner Workbook

FINANCIAL CHALLENGES					
#	**Description**	**Hours**	**Rate**	**Deposit**	**Withdrawal**
1					
2					
3					
4					
5					
		Total:			

MENTAL CHALLENGES					
#	**Description**	**Hours**	**Rate**	**Deposit**	**Withdrawal**
1					
2					
3					
4					
5					
		Total:			

PHYSICAL CHALLENGES					
#	**Description**	**Hours**	**Rate**	**Deposit**	**Withdrawal**
1					
2					
3					
4					
5					
		Total:			

SOCIAL CHALLENGES					
#	**Description**	**Hours**	**Rate**	**Deposit**	**Withdrawal**
1					
2					
3					
4					
5					
		Total:			

SPIRITUAL CHALLENGES					
#	Description	Hours	Rate	Deposit	Withdrawal
1					
2					
3					
4					
5					
		Total:			

DAILY SUMMARY			
#	Description	Yesterday's Balance	Add Today's Balance
1	Financial		
2	Mental		
3	Physical		
4	Social		
5	Spiritual		
Total			

NOTES:______________________________

AFFIRMATIONS:______________________________

SIGNATURE:____________________ DATE:______________

FINANCIAL CHALLENGES					
#	Description	Hours	Rate	Deposit	Withdrawal
1					
2					
3					
4					
5					
		Total:			

MENTAL CHALLENGES					
#	Description	Hours	Rate	Deposit	Withdrawal
1					
2					
3					
4					
5					
		Total:			

PHYSICAL CHALLENGES					
#	Description	Hours	Rate	Deposit	Withdrawal
1					
2					
3					
4					
5					
		Total:			

SOCIAL CHALLENGES					
#	Description	Hours	Rate	Deposit	Withdrawal
1					
2					
3					
4					
5					
		Total:			

SPIRITUAL CHALLENGES					
#	Description	Hours	Rate	Deposit	Withdrawal
1					
2					
3					
4					
5					
			Total:		

DAILY SUMMARY			
#	Description	Yesterday's Balance	Add Today's Balance
1	Financial		
2	Mental		
3	Physical		
4	Social		
5	Spiritual		
Total			

NOTES:____

____

____

____

____

____

AFFIRMATIONS:______________________________________

____

____

____

____

____

____

SIGNATURE:______________________ DATE:____________

FINANCIAL CHALLENGES					
#	Description	Hours	Rate	Deposit	Withdrawal
1					
2					
3					
4					
5					
		Total:			

MENTAL CHALLENGES					
#	Description	Hours	Rate	Deposit	Withdrawal
1					
2					
3					
4					
5					
		Total:			

PHYSICAL CHALLENGES					
#	Description	Hours	Rate	Deposit	Withdrawal
1					
2					
3					
4					
5					
		Total:			

SOCIAL CHALLENGES					
#	Description	Hours	Rate	Deposit	Withdrawal
1					
2					
3					
4					
5					
		Total:			

Prodigy Planner Workbook

SPIRITUAL CHALLENGES					
#	Description	Hours	Rate	Deposit	Withdrawal
1					
2					
3					
4					
5					
			Total:		

DAILY SUMMARY			
#	Description	Yesterday's Balance	Add Today's Balance
1	Financial		
2	Mental		
3	Physical		
4	Social		
5	Spiritual		
Total			

NOTES:______________________________

____

____

____

____

____

AFFIRMATIONS:______________________________

____

____

____

____

____

____

SIGNATURE:______________________ DATE:______________

FINANCIAL CHALLENGES					
#	Description	Hours	Rate	Deposit	Withdrawal
1					
2					
3					
4					
5					
		Total:			

MENTAL CHALLENGES					
#	Description	Hours	Rate	Deposit	Withdrawal
1					
2					
3					
4					
5					
		Total:			

PHYSICAL CHALLENGES					
#	Description	Hours	Rate	Deposit	Withdrawal
1					
2					
3					
4					
5					
		Total:			

SOCIAL CHALLENGES					
#	Description	Hours	Rate	Deposit	Withdrawal
1					
2					
3					
4					
5					
		Total:			

SPIRITUAL CHALLENGES					
#	**Description**	**Hours**	**Rate**	**Deposit**	**Withdrawal**
1					
2					
3					
4					
5					
		Total:			

DAILY SUMMARY			
#	**Description**	**Yesterday's Balance**	**Add Today's Balance**
1	Financial		
2	Mental		
3	Physical		
4	Social		
5	Spiritual		
Total			

NOTES:____

____

____

____

____

____

AFFIRMATIONS:____

____

____

____

____

____

____

SIGNATURE:______________________________ DATE:________________

FINANCIAL CHALLENGES					
#	Description	Hours	Rate	Deposit	Withdrawal
1					
2					
3					
4					
5					
		Total:			

MENTAL CHALLENGES					
#	Description	Hours	Rate	Deposit	Withdrawal
1					
2					
3					
4					
5					
		Total:			

PHYSICAL CHALLENGES					
#	Description	Hours	Rate	Deposit	Withdrawal
1					
2					
3					
4					
5					
		Total:			

SOCIAL CHALLENGES					
#	Description	Hours	Rate	Deposit	Withdrawal
1					
2					
3					
4					
5					
		Total:			

Prodigy Planner Workbook

SPIRITUAL CHALLENGES					
#	Description	Hours	Rate	Deposit	Withdrawal
1					
2					
3					
4					
5					
		Total:			

DAILY SUMMARY			
#	Description	Yesterday's Balance	Add Today's Balance
1	Financial		
2	Mental		
3	Physical		
4	Social		
5	Spiritual		
Total			

NOTES:____

AFFIRMATIONS:__________________________________

SIGNATURE:____________________ DATE:____________

FINANCIAL CHALLENGES					
#	Description	Hours	Rate	Deposit	Withdrawal
1					
2					
3					
4					
5					
		Total:			

MENTAL CHALLENGES					
#	Description	Hours	Rate	Deposit	Withdrawal
1					
2					
3					
4					
5					
		Total:			

PHYSICAL CHALLENGES					
#	Description	Hours	Rate	Deposit	Withdrawal
1					
2					
3					
4					
5					
		Total:			

SOCIAL CHALLENGES					
#	Description	Hours	Rate	Deposit	Withdrawal
1					
2					
3					
4					
5					
		Total:			

SPIRITUAL CHALLENGES					
#	**Description**	**Hours**	**Rate**	**Deposit**	**Withdrawal**
1					
2					
3					
4					
5					
		Total:			

DAILY SUMMARY			
#	**Description**	**Yesterday's Balance**	**Add Today's Balance**
1	Financial		
2	Mental		
3	Physical		
4	Social		
5	Spiritual		
Total			

NOTES:____

AFFIRMATIONS:____

SIGNATURE:______________________________ DATE:________________

FINANCIAL CHALLENGES					
#	Description	Hours	Rate	Deposit	Withdrawal
1					
2					
3					
4					
5					
		Total:			

MENTAL CHALLENGES					
#	Description	Hours	Rate	Deposit	Withdrawal
1					
2					
3					
4					
5					
		Total:			

PHYSICAL CHALLENGES					
#	Description	Hours	Rate	Deposit	Withdrawal
1					
2					
3					
4					
5					
		Total:			

SOCIAL CHALLENGES					
#	Description	Hours	Rate	Deposit	Withdrawal
1					
2					
3					
4					
5					
		Total:			

Prodigy Planner Workbook

SPIRITUAL CHALLENGES					
#	**Description**	**Hours**	**Rate**	**Deposit**	**Withdrawal**
1					
2					
3					
4					
5					
		Total:			

DAILY SUMMARY			
#	**Description**	**Yesterday's Balance**	**Add Today's Balance**
1	Financial		
2	Mental		
3	Physical		
4	Social		
5	Spiritual		
Total			

NOTES:____

____

____

____

____

____

AFFIRMATIONS:____

____

____

____

____

____

____

SIGNATURE:______________________________ DATE:________________

WEALTH LEVEL 1 - Essentials		
#	**Description**	**Deposit**
1	Have Earned Income	
2	Have Investment Income	
3	Have Leveraged Income	
4	Have Residual Income	
5	Have More Than One Type Of Income	
WEALTH LEVEL 2 - Fundamentals		
#	**Description**	**Deposit**
1	10% Of Income Saved Upon Payment	
2	6-Month Emergency Cash Fund Reserved	
3	1-Year Emergency Electronic Fund Reserved	
4	All Monthly Bills Are Paid On Time	
5	Bills Do Not Exceed 50% Of Monthly Income	
6	No Debt – With Exception Of Mortgage	
WEALTH LEVEL 3 - Safety Net		
#	**Description**	**Deposit**
1	Life Insurance – All Dependents	
2	Medical Insurance – All Dependents	
3	Disability Insurance – If Not Retired	
4	Dental Insurance – All Dependents	
5	Optical Insurance - All Dependents	
6	Long Term Care Insurance – If Retired	
7	Umbrella Insurance	
8	Property Insurance – Homeowner/Renters	
9	Auto Insurance	
10	Filed All Bills & Receipts	

WEALTH LEVEL 4 - Look Good On Paper		
#	**Description**	**Deposit**
1	Have A Credit Score Above 760	
2	Have A Secured Credit Cards Only	
3	10% Of Income Invested Upon Payment	
4	Monitor Your Credit Report Monthly	
WEALTH LEVEL 5 - Sustainability		
#	**Description**	**Deposit**
1	Sustainable Power Supply – No Bill	
2	Sustainable Water Supply – No Bill	
3	Recycle & Eliminate Own Waste	
4	Have No Mortgage Or Rent Bill	
5	20-Year Property Tax Funds Reserved	
6	Homestead	
	Total:	

NOTES:____

AFFIRMATIONS:____

SIGNATURE:______________________ DATE:______________

Prodigy Planner Workbook

FINANCIAL CHALLENGES					
#	Description	Hours	Rate	Deposit	Withdrawal
1					
2					
3					
4					
5					
		Total:			

MENTAL CHALLENGES					
#	Description	Hours	Rate	Deposit	Withdrawal
1					
2					
3					
4					
5					
		Total:			

PHYSICAL CHALLENGES					
#	Description	Hours	Rate	Deposit	Withdrawal
1					
2					
3					
4					
5					
		Total:			

SOCIAL CHALLENGES					
#	Description	Hours	Rate	Deposit	Withdrawal
1					
2					
3					
4					
5					
		Total:			

SPIRITUAL CHALLENGES					
#	**Description**	**Hours**	**Rate**	**Deposit**	**Withdrawal**
1					
2					
3					
4					
5					
			Total:		

DAILY SUMMARY			
#	**Description**	**Yesterday's Balance**	**Add Today's Balance**
1	Financial		
2	Mental		
3	Physical		
4	Social		
5	Spiritual		
	Monthly Wealth Bonus		
	Total		

NOTES:____

AFFIRMATIONS:____________________________________

SIGNATURE:________________________ DATE:____________

Prodigy Planner Workbook

FINANCIAL CHALLENGES					
#	Description	Hours	Rate	Deposit	Withdrawal
1					
2					
3					
4					
5					
		Total:			

MENTAL CHALLENGES					
#	Description	Hours	Rate	Deposit	Withdrawal
1					
2					
3					
4					
5					
		Total:			

PHYSICAL CHALLENGES					
#	Description	Hours	Rate	Deposit	Withdrawal
1					
2					
3					
4					
5					
		Total:			

SOCIAL CHALLENGES					
#	Description	Hours	Rate	Deposit	Withdrawal
1					
2					
3					
4					
5					
		Total:			

Prodigy Planner Workbook

SPIRITUAL CHALLENGES					
#	Description	Hours	Rate	Deposit	Withdrawal
1					
2					
3					
4					
5					
			Total:		

DAILY SUMMARY			
#	Description	Yesterday's Balance	Add Today's Balance
1	Financial		
2	Mental		
3	Physical		
4	Social		
5	Spiritual		
		Total	

NOTES:____

AFFIRMATIONS:__________________________________

SIGNATURE:________________________ DATE:____________

FINANCIAL CHALLENGES					
#	Description	Hours	Rate	Deposit	Withdrawal
1					
2					
3					
4					
5					
		Total:			

MENTAL CHALLENGES					
#	Description	Hours	Rate	Deposit	Withdrawal
1					
2					
3					
4					
5					
		Total:			

PHYSICAL CHALLENGES					
#	Description	Hours	Rate	Deposit	Withdrawal
1					
2					
3					
4					
5					
		Total:			

SOCIAL CHALLENGES					
#	Description	Hours	Rate	Deposit	Withdrawal
1					
2					
3					
4					
5					
		Total:			

Prodigy Planner Workbook

SPIRITUAL CHALLENGES					
#	**Description**	**Hours**	**Rate**	**Deposit**	**Withdrawal**
1					
2					
3					
4					
5					
		Total:			

DAILY SUMMARY			
#	**Description**	**Yesterday's Balance**	**Add Today's Balance**
1	Financial		
2	Mental		
3	Physical		
4	Social		
5	Spiritual		
Total			

NOTES:____

AFFIRMATIONS:____

SIGNATURE:__________________________ DATE:_______________

FINANCIAL CHALLENGES					
#	Description	Hours	Rate	Deposit	Withdrawal
1					
2					
3					
4					
5					
		Total:			

MENTAL CHALLENGES					
#	Description	Hours	Rate	Deposit	Withdrawal
1					
2					
3					
4					
5					
		Total:			

PHYSICAL CHALLENGES					
#	Description	Hours	Rate	Deposit	Withdrawal
1					
2					
3					
4					
5					
		Total:			

SOCIAL CHALLENGES					
#	Description	Hours	Rate	Deposit	Withdrawal
1					
2					
3					
4					
5					
		Total:			

Prodigy Planner Workbook

SPIRITUAL CHALLENGES					
#	**Description**	**Hours**	**Rate**	**Deposit**	**Withdrawal**
1					
2					
3					
4					
5					
		Total:			

DAILY SUMMARY			
#	**Description**	**Yesterday's Balance**	**Add Today's Balance**
1	Financial		
2	Mental		
3	Physical		
4	Social		
5	Spiritual		
Total			

NOTES:____

AFFIRMATIONS:__________________________________

SIGNATURE:________________________ DATE:____________

FINANCIAL CHALLENGES					
#	Description	Hours	Rate	Deposit	Withdrawal
1					
2					
3					
4					
5					
		Total:			

MENTAL CHALLENGES					
#	Description	Hours	Rate	Deposit	Withdrawal
1					
2					
3					
4					
5					
		Total:			

PHYSICAL CHALLENGES					
#	Description	Hours	Rate	Deposit	Withdrawal
1					
2					
3					
4					
5					
		Total:			

SOCIAL CHALLENGES					
#	Description	Hours	Rate	Deposit	Withdrawal
1					
2					
3					
4					
5					
		Total:			

Prodigy Planner Workbook

SPIRITUAL CHALLENGES					
#	Description	Hours	Rate	Deposit	Withdrawal
1					
2					
3					
4					
5					
		Total:			

DAILY SUMMARY			
#	Description	Yesterday's Balance	Add Today's Balance
1	Financial		
2	Mental		
3	Physical		
4	Social		
5	Spiritual		
Total			

NOTES:____

____

____

____

____

____

AFFIRMATIONS:_________________________________

____

____

____

____

____

____

SIGNATURE:______________________ DATE:____________

Prodigy Planner Workbook

FINANCIAL CHALLENGES					
#	Description	Hours	Rate	Deposit	Withdrawal
1					
2					
3					
4					
5					
		Total:			

MENTAL CHALLENGES					
#	Description	Hours	Rate	Deposit	Withdrawal
1					
2					
3					
4					
5					
		Total:			

PHYSICAL CHALLENGES					
#	Description	Hours	Rate	Deposit	Withdrawal
1					
2					
3					
4					
5					
		Total:			

SOCIAL CHALLENGES					
#	Description	Hours	Rate	Deposit	Withdrawal
1					
2					
3					
4					
5					
		Total:			

SPIRITUAL CHALLENGES					
#	**Description**	**Hours**	**Rate**	**Deposit**	**Withdrawal**
1					
2					
3					
4					
5					
		Total:			

DAILY SUMMARY			
#	**Description**	**Yesterday's Balance**	**Add Today's Balance**
1	Financial		
2	Mental		
3	Physical		
4	Social		
5	Spiritual		
Total			

NOTES:____

____

____

____

____

____

AFFIRMATIONS:______________________________________

____

____

____

____

____

____

SIGNATURE:______________________ DATE:______________

Prodigy Planner Workbook

FINANCIAL CHALLENGES					
#	Description	Hours	Rate	Deposit	Withdrawal
1					
2					
3					
4					
5					
		Total:			

MENTAL CHALLENGES					
#	Description	Hours	Rate	Deposit	Withdrawal
1					
2					
3					
4					
5					
		Total:			

PHYSICAL CHALLENGES					
#	Description	Hours	Rate	Deposit	Withdrawal
1					
2					
3					
4					
5					
		Total:			

SOCIAL CHALLENGES					
#	Description	Hours	Rate	Deposit	Withdrawal
1					
2					
3					
4					
5					
		Total:			

Prodigy Planner Workbook

SPIRITUAL CHALLENGES					
#	Description	Hours	Rate	Deposit	Withdrawal
1					
2					
3					
4					
5					
		Total:			

DAILY SUMMARY			
#	Description	Yesterday's Balance	Add Today's Balance
1	Financial		
2	Mental		
3	Physical		
4	Social		
5	Spiritual		
Total			

NOTES:____

AFFIRMATIONS:________________________________

SIGNATURE:____________________ DATE:____________

FINANCIAL CHALLENGES					
#	Description	Hours	Rate	Deposit	Withdrawal
1					
2					
3					
4					
5					
		Total:			

MENTAL CHALLENGES					
#	Description	Hours	Rate	Deposit	Withdrawal
1					
2					
3					
4					
5					
		Total:			

PHYSICAL CHALLENGES					
#	Description	Hours	Rate	Deposit	Withdrawal
1					
2					
3					
4					
5					
		Total:			

SOCIAL CHALLENGES					
#	Description	Hours	Rate	Deposit	Withdrawal
1					
2					
3					
4					
5					
		Total:			

SPIRITUAL CHALLENGES					
#	Description	Hours	Rate	Deposit	Withdrawal
1					
2					
3					
4					
5					
		Total:			

DAILY SUMMARY			
#	Description	Yesterday's Balance	Add Today's Balance
1	Financial		
2	Mental		
3	Physical		
4	Social		
5	Spiritual		
Total			

NOTES:____

AFFIRMATIONS:____________________________________

SIGNATURE:____________________ DATE:____________

FINANCIAL CHALLENGES					
#	Description	Hours	Rate	Deposit	Withdrawal
1					
2					
3					
4					
5					
		Total:			

MENTAL CHALLENGES					
#	Description	Hours	Rate	Deposit	Withdrawal
1					
2					
3					
4					
5					
		Total:			

PHYSICAL CHALLENGES					
#	Description	Hours	Rate	Deposit	Withdrawal
1					
2					
3					
4					
5					
		Total:			

SOCIAL CHALLENGES					
#	Description	Hours	Rate	Deposit	Withdrawal
1					
2					
3					
4					
5					
		Total:			

Prodigy Planner Workbook

SPIRITUAL CHALLENGES					
#	Description	Hours	Rate	Deposit	Withdrawal
1					
2					
3					
4					
5					
		Total:			

DAILY SUMMARY			
#	Description	Yesterday's Balance	Add Today's Balance
1	Financial		
2	Mental		
3	Physical		
4	Social		
5	Spiritual		
Total			

NOTES:______________________________

AFFIRMATIONS:______________________________

SIGNATURE:____________________ DATE:__________

FINANCIAL CHALLENGES					
#	Description	Hours	Rate	Deposit	Withdrawal
1					
2					
3					
4					
5					
		Total:			

MENTAL CHALLENGES					
#	Description	Hours	Rate	Deposit	Withdrawal
1					
2					
3					
4					
5					
		Total:			

PHYSICAL CHALLENGES					
#	Description	Hours	Rate	Deposit	Withdrawal
1					
2					
3					
4					
5					
		Total:			

SOCIAL CHALLENGES					
#	Description	Hours	Rate	Deposit	Withdrawal
1					
2					
3					
4					
5					
		Total:			

Prodigy Planner Workbook

SPIRITUAL CHALLENGES					
#	Description	Hours	Rate	Deposit	Withdrawal
1					
2					
3					
4					
5					
		Total:			

DAILY SUMMARY			
#	Description	Yesterday's Balance	Add Today's Balance
1	Financial		
2	Mental		
3	Physical		
4	Social		
5	Spiritual		
Total			

NOTES:____

AFFIRMATIONS:__________________________________

SIGNATURE:________________________ DATE:______________

FINANCIAL CHALLENGES					
#	Description	Hours	Rate	Deposit	Withdrawal
1					
2					
3					
4					
5					
		Total:			

MENTAL CHALLENGES					
#	Description	Hours	Rate	Deposit	Withdrawal
1					
2					
3					
4					
5					
		Total:			

PHYSICAL CHALLENGES					
#	Description	Hours	Rate	Deposit	Withdrawal
1					
2					
3					
4					
5					
		Total:			

SOCIAL CHALLENGES					
#	Description	Hours	Rate	Deposit	Withdrawal
1					
2					
3					
4					
5					
		Total:			

Prodigy Planner Workbook

SPIRITUAL CHALLENGES					
#	Description	Hours	Rate	Deposit	Withdrawal
1					
2					
3					
4					
5					
		Total:			

DAILY SUMMARY			
#	Description	Yesterday's Balance	Add Today's Balance
1	Financial		
2	Mental		
3	Physical		
4	Social		
5	Spiritual		
Total			

NOTES:______________________________

____

____

____

____

____

AFFIRMATIONS:______________________________

____

____

____

____

____

____

SIGNATURE:______________________ DATE:____________

FINANCIAL CHALLENGES					
#	Description	Hours	Rate	Deposit	Withdrawal
1					
2					
3					
4					
5					
		Total:			

MENTAL CHALLENGES					
#	Description	Hours	Rate	Deposit	Withdrawal
1					
2					
3					
4					
5					
		Total:			

PHYSICAL CHALLENGES					
#	Description	Hours	Rate	Deposit	Withdrawal
1					
2					
3					
4					
5					
		Total:			

SOCIAL CHALLENGES					
#	Description	Hours	Rate	Deposit	Withdrawal
1					
2					
3					
4					
5					
		Total:			

SPIRITUAL CHALLENGES					
#	Description	Hours	Rate	Deposit	Withdrawal
1					
2					
3					
4					
5					
		Total:			

DAILY SUMMARY			
#	Description	Yesterday's Balance	Add Today's Balance
1	Financial		
2	Mental		
3	Physical		
4	Social		
5	Spiritual		
Total			

NOTES:____

AFFIRMATIONS:____

SIGNATURE:____________________ DATE:______________

FINANCIAL CHALLENGES					
#	**Description**	**Hours**	**Rate**	**Deposit**	**Withdrawal**
1					
2					
3					
4					
5					
		Total:			

MENTAL CHALLENGES					
#	**Description**	**Hours**	**Rate**	**Deposit**	**Withdrawal**
1					
2					
3					
4					
5					
		Total:			

PHYSICAL CHALLENGES					
#	**Description**	**Hours**	**Rate**	**Deposit**	**Withdrawal**
1					
2					
3					
4					
5					
		Total:			

SOCIAL CHALLENGES					
#	**Description**	**Hours**	**Rate**	**Deposit**	**Withdrawal**
1					
2					
3					
4					
5					
		Total:			

Prodigy Planner Workbook

SPIRITUAL CHALLENGES					
#	**Description**	**Hours**	**Rate**	**Deposit**	**Withdrawal**
1					
2					
3					
4					
5					
		Total:			

DAILY SUMMARY			
#	**Description**	**Yesterday's Balance**	**Add Today's Balance**
1	Financial		
2	Mental		
3	Physical		
4	Social		
5	Spiritual		
Total			

NOTES:____

____

____

____

____

____

AFFIRMATIONS:____

____

____

____

____

____

____

SIGNATURE:______________________________ DATE:________________

FINANCIAL CHALLENGES					
#	Description	Hours	Rate	Deposit	Withdrawal
1					
2					
3					
4					
5					
		Total:			

MENTAL CHALLENGES					
#	Description	Hours	Rate	Deposit	Withdrawal
1					
2					
3					
4					
5					
		Total:			

PHYSICAL CHALLENGES					
#	Description	Hours	Rate	Deposit	Withdrawal
1					
2					
3					
4					
5					
		Total:			

SOCIAL CHALLENGES					
#	Description	Hours	Rate	Deposit	Withdrawal
1					
2					
3					
4					
5					
		Total:			

SPIRITUAL CHALLENGES					
#	**Description**	**Hours**	**Rate**	**Deposit**	**Withdrawal**
1					
2					
3					
4					
5					
		Total:			

DAILY SUMMARY			
#	**Description**	**Yesterday's Balance**	**Add Today's Balance**
1	Financial		
2	Mental		
3	Physical		
4	Social		
5	Spiritual		
Total			

NOTES:____

____

____

____

____

____

AFFIRMATIONS:____

____

____

____

____

____

____

SIGNATURE:____________________________ DATE:______________

FINANCIAL CHALLENGES					
#	Description	Hours	Rate	Deposit	Withdrawal
1					
2					
3					
4					
5					
		Total:			

MENTAL CHALLENGES					
#	Description	Hours	Rate	Deposit	Withdrawal
1					
2					
3					
4					
5					
		Total:			

PHYSICAL CHALLENGES					
#	Description	Hours	Rate	Deposit	Withdrawal
1					
2					
3					
4					
5					
		Total:			

SOCIAL CHALLENGES					
#	Description	Hours	Rate	Deposit	Withdrawal
1					
2					
3					
4					
5					
		Total:			

SPIRITUAL CHALLENGES					
#	**Description**	**Hours**	**Rate**	**Deposit**	**Withdrawal**
1					
2					
3					
4					
5					
		Total:			

DAILY SUMMARY			
#	**Description**	**Yesterday's Balance**	**Add Today's Balance**
1	Financial		
2	Mental		
3	Physical		
4	Social		
5	Spiritual		
Total			

NOTES:____

AFFIRMATIONS:________________________________

SIGNATURE:____________________ DATE:____________

Prodigy Planner Workbook

FINANCIAL CHALLENGES					
#	Description	Hours	Rate	Deposit	Withdrawal
1					
2					
3					
4					
5					
		Total:			

MENTAL CHALLENGES					
#	Description	Hours	Rate	Deposit	Withdrawal
1					
2					
3					
4					
5					
		Total:			

PHYSICAL CHALLENGES					
#	Description	Hours	Rate	Deposit	Withdrawal
1					
2					
3					
4					
5					
		Total:			

SOCIAL CHALLENGES					
#	Description	Hours	Rate	Deposit	Withdrawal
1					
2					
3					
4					
5					
		Total:			

SPIRITUAL CHALLENGES					
#	Description	Hours	Rate	Deposit	Withdrawal
1					
2					
3					
4					
5					
			Total:		

DAILY SUMMARY			
#	Description	Yesterday's Balance	Add Today's Balance
1	Financial		
2	Mental		
3	Physical		
4	Social		
5	Spiritual		
		Total	

NOTES:____

AFFIRMATIONS:____

SIGNATURE:______________________ DATE:______________

Prodigy Planner Workbook

FINANCIAL CHALLENGES					
#	Description	Hours	Rate	Deposit	Withdrawal
1					
2					
3					
4					
5					
		Total:			

MENTAL CHALLENGES					
#	Description	Hours	Rate	Deposit	Withdrawal
1					
2					
3					
4					
5					
		Total:			

PHYSICAL CHALLENGES					
#	Description	Hours	Rate	Deposit	Withdrawal
1					
2					
3					
4					
5					
		Total:			

SOCIAL CHALLENGES					
#	Description	Hours	Rate	Deposit	Withdrawal
1					
2					
3					
4					
5					
		Total:			

Prodigy Planner Workbook

SPIRITUAL CHALLENGES					
#	Description	Hours	Rate	Deposit	Withdrawal
1					
2					
3					
4					
5					
		Total:			

DAILY SUMMARY			
#	Description	Yesterday's Balance	Add Today's Balance
1	Financial		
2	Mental		
3	Physical		
4	Social		
5	Spiritual		
Total			

NOTES:______________________________

____

____

____

____

____

AFFIRMATIONS:______________________________

____

____

____

____

____

____

SIGNATURE:______________________ DATE:______________

FINANCIAL CHALLENGES					
#	Description	Hours	Rate	Deposit	Withdrawal
1					
2					
3					
4					
5					
		Total:			

MENTAL CHALLENGES					
#	Description	Hours	Rate	Deposit	Withdrawal
1					
2					
3					
4					
5					
		Total:			

PHYSICAL CHALLENGES					
#	Description	Hours	Rate	Deposit	Withdrawal
1					
2					
3					
4					
5					
		Total:			

SOCIAL CHALLENGES					
#	Description	Hours	Rate	Deposit	Withdrawal
1					
2					
3					
4					
5					
		Total:			

SPIRITUAL CHALLENGES					
#	Description	Hours	Rate	Deposit	Withdrawal
1					
2					
3					
4					
5					
		Total:			

DAILY SUMMARY			
#	Description	Yesterday's Balance	Add Today's Balance
1	Financial		
2	Mental		
3	Physical		
4	Social		
5	Spiritual		
Total			

NOTES:______________________________

AFFIRMATIONS:______________________________

SIGNATURE:____________________ DATE:______________

FINANCIAL CHALLENGES					
#	Description	Hours	Rate	Deposit	Withdrawal
1					
2					
3					
4					
5					
		Total:			

MENTAL CHALLENGES					
#	Description	Hours	Rate	Deposit	Withdrawal
1					
2					
3					
4					
5					
		Total:			

PHYSICAL CHALLENGES					
#	Description	Hours	Rate	Deposit	Withdrawal
1					
2					
3					
4					
5					
		Total:			

SOCIAL CHALLENGES					
#	Description	Hours	Rate	Deposit	Withdrawal
1					
2					
3					
4					
5					
		Total:			

SPIRITUAL CHALLENGES					
#	Description	Hours	Rate	Deposit	Withdrawal
1					
2					
3					
4					
5					
		Total:			

DAILY SUMMARY			
#	Description	Yesterday's Balance	Add Today's Balance
1	Financial		
2	Mental		
3	Physical		
4	Social		
5	Spiritual		
Total			

NOTES:____

____

____

____

____

____

AFFIRMATIONS:______________________________________

____

____

____

____

____

____

SIGNATURE:____________________________ DATE:________________

Prodigy Planner Workbook

FINANCIAL CHALLENGES					
#	Description	Hours	Rate	Deposit	Withdrawal
1					
2					
3					
4					
5					
		Total:			

MENTAL CHALLENGES					
#	Description	Hours	Rate	Deposit	Withdrawal
1					
2					
3					
4					
5					
		Total:			

PHYSICAL CHALLENGES					
#	Description	Hours	Rate	Deposit	Withdrawal
1					
2					
3					
4					
5					
		Total:			

SOCIAL CHALLENGES					
#	Description	Hours	Rate	Deposit	Withdrawal
1					
2					
3					
4					
5					
		Total:			

SPIRITUAL CHALLENGES					
#	Description	Hours	Rate	Deposit	Withdrawal
1					
2					
3					
4					
5					
		Total:			

DAILY SUMMARY			
#	Description	Yesterday's Balance	Add Today's Balance
1	Financial		
2	Mental		
3	Physical		
4	Social		
5	Spiritual		
Total			

NOTES:____

AFFIRMATIONS:____

SIGNATURE:______________________________ DATE:________________

FINANCIAL CHALLENGES					
#	Description	Hours	Rate	Deposit	Withdrawal
1					
2					
3					
4					
5					
		Total:			

MENTAL CHALLENGES					
#	Description	Hours	Rate	Deposit	Withdrawal
1					
2					
3					
4					
5					
		Total:			

PHYSICAL CHALLENGES					
#	Description	Hours	Rate	Deposit	Withdrawal
1					
2					
3					
4					
5					
		Total:			

SOCIAL CHALLENGES					
#	Description	Hours	Rate	Deposit	Withdrawal
1					
2					
3					
4					
5					
		Total:			

Prodigy Planner Workbook

SPIRITUAL CHALLENGES					
#	Description	Hours	Rate	Deposit	Withdrawal
1					
2					
3					
4					
5					
		Total:			

DAILY SUMMARY			
#	Description	Yesterday's Balance	Add Today's Balance
1	Financial		
2	Mental		
3	Physical		
4	Social		
5	Spiritual		
Total			

NOTES:____

AFFIRMATIONS:__________________________________

SIGNATURE:____________________ DATE:____________

FINANCIAL CHALLENGES					
#	Description	Hours	Rate	Deposit	Withdrawal
1					
2					
3					
4					
5					
		Total:			

MENTAL CHALLENGES					
#	Description	Hours	Rate	Deposit	Withdrawal
1					
2					
3					
4					
5					
		Total:			

PHYSICAL CHALLENGES					
#	Description	Hours	Rate	Deposit	Withdrawal
1					
2					
3					
4					
5					
		Total:			

SOCIAL CHALLENGES					
#	Description	Hours	Rate	Deposit	Withdrawal
1					
2					
3					
4					
5					
		Total:			

SPIRITUAL CHALLENGES					
#	Description	Hours	Rate	Deposit	Withdrawal
1					
2					
3					
4					
5					
			Total:		

DAILY SUMMARY			
#	Description	Yesterday's Balance	Add Today's Balance
1	Financial		
2	Mental		
3	Physical		
4	Social		
5	Spiritual		
Total			

NOTES:____

____

____

____

____

____

AFFIRMATIONS:_______________________________________

____

____

____

____

____

____

SIGNATURE:____________________________ DATE:________________

FINANCIAL CHALLENGES					
#	Description	Hours	Rate	Deposit	Withdrawal
1					
2					
3					
4					
5					
		Total:			

MENTAL CHALLENGES					
#	Description	Hours	Rate	Deposit	Withdrawal
1					
2					
3					
4					
5					
		Total:			

PHYSICAL CHALLENGES					
#	Description	Hours	Rate	Deposit	Withdrawal
1					
2					
3					
4					
5					
		Total:			

SOCIAL CHALLENGES					
#	Description	Hours	Rate	Deposit	Withdrawal
1					
2					
3					
4					
5					
		Total:			

Prodigy Planner Workbook

SPIRITUAL CHALLENGES					
#	**Description**	**Hours**	**Rate**	**Deposit**	**Withdrawal**
1					
2					
3					
4					
5					
		Total:			

DAILY SUMMARY			
#	**Description**	**Yesterday's Balance**	**Add Today's Balance**
1	Financial		
2	Mental		
3	Physical		
4	Social		
5	Spiritual		
Total			

NOTES:____

AFFIRMATIONS:__________________________________

SIGNATURE:________________________ DATE:______________

FINANCIAL CHALLENGES					
#	Description	Hours	Rate	Deposit	Withdrawal
1					
2					
3					
4					
5					
		Total:			

MENTAL CHALLENGES					
#	Description	Hours	Rate	Deposit	Withdrawal
1					
2					
3					
4					
5					
		Total:			

PHYSICAL CHALLENGES					
#	Description	Hours	Rate	Deposit	Withdrawal
1					
2					
3					
4					
5					
		Total:			

SOCIAL CHALLENGES					
#	Description	Hours	Rate	Deposit	Withdrawal
1					
2					
3					
4					
5					
		Total:			

Prodigy Planner Workbook

SPIRITUAL CHALLENGES					
#	**Description**	**Hours**	**Rate**	**Deposit**	**Withdrawal**
1					
2					
3					
4					
5					
		Total:			

DAILY SUMMARY			
#	**Description**	**Yesterday's Balance**	**Add Today's Balance**
1	Financial		
2	Mental		
3	Physical		
4	Social		
5	Spiritual		
Total			

NOTES:____

AFFIRMATIONS:____

SIGNATURE:______________________ DATE:______________

FINANCIAL CHALLENGES					
#	Description	Hours	Rate	Deposit	Withdrawal
1					
2					
3					
4					
5					
		Total:			

MENTAL CHALLENGES					
#	Description	Hours	Rate	Deposit	Withdrawal
1					
2					
3					
4					
5					
		Total:			

PHYSICAL CHALLENGES					
#	Description	Hours	Rate	Deposit	Withdrawal
1					
2					
3					
4					
5					
		Total:			

SOCIAL CHALLENGES					
#	Description	Hours	Rate	Deposit	Withdrawal
1					
2					
3					
4					
5					
		Total:			

SPIRITUAL CHALLENGES					
#	**Description**	**Hours**	**Rate**	**Deposit**	**Withdrawal**
1					
2					
3					
4					
5					
		Total:			

DAILY SUMMARY			
#	**Description**	**Yesterday's Balance**	**Add Today's Balance**
1	Financial		
2	Mental		
3	Physical		
4	Social		
5	Spiritual		
Total			

NOTES:____

____

____

____

____

____

AFFIRMATIONS:____

____

____

____

____

____

____

SIGNATURE:______________________________ DATE:________________

FINANCIAL CHALLENGES					
#	Description	Hours	Rate	Deposit	Withdrawal
1					
2					
3					
4					
5					
		Total:			

MENTAL CHALLENGES					
#	Description	Hours	Rate	Deposit	Withdrawal
1					
2					
3					
4					
5					
		Total:			

PHYSICAL CHALLENGES					
#	Description	Hours	Rate	Deposit	Withdrawal
1					
2					
3					
4					
5					
		Total:			

SOCIAL CHALLENGES					
#	Description	Hours	Rate	Deposit	Withdrawal
1					
2					
3					
4					
5					
		Total:			

SPIRITUAL CHALLENGES					
#	Description	Hours	Rate	Deposit	Withdrawal
1					
2					
3					
4					
5					
		Total:			

DAILY SUMMARY			
#	Description	Yesterday's Balance	Add Today's Balance
1	Financial		
2	Mental		
3	Physical		
4	Social		
5	Spiritual		
Total			

NOTES:______________________________

____

____

____

____

____

AFFIRMATIONS:______________________________

____

____

____

____

____

____

SIGNATURE:______________________ DATE:______________

FINANCIAL CHALLENGES					
#	Description	Hours	Rate	Deposit	Withdrawal
1					
2					
3					
4					
5					
		Total:			

MENTAL CHALLENGES					
#	Description	Hours	Rate	Deposit	Withdrawal
1					
2					
3					
4					
5					
		Total:			

PHYSICAL CHALLENGES					
#	Description	Hours	Rate	Deposit	Withdrawal
1					
2					
3					
4					
5					
		Total:			

SOCIAL CHALLENGES					
#	Description	Hours	Rate	Deposit	Withdrawal
1					
2					
3					
4					
5					
		Total:			

Prodigy Planner Workbook

SPIRITUAL CHALLENGES					
#	**Description**	**Hours**	**Rate**	**Deposit**	**Withdrawal**
1					
2					
3					
4					
5					
		Total:			

DAILY SUMMARY			
#	**Description**	**Yesterday's Balance**	**Add Today's Balance**
1	Financial		
2	Mental		
3	Physical		
4	Social		
5	Spiritual		
	Total		

NOTES:____

AFFIRMATIONS:_______________________________________

SIGNATURE:_________________________ DATE:_______________

FINANCIAL CHALLENGES					
#	Description	Hours	Rate	Deposit	Withdrawal
1					
2					
3					
4					
5					
		Total:			

MENTAL CHALLENGES					
#	Description	Hours	Rate	Deposit	Withdrawal
1					
2					
3					
4					
5					
		Total:			

PHYSICAL CHALLENGES					
#	Description	Hours	Rate	Deposit	Withdrawal
1					
2					
3					
4					
5					
		Total:			

SOCIAL CHALLENGES					
#	Description	Hours	Rate	Deposit	Withdrawal
1					
2					
3					
4					
5					
		Total:			

Prodigy Planner Workbook

SPIRITUAL CHALLENGES					
#	Description	Hours	Rate	Deposit	Withdrawal
1					
2					
3					
4					
5					
		Total:			

DAILY SUMMARY			
#	Description	Yesterday's Balance	Add Today's Balance
1	Financial		
2	Mental		
3	Physical		
4	Social		
5	Spiritual		
Total			

NOTES:____

____

____

____

____

____

AFFIRMATIONS:______________________________________

____

____

____

____

____

____

SIGNATURE:______________________ DATE:____________

WEALTH LEVEL 1 - Essentials		
#	**Description**	**Deposit**
1	Have Earned Income	
2	Have Investment Income	
3	Have Leveraged Income	
4	Have Residual Income	
5	Have More Than One Type Of Income	

WEALTH LEVEL 2 - Fundamentals		
#	**Description**	**Deposit**
1	10% Of Income Saved Upon Payment	
2	6-Month Emergency Cash Fund Reserved	
3	1-Year Emergency Electronic Fund Reserved	
4	All Monthly Bills Are Paid On Time	
5	Bills Do Not Exceed 50% Of Monthly Income	
6	No Debt – With Exception Of Mortgage	

WEALTH LEVEL 3 - Safety Net		
#	**Description**	**Deposit**
1	Life Insurance – All Dependents	
2	Medical Insurance – All Dependents	
3	Disability Insurance – If Not Retired	
4	Dental Insurance – All Dependents	
5	Optical Insurance - All Dependents	
6	Long Term Care Insurance – If Retired	
7	Umbrella Insurance	
8	Property Insurance – Homeowner/Renters	
9	Auto Insurance	
10	Filed All Bills & Receipts	

WEALTH LEVEL 4 - Look Good On Paper		
#	**Description**	**Deposit**
1	Have A Credit Score Above 760	
2	Have A Secured Credit Cards Only	
3	10% Of Income Invested Upon Payment	
4	Monitor Your Credit Report Monthly	
WEALTH LEVEL 5 - Sustainability		
#	**Description**	**Deposit**
1	Sustainable Power Supply – No Bill	
2	Sustainable Water Supply – No Bill	
3	Recycle & Eliminate Own Waste	
4	Have No Mortgage Or Rent Bill	
5	20-Year Property Tax Funds Reserved	
6	Homestead	
	Total:	

NOTES:____

AFFIRMATIONS:__________________________________

SIGNATURE:__________________________ DATE:_______________

FINANCIAL CHALLENGES					
#	Description	Hours	Rate	Deposit	Withdrawal
1					
2					
3					
4					
5					
		Total:			

MENTAL CHALLENGES					
#	Description	Hours	Rate	Deposit	Withdrawal
1					
2					
3					
4					
5					
		Total:			

PHYSICAL CHALLENGES					
#	Description	Hours	Rate	Deposit	Withdrawal
1					
2					
3					
4					
5					
		Total:			

SOCIAL CHALLENGES					
#	Description	Hours	Rate	Deposit	Withdrawal
1					
2					
3					
4					
5					
		Total:			

SPIRITUAL CHALLENGES					
#	**Description**	**Hours**	**Rate**	**Deposit**	**Withdrawal**
1					
2					
3					
4					
5					
		Total:			

DAILY SUMMARY			
#	**Description**	**Yesterday's Balance**	**Add Today's Balance**
1	Financial		
2	Mental		
3	Physical		
4	Social		
5	Spiritual		
Monthly Wealth Bonus			
Total			

NOTES:______________________________

____

____

____

____

____

AFFIRMATIONS:______________________________

____

____

____

____

____

SIGNATURE:______________________ DATE:______________

FINANCIAL CHALLENGES					
#	Description	Hours	Rate	Deposit	Withdrawal
1					
2					
3					
4					
5					
		Total:			

MENTAL CHALLENGES					
#	Description	Hours	Rate	Deposit	Withdrawal
1					
2					
3					
4					
5					
		Total:			

PHYSICAL CHALLENGES					
#	Description	Hours	Rate	Deposit	Withdrawal
1					
2					
3					
4					
5					
		Total:			

SOCIAL CHALLENGES					
#	Description	Hours	Rate	Deposit	Withdrawal
1					
2					
3					
4					
5					
		Total:			

Prodigy Planner Workbook

SPIRITUAL CHALLENGES					
#	Description	Hours	Rate	Deposit	Withdrawal
1					
2					
3					
4					
5					
		Total:			

DAILY SUMMARY			
#	Description	Yesterday's Balance	Add Today's Balance
1	Financial		
2	Mental		
3	Physical		
4	Social		
5	Spiritual		
Total			

NOTES:____

AFFIRMATIONS:__________________________________

SIGNATURE:________________________ DATE:______________

Prodigy Planner Workbook

FINANCIAL CHALLENGES					
#	Description	Hours	Rate	Deposit	Withdrawal
1					
2					
3					
4					
5					
		Total:			

MENTAL CHALLENGES					
#	Description	Hours	Rate	Deposit	Withdrawal
1					
2					
3					
4					
5					
		Total:			

PHYSICAL CHALLENGES					
#	Description	Hours	Rate	Deposit	Withdrawal
1					
2					
3					
4					
5					
		Total:			

SOCIAL CHALLENGES					
#	Description	Hours	Rate	Deposit	Withdrawal
1					
2					
3					
4					
5					
		Total:			

SPIRITUAL CHALLENGES					
#	Description	Hours	Rate	Deposit	Withdrawal
1					
2					
3					
4					
5					
		Total:			

DAILY SUMMARY			
#	Description	Yesterday's Balance	Add Today's Balance
1	Financial		
2	Mental		
3	Physical		
4	Social		
5	Spiritual		
Total			

NOTES:______________________________

AFFIRMATIONS:______________________________

SIGNATURE:____________________ DATE:______________

Prodigy Planner Workbook

FINANCIAL CHALLENGES					
#	Description	Hours	Rate	Deposit	Withdrawal
1					
2					
3					
4					
5					
		Total:			

MENTAL CHALLENGES					
#	Description	Hours	Rate	Deposit	Withdrawal
1					
2					
3					
4					
5					
		Total:			

PHYSICAL CHALLENGES					
#	Description	Hours	Rate	Deposit	Withdrawal
1					
2					
3					
4					
5					
		Total:			

SOCIAL CHALLENGES					
#	Description	Hours	Rate	Deposit	Withdrawal
1					
2					
3					
4					
5					
		Total:			

Prodigy Planner Workbook

SPIRITUAL CHALLENGES					
#	Description	Hours	Rate	Deposit	Withdrawal
1					
2					
3					
4					
5					
		Total:			

DAILY SUMMARY			
#	Description	Yesterday's Balance	Add Today's Balance
1	Financial		
2	Mental		
3	Physical		
4	Social		
5	Spiritual		
	Total		

NOTES:______________________________________

AFFIRMATIONS:________________________________

SIGNATURE:____________________ DATE:____________

FINANCIAL CHALLENGES					
#	Description	Hours	Rate	Deposit	Withdrawal
1					
2					
3					
4					
5					
		Total:			

MENTAL CHALLENGES					
#	Description	Hours	Rate	Deposit	Withdrawal
1					
2					
3					
4					
5					
		Total:			

PHYSICAL CHALLENGES					
#	Description	Hours	Rate	Deposit	Withdrawal
1					
2					
3					
4					
5					
		Total:			

SOCIAL CHALLENGES					
#	Description	Hours	Rate	Deposit	Withdrawal
1					
2					
3					
4					
5					
		Total:			

Prodigy Planner Workbook

SPIRITUAL CHALLENGES					
#	**Description**	**Hours**	**Rate**	**Deposit**	**Withdrawal**
1					
2					
3					
4					
5					
		Total:			

DAILY SUMMARY			
#	**Description**	**Yesterday's Balance**	**Add Today's Balance**
1	Financial		
2	Mental		
3	Physical		
4	Social		
5	Spiritual		
Total			

NOTES:____

AFFIRMATIONS:______________________________________

SIGNATURE:__________________________ DATE:______________

FINANCIAL CHALLENGES					
#	Description	Hours	Rate	Deposit	Withdrawal
1					
2					
3					
4					
5					
		Total:			

MENTAL CHALLENGES					
#	Description	Hours	Rate	Deposit	Withdrawal
1					
2					
3					
4					
5					
		Total:			

PHYSICAL CHALLENGES					
#	Description	Hours	Rate	Deposit	Withdrawal
1					
2					
3					
4					
5					
		Total:			

SOCIAL CHALLENGES					
#	Description	Hours	Rate	Deposit	Withdrawal
1					
2					
3					
4					
5					
		Total:			

SPIRITUAL CHALLENGES					
#	Description	Hours	Rate	Deposit	Withdrawal
1					
2					
3					
4					
5					
		Total:			

DAILY SUMMARY			
#	Description	Yesterday's Balance	Add Today's Balance
1	Financial		
2	Mental		
3	Physical		
4	Social		
5	Spiritual		
	Total		

NOTES:____

AFFIRMATIONS:____________________________________

SIGNATURE:________________________ DATE:______________

FINANCIAL CHALLENGES					
#	Description	Hours	Rate	Deposit	Withdrawal
1					
2					
3					
4					
5					
		Total:			

MENTAL CHALLENGES					
#	Description	Hours	Rate	Deposit	Withdrawal
1					
2					
3					
4					
5					
		Total:			

PHYSICAL CHALLENGES					
#	Description	Hours	Rate	Deposit	Withdrawal
1					
2					
3					
4					
5					
		Total:			

SOCIAL CHALLENGES					
#	Description	Hours	Rate	Deposit	Withdrawal
1					
2					
3					
4					
5					
		Total:			

SPIRITUAL CHALLENGES					
#	**Description**	**Hours**	**Rate**	**Deposit**	**Withdrawal**
1					
2					
3					
4					
5					
		Total:			

DAILY SUMMARY			
#	**Description**	**Yesterday's Balance**	**Add Today's Balance**
1	Financial		
2	Mental		
3	Physical		
4	Social		
5	Spiritual		
Total			

NOTES:____

AFFIRMATIONS:____________________________________

SIGNATURE:__________________________ DATE:______________

FINANCIAL CHALLENGES					
#	Description	Hours	Rate	Deposit	Withdrawal
1					
2					
3					
4					
5					
		Total:			

MENTAL CHALLENGES					
#	Description	Hours	Rate	Deposit	Withdrawal
1					
2					
3					
4					
5					
		Total:			

PHYSICAL CHALLENGES					
#	Description	Hours	Rate	Deposit	Withdrawal
1					
2					
3					
4					
5					
		Total:			

SOCIAL CHALLENGES					
#	Description	Hours	Rate	Deposit	Withdrawal
1					
2					
3					
4					
5					
		Total:			

SPIRITUAL CHALLENGES					
#	Description	Hours	Rate	Deposit	Withdrawal
1					
2					
3					
4					
5					
		Total:			

DAILY SUMMARY			
#	Description	Yesterday's Balance	Add Today's Balance
1	Financial		
2	Mental		
3	Physical		
4	Social		
5	Spiritual		
	Total		

NOTES:____

AFFIRMATIONS:____

SIGNATURE:______________________ DATE:______________

FINANCIAL CHALLENGES					
#	Description	Hours	Rate	Deposit	Withdrawal
1					
2					
3					
4					
5					
		Total:			

MENTAL CHALLENGES					
#	Description	Hours	Rate	Deposit	Withdrawal
1					
2					
3					
4					
5					
		Total:			

PHYSICAL CHALLENGES					
#	Description	Hours	Rate	Deposit	Withdrawal
1					
2					
3					
4					
5					
		Total:			

SOCIAL CHALLENGES					
#	Description	Hours	Rate	Deposit	Withdrawal
1					
2					
3					
4					
5					
		Total:			

Prodigy Planner Workbook

SPIRITUAL CHALLENGES					
#	**Description**	**Hours**	**Rate**	**Deposit**	**Withdrawal**
1					
2					
3					
4					
5					
		Total:			

DAILY SUMMARY			
#	**Description**	**Yesterday's Balance**	**Add Today's Balance**
1	Financial		
2	Mental		
3	Physical		
4	Social		
5	Spiritual		
Total			

NOTES:____

AFFIRMATIONS:__________________________________

SIGNATURE:__________________________ DATE:_______________

Prodigy Planner Workbook

FINANCIAL CHALLENGES					
#	**Description**	**Hours**	**Rate**	**Deposit**	**Withdrawal**
1					
2					
3					
4					
5					
		Total:			

MENTAL CHALLENGES					
#	**Description**	**Hours**	**Rate**	**Deposit**	**Withdrawal**
1					
2					
3					
4					
5					
		Total:			

PHYSICAL CHALLENGES					
#	**Description**	**Hours**	**Rate**	**Deposit**	**Withdrawal**
1					
2					
3					
4					
5					
		Total:			

SOCIAL CHALLENGES					
#	**Description**	**Hours**	**Rate**	**Deposit**	**Withdrawal**
1					
2					
3					
4					
5					
		Total:			

Prodigy Planner Workbook

SPIRITUAL CHALLENGES					
#	Description	Hours	Rate	Deposit	Withdrawal
1					
2					
3					
4					
5					
		Total:			

DAILY SUMMARY			
#	Description	Yesterday's Balance	Add Today's Balance
1	Financial		
2	Mental		
3	Physical		
4	Social		
5	Spiritual		
Total			

NOTES:________________________________

AFFIRMATIONS:________________________________

SIGNATURE:____________________ DATE:____________

FINANCIAL CHALLENGES					
#	**Description**	**Hours**	**Rate**	**Deposit**	**Withdrawal**
1					
2					
3					
4					
5					
		Total:			

MENTAL CHALLENGES					
#	**Description**	**Hours**	**Rate**	**Deposit**	**Withdrawal**
1					
2					
3					
4					
5					
		Total:			

PHYSICAL CHALLENGES					
#	**Description**	**Hours**	**Rate**	**Deposit**	**Withdrawal**
1					
2					
3					
4					
5					
		Total:			

SOCIAL CHALLENGES					
#	**Description**	**Hours**	**Rate**	**Deposit**	**Withdrawal**
1					
2					
3					
4					
5					
		Total:			

SPIRITUAL CHALLENGES					
#	Description	Hours	Rate	Deposit	Withdrawal
1					
2					
3					
4					
5					
			Total:		

DAILY SUMMARY			
#	Description	Yesterday's Balance	Add Today's Balance
1	Financial		
2	Mental		
3	Physical		
4	Social		
5	Spiritual		
	Total		

NOTES:____

AFFIRMATIONS:____________________________________

SIGNATURE:____________________ DATE:____________

FINANCIAL CHALLENGES					
#	Description	Hours	Rate	Deposit	Withdrawal
1					
2					
3					
4					
5					
		Total:			

MENTAL CHALLENGES					
#	Description	Hours	Rate	Deposit	Withdrawal
1					
2					
3					
4					
5					
		Total:			

PHYSICAL CHALLENGES					
#	Description	Hours	Rate	Deposit	Withdrawal
1					
2					
3					
4					
5					
		Total:			

SOCIAL CHALLENGES					
#	Description	Hours	Rate	Deposit	Withdrawal
1					
2					
3					
4					
5					
		Total:			

Prodigy Planner Workbook

SPIRITUAL CHALLENGES					
#	**Description**	**Hours**	**Rate**	**Deposit**	**Withdrawal**
1					
2					
3					
4					
5					
		Total:			

DAILY SUMMARY			
#	**Description**	**Yesterday's Balance**	**Add Today's Balance**
1	Financial		
2	Mental		
3	Physical		
4	Social		
5	Spiritual		
Total			

NOTES:______________________________

AFFIRMATIONS:______________________________

SIGNATURE:____________________ DATE:____________

FINANCIAL CHALLENGES					
#	Description	Hours	Rate	Deposit	Withdrawal
1					
2					
3					
4					
5					
		Total:			

MENTAL CHALLENGES					
#	Description	Hours	Rate	Deposit	Withdrawal
1					
2					
3					
4					
5					
		Total:			

PHYSICAL CHALLENGES					
#	Description	Hours	Rate	Deposit	Withdrawal
1					
2					
3					
4					
5					
		Total:			

SOCIAL CHALLENGES					
#	Description	Hours	Rate	Deposit	Withdrawal
1					
2					
3					
4					
5					
		Total:			

SPIRITUAL CHALLENGES					
#	**Description**	**Hours**	**Rate**	**Deposit**	**Withdrawal**
1					
2					
3					
4					
5					
		Total:			

DAILY SUMMARY			
#	**Description**	**Yesterday's Balance**	**Add Today's Balance**
1	Financial		
2	Mental		
3	Physical		
4	Social		
5	Spiritual		
Total			

NOTES:______________________________________

____

____

____

____

____

AFFIRMATIONS:______________________________________

____

____

____

____

____

____

SIGNATURE:________________________ DATE:______________

FINANCIAL CHALLENGES					
#	Description	Hours	Rate	Deposit	Withdrawal
1					
2					
3					
4					
5					
		Total:			

MENTAL CHALLENGES					
#	Description	Hours	Rate	Deposit	Withdrawal
1					
2					
3					
4					
5					
		Total:			

PHYSICAL CHALLENGES					
#	Description	Hours	Rate	Deposit	Withdrawal
1					
2					
3					
4					
5					
		Total:			

SOCIAL CHALLENGES					
#	Description	Hours	Rate	Deposit	Withdrawal
1					
2					
3					
4					
5					
		Total:			

Prodigy Planner Workbook

SPIRITUAL CHALLENGES					
#	Description	Hours	Rate	Deposit	Withdrawal
1					
2					
3					
4					
5					
		Total:			

DAILY SUMMARY			
#	Description	Yesterday's Balance	Add Today's Balance
1	Financial		
2	Mental		
3	Physical		
4	Social		
5	Spiritual		
Total			

NOTES:____

AFFIRMATIONS:____

SIGNATURE:____________________________ DATE:________________

FINANCIAL CHALLENGES					
#	Description	Hours	Rate	Deposit	Withdrawal
1					
2					
3					
4					
5					
		Total:			

MENTAL CHALLENGES					
#	Description	Hours	Rate	Deposit	Withdrawal
1					
2					
3					
4					
5					
		Total:			

PHYSICAL CHALLENGES					
#	Description	Hours	Rate	Deposit	Withdrawal
1					
2					
3					
4					
5					
		Total:			

SOCIAL CHALLENGES					
#	Description	Hours	Rate	Deposit	Withdrawal
1					
2					
3					
4					
5					
		Total:			

SPIRITUAL CHALLENGES					
#	**Description**	**Hours**	**Rate**	**Deposit**	**Withdrawal**
1					
2					
3					
4					
5					
		Total:			

DAILY SUMMARY			
#	**Description**	**Yesterday's Balance**	**Add Today's Balance**
1	Financial		
2	Mental		
3	Physical		
4	Social		
5	Spiritual		
Total			

NOTES:____

____

____

____

____

____

AFFIRMATIONS:____

____

____

____

____

____

____

SIGNATURE:______________________________ DATE:________________

FINANCIAL CHALLENGES					
#	Description	Hours	Rate	Deposit	Withdrawal
1					
2					
3					
4					
5					
		Total:			

MENTAL CHALLENGES					
#	Description	Hours	Rate	Deposit	Withdrawal
1					
2					
3					
4					
5					
		Total:			

PHYSICAL CHALLENGES					
#	Description	Hours	Rate	Deposit	Withdrawal
1					
2					
3					
4					
5					
		Total:			

SOCIAL CHALLENGES					
#	Description	Hours	Rate	Deposit	Withdrawal
1					
2					
3					
4					
5					
		Total:			

Prodigy Planner Workbook

SPIRITUAL CHALLENGES					
#	Description	Hours	Rate	Deposit	Withdrawal
1					
2					
3					
4					
5					
		Total:			

DAILY SUMMARY			
#	Description	Yesterday's Balance	Add Today's Balance
1	Financial		
2	Mental		
3	Physical		
4	Social		
5	Spiritual		
Total			

NOTES:____

AFFIRMATIONS:__________________________________

SIGNATURE:________________________ DATE:____________

FINANCIAL CHALLENGES					
#	Description	Hours	Rate	Deposit	Withdrawal
1					
2					
3					
4					
5					
		Total:			

MENTAL CHALLENGES					
#	Description	Hours	Rate	Deposit	Withdrawal
1					
2					
3					
4					
5					
		Total:			

PHYSICAL CHALLENGES					
#	Description	Hours	Rate	Deposit	Withdrawal
1					
2					
3					
4					
5					
		Total:			

SOCIAL CHALLENGES					
#	Description	Hours	Rate	Deposit	Withdrawal
1					
2					
3					
4					
5					
		Total:			

Prodigy Planner Workbook

SPIRITUAL CHALLENGES					
#	**Description**	**Hours**	**Rate**	**Deposit**	**Withdrawal**
1					
2					
3					
4					
5					
		Total:			

DAILY SUMMARY			
#	**Description**	**Yesterday's Balance**	**Add Today's Balance**
1	Financial		
2	Mental		
3	Physical		
4	Social		
5	Spiritual		
Total			

NOTES:____

AFFIRMATIONS:____________________________________

SIGNATURE:________________________ DATE:______________

FINANCIAL CHALLENGES					
#	Description	Hours	Rate	Deposit	Withdrawal
1					
2					
3					
4					
5					
		Total:			

MENTAL CHALLENGES					
#	Description	Hours	Rate	Deposit	Withdrawal
1					
2					
3					
4					
5					
		Total:			

PHYSICAL CHALLENGES					
#	Description	Hours	Rate	Deposit	Withdrawal
1					
2					
3					
4					
5					
		Total:			

SOCIAL CHALLENGES					
#	Description	Hours	Rate	Deposit	Withdrawal
1					
2					
3					
4					
5					
		Total:			

SPIRITUAL CHALLENGES					
#	**Description**	**Hours**	**Rate**	**Deposit**	**Withdrawal**
1					
2					
3					
4					
5					
		Total:			

DAILY SUMMARY			
#	**Description**	**Yesterday's Balance**	**Add Today's Balance**
1	Financial		
2	Mental		
3	Physical		
4	Social		
5	Spiritual		
Total			

NOTES:____

AFFIRMATIONS:____________________________________

SIGNATURE:________________________ DATE:______________

FINANCIAL CHALLENGES					
#	Description	Hours	Rate	Deposit	Withdrawal
1					
2					
3					
4					
5					
		Total:			

MENTAL CHALLENGES					
#	Description	Hours	Rate	Deposit	Withdrawal
1					
2					
3					
4					
5					
		Total:			

PHYSICAL CHALLENGES					
#	Description	Hours	Rate	Deposit	Withdrawal
1					
2					
3					
4					
5					
		Total:			

SOCIAL CHALLENGES					
#	Description	Hours	Rate	Deposit	Withdrawal
1					
2					
3					
4					
5					
		Total:			

SPIRITUAL CHALLENGES					
#	**Description**	**Hours**	**Rate**	**Deposit**	**Withdrawal**
1					
2					
3					
4					
5					
			Total:		

DAILY SUMMARY			
#	**Description**	**Yesterday's Balance**	**Add Today's Balance**
1	Financial		
2	Mental		
3	Physical		
4	Social		
5	Spiritual		
Total			

NOTES:____

____

____

____

____

____

AFFIRMATIONS:______________________________________

____

____

____

____

____

____

SIGNATURE:_____________________________ DATE:________________

FINANCIAL CHALLENGES					
#	Description	Hours	Rate	Deposit	Withdrawal
1					
2					
3					
4					
5					
		Total:			

MENTAL CHALLENGES					
#	Description	Hours	Rate	Deposit	Withdrawal
1					
2					
3					
4					
5					
		Total:			

PHYSICAL CHALLENGES					
#	Description	Hours	Rate	Deposit	Withdrawal
1					
2					
3					
4					
5					
		Total:			

SOCIAL CHALLENGES					
#	Description	Hours	Rate	Deposit	Withdrawal
1					
2					
3					
4					
5					
		Total:			

Prodigy Planner Workbook

SPIRITUAL CHALLENGES					
#	**Description**	**Hours**	**Rate**	**Deposit**	**Withdrawal**
1					
2					
3					
4					
5					
		Total:			

DAILY SUMMARY			
#	**Description**	**Yesterday's Balance**	**Add Today's Balance**
1	Financial		
2	Mental		
3	Physical		
4	Social		
5	Spiritual		
	Total		

NOTES:____

____

____

____

____

____

AFFIRMATIONS:______________________________________

____

____

____

____

____

____

SIGNATURE:______________________ DATE:______________

FINANCIAL CHALLENGES					
#	Description	Hours	Rate	Deposit	Withdrawal
1					
2					
3					
4					
5					
		Total:			

MENTAL CHALLENGES					
#	Description	Hours	Rate	Deposit	Withdrawal
1					
2					
3					
4					
5					
		Total:			

PHYSICAL CHALLENGES					
#	Description	Hours	Rate	Deposit	Withdrawal
1					
2					
3					
4					
5					
		Total:			

SOCIAL CHALLENGES					
#	Description	Hours	Rate	Deposit	Withdrawal
1					
2					
3					
4					
5					
		Total:			

SPIRITUAL CHALLENGES					
#	Description	Hours	Rate	Deposit	Withdrawal
1					
2					
3					
4					
5					
			Total:		

DAILY SUMMARY			
#	Description	Yesterday's Balance	Add Today's Balance
1	Financial		
2	Mental		
3	Physical		
4	Social		
5	Spiritual		
Total			

NOTES:______________________________

AFFIRMATIONS:______________________________

SIGNATURE:____________________ DATE:____________

FINANCIAL CHALLENGES					
#	Description	Hours	Rate	Deposit	Withdrawal
1					
2					
3					
4					
5					
		Total:			

MENTAL CHALLENGES					
#	Description	Hours	Rate	Deposit	Withdrawal
1					
2					
3					
4					
5					
		Total:			

PHYSICAL CHALLENGES					
#	Description	Hours	Rate	Deposit	Withdrawal
1					
2					
3					
4					
5					
		Total:			

SOCIAL CHALLENGES					
#	Description	Hours	Rate	Deposit	Withdrawal
1					
2					
3					
4					
5					
		Total:			

SPIRITUAL CHALLENGES					
#	**Description**	**Hours**	**Rate**	**Deposit**	**Withdrawal**
1					
2					
3					
4					
5					
		Total:			

DAILY SUMMARY			
#	**Description**	**Yesterday's Balance**	**Add Today's Balance**
1	Financial		
2	Mental		
3	Physical		
4	Social		
5	Spiritual		
Total			

NOTES:____

AFFIRMATIONS:__________________________________

SIGNATURE:________________________ DATE:____________

FINANCIAL CHALLENGES					
#	Description	Hours	Rate	Deposit	Withdrawal
1					
2					
3					
4					
5					
		Total:			

MENTAL CHALLENGES					
#	Description	Hours	Rate	Deposit	Withdrawal
1					
2					
3					
4					
5					
		Total:			

PHYSICAL CHALLENGES					
#	Description	Hours	Rate	Deposit	Withdrawal
1					
2					
3					
4					
5					
		Total:			

SOCIAL CHALLENGES					
#	Description	Hours	Rate	Deposit	Withdrawal
1					
2					
3					
4					
5					
		Total:			

SPIRITUAL CHALLENGES					
#	**Description**	**Hours**	**Rate**	**Deposit**	**Withdrawal**
1					
2					
3					
4					
5					
			Total:		

DAILY SUMMARY			
#	**Description**	**Yesterday's Balance**	**Add Today's Balance**
1	Financial		
2	Mental		
3	Physical		
4	Social		
5	Spiritual		
Total			

NOTES:____

____

____

____

____

____

AFFIRMATIONS:_______________________________________

____

____

____

____

____

____

SIGNATURE:______________________ DATE:______________

FINANCIAL CHALLENGES					
#	Description	Hours	Rate	Deposit	Withdrawal
1					
2					
3					
4					
5					
		Total:			

MENTAL CHALLENGES					
#	Description	Hours	Rate	Deposit	Withdrawal
1					
2					
3					
4					
5					
		Total:			

PHYSICAL CHALLENGES					
#	Description	Hours	Rate	Deposit	Withdrawal
1					
2					
3					
4					
5					
		Total:			

SOCIAL CHALLENGES					
#	Description	Hours	Rate	Deposit	Withdrawal
1					
2					
3					
4					
5					
		Total:			

Prodigy Planner Workbook

SPIRITUAL CHALLENGES					
#	**Description**	**Hours**	**Rate**	**Deposit**	**Withdrawal**
1					
2					
3					
4					
5					
		Total:			

DAILY SUMMARY			
#	**Description**	**Yesterday's Balance**	**Add Today's Balance**
1	Financial		
2	Mental		
3	Physical		
4	Social		
5	Spiritual		
Total			

NOTES:____

____

____

____

____

____

AFFIRMATIONS:______________________________________

____

____

____

____

____

____

SIGNATURE:______________________________ DATE:________________

FINANCIAL CHALLENGES					
#	Description	Hours	Rate	Deposit	Withdrawal
1					
2					
3					
4					
5					
		Total:			

MENTAL CHALLENGES					
#	Description	Hours	Rate	Deposit	Withdrawal
1					
2					
3					
4					
5					
		Total:			

PHYSICAL CHALLENGES					
#	Description	Hours	Rate	Deposit	Withdrawal
1					
2					
3					
4					
5					
		Total:			

SOCIAL CHALLENGES					
#	Description	Hours	Rate	Deposit	Withdrawal
1					
2					
3					
4					
5					
		Total:			

SPIRITUAL CHALLENGES					
#	Description	Hours	Rate	Deposit	Withdrawal
1					
2					
3					
4					
5					
		Total:			

DAILY SUMMARY			
#	Description	Yesterday's Balance	Add Today's Balance
1	Financial		
2	Mental		
3	Physical		
4	Social		
5	Spiritual		
Total			

NOTES:____

____

____

____

____

____

AFFIRMATIONS:______________________________________

____

____

____

____

____

____

SIGNATURE:______________________________ DATE:________________

FINANCIAL CHALLENGES					
#	Description	Hours	Rate	Deposit	Withdrawal
1					
2					
3					
4					
5					
		Total:			

MENTAL CHALLENGES					
#	Description	Hours	Rate	Deposit	Withdrawal
1					
2					
3					
4					
5					
		Total:			

PHYSICAL CHALLENGES					
#	Description	Hours	Rate	Deposit	Withdrawal
1					
2					
3					
4					
5					
		Total:			

SOCIAL CHALLENGES					
#	Description	Hours	Rate	Deposit	Withdrawal
1					
2					
3					
4					
5					
		Total:			

Prodigy Planner Workbook

SPIRITUAL CHALLENGES					
#	**Description**	**Hours**	**Rate**	**Deposit**	**Withdrawal**
1					
2					
3					
4					
5					
		Total:			

DAILY SUMMARY			
#	**Description**	**Yesterday's Balance**	**Add Today's Balance**
1	Financial		
2	Mental		
3	Physical		
4	Social		
5	Spiritual		
Total			

NOTES:____

AFFIRMATIONS:______________________________________

SIGNATURE:__________________________ DATE:_______________

FINANCIAL CHALLENGES					
#	Description	Hours	Rate	Deposit	Withdrawal
1					
2					
3					
4					
5					
		Total:			

MENTAL CHALLENGES					
#	Description	Hours	Rate	Deposit	Withdrawal
1					
2					
3					
4					
5					
		Total:			

PHYSICAL CHALLENGES					
#	Description	Hours	Rate	Deposit	Withdrawal
1					
2					
3					
4					
5					
		Total:			

SOCIAL CHALLENGES					
#	Description	Hours	Rate	Deposit	Withdrawal
1					
2					
3					
4					
5					
		Total:			

SPIRITUAL CHALLENGES					
#	**Description**	**Hours**	**Rate**	**Deposit**	**Withdrawal**
1					
2					
3					
4					
5					
			Total:		

DAILY SUMMARY			
#	**Description**	**Yesterday's Balance**	**Add Today's Balance**
1	Financial		
2	Mental		
3	Physical		
4	Social		
5	Spiritual		
		Total	

NOTES:____

____

____

____

____

____

AFFIRMATIONS:____

____

____

____

____

____

____

SIGNATURE:______________________________ DATE:________________

FINANCIAL CHALLENGES					
#	Description	Hours	Rate	Deposit	Withdrawal
1					
2					
3					
4					
5					
		Total:			

MENTAL CHALLENGES					
#	Description	Hours	Rate	Deposit	Withdrawal
1					
2					
3					
4					
5					
		Total:			

PHYSICAL CHALLENGES					
#	Description	Hours	Rate	Deposit	Withdrawal
1					
2					
3					
4					
5					
		Total:			

SOCIAL CHALLENGES					
#	Description	Hours	Rate	Deposit	Withdrawal
1					
2					
3					
4					
5					
		Total:			

SPIRITUAL CHALLENGES					
#	**Description**	**Hours**	**Rate**	**Deposit**	**Withdrawal**
1					
2					
3					
4					
5					
		Total:			

DAILY SUMMARY			
#	**Description**	**Yesterday's Balance**	**Add Today's Balance**
1	Financial		
2	Mental		
3	Physical		
4	Social		
5	Spiritual		
	Total		

NOTES:____

AFFIRMATIONS:____________________________________

SIGNATURE:________________________ DATE:______________

WEALTH LEVEL 1 - Essentials		
#	**Description**	**Deposit**
1	Have Earned Income	
2	Have Investment Income	
3	Have Leveraged Income	
4	Have Residual Income	
5	Have More Than One Type Of Income	

WEALTH LEVEL 2 - Fundamentals		
#	**Description**	**Deposit**
1	10% Of Income Saved Upon Payment	
2	6-Month Emergency Cash Fund Reserved	
3	1-Year Emergency Electronic Fund Reserved	
4	All Monthly Bills Are Paid On Time	
5	Bills Do Not Exceed 50% Of Monthly Income	
6	No Debt – With Exception Of Mortgage	

WEALTH LEVEL 3 - Safety Net		
#	**Description**	**Deposit**
1	Life Insurance – All Dependents	
2	Medical Insurance – All Dependents	
3	Disability Insurance – If Not Retired	
4	Dental Insurance – All Dependents	
5	Optical Insurance - All Dependents	
6	Long Term Care Insurance – If Retired	
7	Umbrella Insurance	
8	Property Insurance – Homeowner/Renters	
9	Auto Insurance	
10	Filed All Bills & Receipts	

WEALTH LEVEL 4 - Look Good On Paper		
#	**Description**	**Deposit**
1	Have A Credit Score Above 760	
2	Have A Secured Credit Cards Only	
3	10% Of Income Invested Upon Payment	
4	Monitor Your Credit Report Monthly	
WEALTH LEVEL 5 - Sustainability		
#	**Description**	**Deposit**
1	Sustainable Power Supply – No Bill	
2	Sustainable Water Supply – No Bill	
3	Recycle & Eliminate Own Waste	
4	Have No Mortgage Or Rent Bill	
5	20-Year Property Tax Funds Reserved	
6	Homestead	
	Total:	

NOTES:____

AFFIRMATIONS:_______________________________________

SIGNATURE:______________________ DATE:______________

FINANCIAL CHALLENGES					
#	Description	Hours	Rate	Deposit	Withdrawal
1					
2					
3					
4					
5					
		Total:			

MENTAL CHALLENGES					
#	Description	Hours	Rate	Deposit	Withdrawal
1					
2					
3					
4					
5					
		Total:			

PHYSICAL CHALLENGES					
#	Description	Hours	Rate	Deposit	Withdrawal
1					
2					
3					
4					
5					
		Total:			

SOCIAL CHALLENGES					
#	Description	Hours	Rate	Deposit	Withdrawal
1					
2					
3					
4					
5					
		Total:			

Prodigy Planner Workbook

SPIRITUAL CHALLENGES					
#	Description	Hours	Rate	Deposit	Withdrawal
1					
2					
3					
4					
5					
			Total:		

DAILY SUMMARY			
#	Description	Yesterday's Balance	Add Today's Balance
1	Financial		
2	Mental		
3	Physical		
4	Social		
5	Spiritual		
	Monthly Wealth Bonus		
	Total		

NOTES:____

AFFIRMATIONS:______________________________________

SIGNATURE:________________________ DATE:______________

FINANCIAL CHALLENGES					
#	Description	Hours	Rate	Deposit	Withdrawal
1					
2					
3					
4					
5					
		Total:			

MENTAL CHALLENGES					
#	Description	Hours	Rate	Deposit	Withdrawal
1					
2					
3					
4					
5					
		Total:			

PHYSICAL CHALLENGES					
#	Description	Hours	Rate	Deposit	Withdrawal
1					
2					
3					
4					
5					
		Total:			

SOCIAL CHALLENGES					
#	Description	Hours	Rate	Deposit	Withdrawal
1					
2					
3					
4					
5					
		Total:			

Prodigy Planner Workbook

SPIRITUAL CHALLENGES					
#	Description	Hours	Rate	Deposit	Withdrawal
1					
2					
3					
4					
5					
		Total:			

DAILY SUMMARY			
#	Description	Yesterday's Balance	Add Today's Balance
1	Financial		
2	Mental		
3	Physical		
4	Social		
5	Spiritual		
Total			

NOTES:____

____

____

____

____

____

AFFIRMATIONS:____

____

____

____

____

____

____

SIGNATURE:______________________________ DATE:________________

FINANCIAL CHALLENGES					
#	Description	Hours	Rate	Deposit	Withdrawal
1					
2					
3					
4					
5					
		Total:			

MENTAL CHALLENGES					
#	Description	Hours	Rate	Deposit	Withdrawal
1					
2					
3					
4					
5					
		Total:			

PHYSICAL CHALLENGES					
#	Description	Hours	Rate	Deposit	Withdrawal
1					
2					
3					
4					
5					
		Total:			

SOCIAL CHALLENGES					
#	Description	Hours	Rate	Deposit	Withdrawal
1					
2					
3					
4					
5					
		Total:			

SPIRITUAL CHALLENGES					
#	**Description**	**Hours**	**Rate**	**Deposit**	**Withdrawal**
1					
2					
3					
4					
5					
		Total:			

DAILY SUMMARY			
#	**Description**	**Yesterday's Balance**	**Add Today's Balance**
1	Financial		
2	Mental		
3	Physical		
4	Social		
5	Spiritual		
Total			

NOTES:______________________________________

____

____

____

____

____

AFFIRMATIONS:______________________________________

____

____

____

____

____

____

SIGNATURE:______________________ DATE:______________

FINANCIAL CHALLENGES					
#	Description	Hours	Rate	Deposit	Withdrawal
1					
2					
3					
4					
5					
		Total:			

MENTAL CHALLENGES					
#	Description	Hours	Rate	Deposit	Withdrawal
1					
2					
3					
4					
5					
		Total:			

PHYSICAL CHALLENGES					
#	Description	Hours	Rate	Deposit	Withdrawal
1					
2					
3					
4					
5					
		Total:			

SOCIAL CHALLENGES					
#	Description	Hours	Rate	Deposit	Withdrawal
1					
2					
3					
4					
5					
		Total:			

SPIRITUAL CHALLENGES					
#	**Description**	**Hours**	**Rate**	**Deposit**	**Withdrawal**
1					
2					
3					
4					
5					
			Total:		

DAILY SUMMARY			
#	**Description**	**Yesterday's Balance**	**Add Today's Balance**
1	Financial		
2	Mental		
3	Physical		
4	Social		
5	Spiritual		
Total			

NOTES:______________________________

AFFIRMATIONS:______________________________

SIGNATURE:____________________ DATE:____________

FINANCIAL CHALLENGES					
#	Description	Hours	Rate	Deposit	Withdrawal
1					
2					
3					
4					
5					
		Total:			

MENTAL CHALLENGES					
#	Description	Hours	Rate	Deposit	Withdrawal
1					
2					
3					
4					
5					
		Total:			

PHYSICAL CHALLENGES					
#	Description	Hours	Rate	Deposit	Withdrawal
1					
2					
3					
4					
5					
		Total:			

SOCIAL CHALLENGES					
#	Description	Hours	Rate	Deposit	Withdrawal
1					
2					
3					
4					
5					
		Total:			

SPIRITUAL CHALLENGES					
#	**Description**	**Hours**	**Rate**	**Deposit**	**Withdrawal**
1					
2					
3					
4					
5					
		Total:			

DAILY SUMMARY			
#	**Description**	**Yesterday's Balance**	**Add Today's Balance**
1	Financial		
2	Mental		
3	Physical		
4	Social		
5	Spiritual		
Total			

NOTES:____

AFFIRMATIONS:____

SIGNATURE:______________________________ DATE:________________

FINANCIAL CHALLENGES					
#	Description	Hours	Rate	Deposit	Withdrawal
1					
2					
3					
4					
5					
		Total:			

MENTAL CHALLENGES					
#	Description	Hours	Rate	Deposit	Withdrawal
1					
2					
3					
4					
5					
		Total:			

PHYSICAL CHALLENGES					
#	Description	Hours	Rate	Deposit	Withdrawal
1					
2					
3					
4					
5					
		Total:			

SOCIAL CHALLENGES					
#	Description	Hours	Rate	Deposit	Withdrawal
1					
2					
3					
4					
5					
		Total:			

SPIRITUAL CHALLENGES					
#	Description	Hours	Rate	Deposit	Withdrawal
1					
2					
3					
4					
5					
		Total:			

DAILY SUMMARY			
#	Description	Yesterday's Balance	Add Today's Balance
1	Financial		
2	Mental		
3	Physical		
4	Social		
5	Spiritual		
Total			

NOTES:____

____

____

____

____

____

AFFIRMATIONS:______________________________________

____

____

____

____

____

____

SIGNATURE:______________________________ DATE:________________

FINANCIAL CHALLENGES					
#	Description	Hours	Rate	Deposit	Withdrawal
1					
2					
3					
4					
5					
		Total:			

MENTAL CHALLENGES					
#	Description	Hours	Rate	Deposit	Withdrawal
1					
2					
3					
4					
5					
		Total:			

PHYSICAL CHALLENGES					
#	Description	Hours	Rate	Deposit	Withdrawal
1					
2					
3					
4					
5					
		Total:			

SOCIAL CHALLENGES					
#	Description	Hours	Rate	Deposit	Withdrawal
1					
2					
3					
4					
5					
		Total:			

SPIRITUAL CHALLENGES					
#	**Description**	**Hours**	**Rate**	**Deposit**	**Withdrawal**
1					
2					
3					
4					
5					
		Total:			

DAILY SUMMARY			
#	**Description**	**Yesterday's Balance**	**Add Today's Balance**
1	Financial		
2	Mental		
3	Physical		
4	Social		
5	Spiritual		
Total			

NOTES:______________________________

____

____

____

____

____

AFFIRMATIONS:______________________________

____

____

____

____

____

____

SIGNATURE:______________________ DATE:______________

FINANCIAL CHALLENGES					
#	Description	Hours	Rate	Deposit	Withdrawal
1					
2					
3					
4					
5					
		Total:			

MENTAL CHALLENGES					
#	Description	Hours	Rate	Deposit	Withdrawal
1					
2					
3					
4					
5					
		Total:			

PHYSICAL CHALLENGES					
#	Description	Hours	Rate	Deposit	Withdrawal
1					
2					
3					
4					
5					
		Total:			

SOCIAL CHALLENGES					
#	Description	Hours	Rate	Deposit	Withdrawal
1					
2					
3					
4					
5					
		Total:			

SPIRITUAL CHALLENGES					
#	**Description**	**Hours**	**Rate**	**Deposit**	**Withdrawal**
1					
2					
3					
4					
5					
		Total:			

DAILY SUMMARY			
#	**Description**	**Yesterday's Balance**	**Add Today's Balance**
1	Financial		
2	Mental		
3	Physical		
4	Social		
5	Spiritual		
Total			

NOTES:______________________________

AFFIRMATIONS:______________________________

SIGNATURE:____________________ DATE:__________

Prodigy Planner Workbook

FINANCIAL CHALLENGES					
#	Description	Hours	Rate	Deposit	Withdrawal
1					
2					
3					
4					
5					
		Total:			

MENTAL CHALLENGES					
#	Description	Hours	Rate	Deposit	Withdrawal
1					
2					
3					
4					
5					
		Total:			

PHYSICAL CHALLENGES					
#	Description	Hours	Rate	Deposit	Withdrawal
1					
2					
3					
4					
5					
		Total:			

SOCIAL CHALLENGES					
#	Description	Hours	Rate	Deposit	Withdrawal
1					
2					
3					
4					
5					
		Total:			

SPIRITUAL CHALLENGES					
#	**Description**	**Hours**	**Rate**	**Deposit**	**Withdrawal**
1					
2					
3					
4					
5					
			Total:		

DAILY SUMMARY			
#	**Description**	**Yesterday's Balance**	**Add Today's Balance**
1	Financial		
2	Mental		
3	Physical		
4	Social		
5	Spiritual		
	Total		

NOTES:____

AFFIRMATIONS:_______________________________________

SIGNATURE:______________________ DATE:______________

FINANCIAL CHALLENGES					
#	Description	Hours	Rate	Deposit	Withdrawal
1					
2					
3					
4					
5					
		Total:			

MENTAL CHALLENGES					
#	Description	Hours	Rate	Deposit	Withdrawal
1					
2					
3					
4					
5					
		Total:			

PHYSICAL CHALLENGES					
#	Description	Hours	Rate	Deposit	Withdrawal
1					
2					
3					
4					
5					
		Total:			

SOCIAL CHALLENGES					
#	Description	Hours	Rate	Deposit	Withdrawal
1					
2					
3					
4					
5					
		Total:			

SPIRITUAL CHALLENGES					
#	**Description**	**Hours**	**Rate**	**Deposit**	**Withdrawal**
1					
2					
3					
4					
5					
			Total:		

DAILY SUMMARY			
#	**Description**	**Yesterday's Balance**	**Add Today's Balance**
1	Financial		
2	Mental		
3	Physical		
4	Social		
5	Spiritual		
	Total		

NOTES:____

____

____

____

____

____

AFFIRMATIONS:____

____

____

____

____

____

____

SIGNATURE:______________________________ DATE:____________________

FINANCIAL CHALLENGES					
#	Description	Hours	Rate	Deposit	Withdrawal
1					
2					
3					
4					
5					
		Total:			

MENTAL CHALLENGES					
#	Description	Hours	Rate	Deposit	Withdrawal
1					
2					
3					
4					
5					
		Total:			

PHYSICAL CHALLENGES					
#	Description	Hours	Rate	Deposit	Withdrawal
1					
2					
3					
4					
5					
		Total:			

SOCIAL CHALLENGES					
#	Description	Hours	Rate	Deposit	Withdrawal
1					
2					
3					
4					
5					
		Total:			

SPIRITUAL CHALLENGES					
#	Description	Hours	Rate	Deposit	Withdrawal
1					
2					
3					
4					
5					
		Total:			

DAILY SUMMARY			
#	Description	Yesterday's Balance	Add Today's Balance
1	Financial		
2	Mental		
3	Physical		
4	Social		
5	Spiritual		
Total			

NOTES:____

AFFIRMATIONS:__________________________________

SIGNATURE:____________________ DATE:____________

Prodigy Planner Workbook

FINANCIAL CHALLENGES					
#	**Description**	**Hours**	**Rate**	**Deposit**	**Withdrawal**
1					
2					
3					
4					
5					
		Total:			

MENTAL CHALLENGES					
#	**Description**	**Hours**	**Rate**	**Deposit**	**Withdrawal**
1					
2					
3					
4					
5					
		Total:			

PHYSICAL CHALLENGES					
#	**Description**	**Hours**	**Rate**	**Deposit**	**Withdrawal**
1					
2					
3					
4					
5					
		Total:			

SOCIAL CHALLENGES					
#	**Description**	**Hours**	**Rate**	**Deposit**	**Withdrawal**
1					
2					
3					
4					
5					
		Total:			

Prodigy Planner Workbook

SPIRITUAL CHALLENGES					
#	Description	Hours	Rate	Deposit	Withdrawal
1					
2					
3					
4					
5					
		Total:			

DAILY SUMMARY			
#	Description	Yesterday's Balance	Add Today's Balance
1	Financial		
2	Mental		
3	Physical		
4	Social		
5	Spiritual		
Total			

NOTES:______________________________

AFFIRMATIONS:______________________________

SIGNATURE:____________________ DATE:____________

FINANCIAL CHALLENGES					
#	Description	Hours	Rate	Deposit	Withdrawal
1					
2					
3					
4					
5					
		Total:			

MENTAL CHALLENGES					
#	Description	Hours	Rate	Deposit	Withdrawal
1					
2					
3					
4					
5					
		Total:			

PHYSICAL CHALLENGES					
#	Description	Hours	Rate	Deposit	Withdrawal
1					
2					
3					
4					
5					
		Total:			

SOCIAL CHALLENGES					
#	Description	Hours	Rate	Deposit	Withdrawal
1					
2					
3					
4					
5					
		Total:			

SPIRITUAL CHALLENGES					
#	**Description**	**Hours**	**Rate**	**Deposit**	**Withdrawal**
1					
2					
3					
4					
5					
		Total:			

DAILY SUMMARY			
#	**Description**	**Yesterday's Balance**	**Add Today's Balance**
1	Financial		
2	Mental		
3	Physical		
4	Social		
5	Spiritual		
Total			

NOTES:____

AFFIRMATIONS:__________________________________

SIGNATURE:____________________ DATE:____________

FINANCIAL CHALLENGES					
#	Description	Hours	Rate	Deposit	Withdrawal
1					
2					
3					
4					
5					
		Total:			

MENTAL CHALLENGES					
#	Description	Hours	Rate	Deposit	Withdrawal
1					
2					
3					
4					
5					
		Total:			

PHYSICAL CHALLENGES					
#	Description	Hours	Rate	Deposit	Withdrawal
1					
2					
3					
4					
5					
		Total:			

SOCIAL CHALLENGES					
#	Description	Hours	Rate	Deposit	Withdrawal
1					
2					
3					
4					
5					
		Total:			

SPIRITUAL CHALLENGES					
#	Description	Hours	Rate	Deposit	Withdrawal
1					
2					
3					
4					
5					
		Total:			

DAILY SUMMARY			
#	Description	Yesterday's Balance	Add Today's Balance
1	Financial		
2	Mental		
3	Physical		
4	Social		
5	Spiritual		
Total			

NOTES:______________________________________

AFFIRMATIONS:______________________________________

SIGNATURE:____________________ DATE:____________

FINANCIAL CHALLENGES					
#	Description	Hours	Rate	Deposit	Withdrawal
1					
2					
3					
4					
5					
		Total:			

MENTAL CHALLENGES					
#	Description	Hours	Rate	Deposit	Withdrawal
1					
2					
3					
4					
5					
		Total:			

PHYSICAL CHALLENGES					
#	Description	Hours	Rate	Deposit	Withdrawal
1					
2					
3					
4					
5					
		Total:			

SOCIAL CHALLENGES					
#	Description	Hours	Rate	Deposit	Withdrawal
1					
2					
3					
4					
5					
		Total:			

SPIRITUAL CHALLENGES					
#	Description	Hours	Rate	Deposit	Withdrawal
1					
2					
3					
4					
5					
		Total:			

DAILY SUMMARY			
#	Description	Yesterday's Balance	Add Today's Balance
1	Financial		
2	Mental		
3	Physical		
4	Social		
5	Spiritual		
Total			

NOTES:____

AFFIRMATIONS:____________________________________

SIGNATURE:____________________ DATE:____________

FINANCIAL CHALLENGES					
#	Description	Hours	Rate	Deposit	Withdrawal
1					
2					
3					
4					
5					
		Total:			

MENTAL CHALLENGES					
#	Description	Hours	Rate	Deposit	Withdrawal
1					
2					
3					
4					
5					
		Total:			

PHYSICAL CHALLENGES					
#	Description	Hours	Rate	Deposit	Withdrawal
1					
2					
3					
4					
5					
		Total:			

SOCIAL CHALLENGES					
#	Description	Hours	Rate	Deposit	Withdrawal
1					
2					
3					
4					
5					
		Total:			

SPIRITUAL CHALLENGES					
#	**Description**	**Hours**	**Rate**	**Deposit**	**Withdrawal**
1					
2					
3					
4					
5					
		Total:			

DAILY SUMMARY			
#	**Description**	**Yesterday's Balance**	**Add Today's Balance**
1	Financial		
2	Mental		
3	Physical		
4	Social		
5	Spiritual		
Total			

NOTES:____________________________________

AFFIRMATIONS:____________________________________

SIGNATURE:________________________ DATE:______________

FINANCIAL CHALLENGES					
#	Description	Hours	Rate	Deposit	Withdrawal
1					
2					
3					
4					
5					
		Total:			

MENTAL CHALLENGES					
#	Description	Hours	Rate	Deposit	Withdrawal
1					
2					
3					
4					
5					
		Total:			

PHYSICAL CHALLENGES					
#	Description	Hours	Rate	Deposit	Withdrawal
1					
2					
3					
4					
5					
		Total:			

SOCIAL CHALLENGES					
#	Description	Hours	Rate	Deposit	Withdrawal
1					
2					
3					
4					
5					
		Total:			

SPIRITUAL CHALLENGES					
#	**Description**	**Hours**	**Rate**	**Deposit**	**Withdrawal**
1					
2					
3					
4					
5					
		Total:			

DAILY SUMMARY			
#	**Description**	**Yesterday's Balance**	**Add Today's Balance**
1	Financial		
2	Mental		
3	Physical		
4	Social		
5	Spiritual		
Total			

NOTES: ______________________________

AFFIRMATIONS: ______________________________

SIGNATURE: ______________________ DATE: ______________

FINANCIAL CHALLENGES					
#	Description	Hours	Rate	Deposit	Withdrawal
1					
2					
3					
4					
5					
		Total:			

MENTAL CHALLENGES					
#	Description	Hours	Rate	Deposit	Withdrawal
1					
2					
3					
4					
5					
		Total:			

PHYSICAL CHALLENGES					
#	Description	Hours	Rate	Deposit	Withdrawal
1					
2					
3					
4					
5					
		Total:			

SOCIAL CHALLENGES					
#	Description	Hours	Rate	Deposit	Withdrawal
1					
2					
3					
4					
5					
		Total:			

SPIRITUAL CHALLENGES					
#	**Description**	**Hours**	**Rate**	**Deposit**	**Withdrawal**
1					
2					
3					
4					
5					
		Total:			

DAILY SUMMARY			
#	**Description**	**Yesterday's Balance**	**Add Today's Balance**
1	Financial		
2	Mental		
3	Physical		
4	Social		
5	Spiritual		
Total			

NOTES:____

AFFIRMATIONS:__________________________________

SIGNATURE:________________________ DATE:______________

FINANCIAL CHALLENGES					
#	Description	Hours	Rate	Deposit	Withdrawal
1					
2					
3					
4					
5					
		Total:			

MENTAL CHALLENGES					
#	Description	Hours	Rate	Deposit	Withdrawal
1					
2					
3					
4					
5					
		Total:			

PHYSICAL CHALLENGES					
#	Description	Hours	Rate	Deposit	Withdrawal
1					
2					
3					
4					
5					
		Total:			

SOCIAL CHALLENGES					
#	Description	Hours	Rate	Deposit	Withdrawal
1					
2					
3					
4					
5					
		Total:			

SPIRITUAL CHALLENGES					
#	**Description**	**Hours**	**Rate**	**Deposit**	**Withdrawal**
1					
2					
3					
4					
5					
		Total:			

DAILY SUMMARY			
#	**Description**	**Yesterday's Balance**	**Add Today's Balance**
1	Financial		
2	Mental		
3	Physical		
4	Social		
5	Spiritual		
Total			

NOTES:______________________________

AFFIRMATIONS:______________________________

SIGNATURE:____________________ DATE:____________

FINANCIAL CHALLENGES					
#	Description	Hours	Rate	Deposit	Withdrawal
1					
2					
3					
4					
5					
		Total:			

MENTAL CHALLENGES					
#	Description	Hours	Rate	Deposit	Withdrawal
1					
2					
3					
4					
5					
		Total:			

PHYSICAL CHALLENGES					
#	Description	Hours	Rate	Deposit	Withdrawal
1					
2					
3					
4					
5					
		Total:			

SOCIAL CHALLENGES					
#	Description	Hours	Rate	Deposit	Withdrawal
1					
2					
3					
4					
5					
		Total:			

Prodigy Planner Workbook

SPIRITUAL CHALLENGES					
#	Description	Hours	Rate	Deposit	Withdrawal
1					
2					
3					
4					
5					
		Total:			

DAILY SUMMARY			
#	Description	Yesterday's Balance	Add Today's Balance
1	Financial		
2	Mental		
3	Physical		
4	Social		
5	Spiritual		
Total			

NOTES:____

AFFIRMATIONS:____

SIGNATURE:______________________ DATE:____________

FINANCIAL CHALLENGES					
#	Description	Hours	Rate	Deposit	Withdrawal
1					
2					
3					
4					
5					
		Total:			

MENTAL CHALLENGES					
#	Description	Hours	Rate	Deposit	Withdrawal
1					
2					
3					
4					
5					
		Total:			

PHYSICAL CHALLENGES					
#	Description	Hours	Rate	Deposit	Withdrawal
1					
2					
3					
4					
5					
		Total:			

SOCIAL CHALLENGES					
#	Description	Hours	Rate	Deposit	Withdrawal
1					
2					
3					
4					
5					
		Total:			

SPIRITUAL CHALLENGES					
#	Description	Hours	Rate	Deposit	Withdrawal
1					
2					
3					
4					
5					
		Total:			

DAILY SUMMARY			
#	Description	Yesterday's Balance	Add Today's Balance
1	Financial		
2	Mental		
3	Physical		
4	Social		
5	Spiritual		
Total			

NOTES:______________________________

AFFIRMATIONS:______________________________

SIGNATURE:____________________ DATE:______________

FINANCIAL CHALLENGES					
#	Description	Hours	Rate	Deposit	Withdrawal
1					
2					
3					
4					
5					
		Total:			

MENTAL CHALLENGES					
#	Description	Hours	Rate	Deposit	Withdrawal
1					
2					
3					
4					
5					
		Total:			

PHYSICAL CHALLENGES					
#	Description	Hours	Rate	Deposit	Withdrawal
1					
2					
3					
4					
5					
		Total:			

SOCIAL CHALLENGES					
#	Description	Hours	Rate	Deposit	Withdrawal
1					
2					
3					
4					
5					
		Total:			

SPIRITUAL CHALLENGES					
#	Description	Hours	Rate	Deposit	Withdrawal
1					
2					
3					
4					
5					
		Total:			

DAILY SUMMARY			
#	Description	Yesterday's Balance	Add Today's Balance
1	Financial		
2	Mental		
3	Physical		
4	Social		
5	Spiritual		
Total			

NOTES:____

AFFIRMATIONS:____

SIGNATURE:______________________ DATE:______________

FINANCIAL CHALLENGES					
#	Description	Hours	Rate	Deposit	Withdrawal
1					
2					
3					
4					
5					
		Total:			

MENTAL CHALLENGES					
#	Description	Hours	Rate	Deposit	Withdrawal
1					
2					
3					
4					
5					
		Total:			

PHYSICAL CHALLENGES					
#	Description	Hours	Rate	Deposit	Withdrawal
1					
2					
3					
4					
5					
		Total:			

SOCIAL CHALLENGES					
#	Description	Hours	Rate	Deposit	Withdrawal
1					
2					
3					
4					
5					
		Total:			

Prodigy Planner Workbook

SPIRITUAL CHALLENGES					
#	**Description**	**Hours**	**Rate**	**Deposit**	**Withdrawal**
1					
2					
3					
4					
5					
		Total:			

DAILY SUMMARY			
#	**Description**	**Yesterday's Balance**	**Add Today's Balance**
1	Financial		
2	Mental		
3	Physical		
4	Social		
5	Spiritual		
Total			

NOTES:____

____

____

____

____

____

AFFIRMATIONS:____

____

____

____

____

____

____

SIGNATURE:______________________________ DATE:________________

FINANCIAL CHALLENGES					
#	Description	Hours	Rate	Deposit	Withdrawal
1					
2					
3					
4					
5					
		Total:			

MENTAL CHALLENGES					
#	Description	Hours	Rate	Deposit	Withdrawal
1					
2					
3					
4					
5					
		Total:			

PHYSICAL CHALLENGES					
#	Description	Hours	Rate	Deposit	Withdrawal
1					
2					
3					
4					
5					
		Total:			

SOCIAL CHALLENGES					
#	Description	Hours	Rate	Deposit	Withdrawal
1					
2					
3					
4					
5					
		Total:			

Prodigy Planner Workbook

SPIRITUAL CHALLENGES					
#	Description	Hours	Rate	Deposit	Withdrawal
1					
2					
3					
4					
5					
			Total:		

DAILY SUMMARY			
#	Description	Yesterday's Balance	Add Today's Balance
1	Financial		
2	Mental		
3	Physical		
4	Social		
5	Spiritual		
Total			

NOTES:____

____

____

____

____

____

AFFIRMATIONS:______________________________________

____

____

____

____

____

____

SIGNATURE:______________________________ DATE:________________

FINANCIAL CHALLENGES					
#	Description	Hours	Rate	Deposit	Withdrawal
1					
2					
3					
4					
5					
		Total:			

MENTAL CHALLENGES					
#	Description	Hours	Rate	Deposit	Withdrawal
1					
2					
3					
4					
5					
		Total:			

PHYSICAL CHALLENGES					
#	Description	Hours	Rate	Deposit	Withdrawal
1					
2					
3					
4					
5					
		Total:			

SOCIAL CHALLENGES					
#	Description	Hours	Rate	Deposit	Withdrawal
1					
2					
3					
4					
5					
		Total:			

Prodigy Planner Workbook

SPIRITUAL CHALLENGES					
#	Description	Hours	Rate	Deposit	Withdrawal
1					
2					
3					
4					
5					
		Total:			

DAILY SUMMARY			
#	Description	Yesterday's Balance	Add Today's Balance
1	Financial		
2	Mental		
3	Physical		
4	Social		
5	Spiritual		
Total			

NOTES:____

AFFIRMATIONS:____

SIGNATURE:______________________ DATE:______________

FINANCIAL CHALLENGES					
#	Description	Hours	Rate	Deposit	Withdrawal
1					
2					
3					
4					
5					
		Total:			

MENTAL CHALLENGES					
#	Description	Hours	Rate	Deposit	Withdrawal
1					
2					
3					
4					
5					
		Total:			

PHYSICAL CHALLENGES					
#	Description	Hours	Rate	Deposit	Withdrawal
1					
2					
3					
4					
5					
		Total:			

SOCIAL CHALLENGES					
#	Description	Hours	Rate	Deposit	Withdrawal
1					
2					
3					
4					
5					
		Total:			

Prodigy Planner Workbook

SPIRITUAL CHALLENGES					
#	Description	Hours	Rate	Deposit	Withdrawal
1					
2					
3					
4					
5					
		Total:			

DAILY SUMMARY			
#	Description	Yesterday's Balance	Add Today's Balance
1	Financial		
2	Mental		
3	Physical		
4	Social		
5	Spiritual		
Total			

NOTES:____

AFFIRMATIONS:________________________________

SIGNATURE:________________________ DATE:______________

FINANCIAL CHALLENGES					
#	Description	Hours	Rate	Deposit	Withdrawal
1					
2					
3					
4					
5					
		Total:			

MENTAL CHALLENGES					
#	Description	Hours	Rate	Deposit	Withdrawal
1					
2					
3					
4					
5					
		Total:			

PHYSICAL CHALLENGES					
#	Description	Hours	Rate	Deposit	Withdrawal
1					
2					
3					
4					
5					
		Total:			

SOCIAL CHALLENGES					
#	Description	Hours	Rate	Deposit	Withdrawal
1					
2					
3					
4					
5					
		Total:			

Prodigy Planner Workbook

SPIRITUAL CHALLENGES					
#	**Description**	**Hours**	**Rate**	**Deposit**	**Withdrawal**
1					
2					
3					
4					
5					
		Total:			

DAILY SUMMARY			
#	**Description**	**Yesterday's Balance**	**Add Today's Balance**
1	Financial		
2	Mental		
3	Physical		
4	Social		
5	Spiritual		
	Total		

NOTES:______________________________

AFFIRMATIONS:______________________________

SIGNATURE:____________________ DATE:__________

FINANCIAL CHALLENGES					
#	Description	Hours	Rate	Deposit	Withdrawal
1					
2					
3					
4					
5					
		Total:			

MENTAL CHALLENGES					
#	Description	Hours	Rate	Deposit	Withdrawal
1					
2					
3					
4					
5					
		Total:			

PHYSICAL CHALLENGES					
#	Description	Hours	Rate	Deposit	Withdrawal
1					
2					
3					
4					
5					
		Total:			

SOCIAL CHALLENGES					
#	Description	Hours	Rate	Deposit	Withdrawal
1					
2					
3					
4					
5					
		Total:			

SPIRITUAL CHALLENGES					
#	Description	Hours	Rate	Deposit	Withdrawal
1					
2					
3					
4					
5					
			Total:		

DAILY SUMMARY			
#	Description	Yesterday's Balance	Add Today's Balance
1	Financial		
2	Mental		
3	Physical		
4	Social		
5	Spiritual		
Total			

NOTES:______________________________

AFFIRMATIONS:______________________________

SIGNATURE:____________________ DATE:____________

WEALTH LEVEL 1 - Essentials		
#	**Description**	**Deposit**
1	Have Earned Income	
2	Have Investment Income	
3	Have Leveraged Income	
4	Have Residual Income	
5	Have More Than One Type Of Income	

WEALTH LEVEL 2 - Fundamentals		
#	**Description**	**Deposit**
1	10% Of Income Saved Upon Payment	
2	6-Month Emergency Cash Fund Reserved	
3	1-Year Emergency Electronic Fund Reserved	
4	All Monthly Bills Are Paid On Time	
5	Bills Do Not Exceed 50% Of Monthly Income	
6	No Debt – With Exception Of Mortgage	

WEALTH LEVEL 3 - Safety Net		
#	**Description**	**Deposit**
1	Life Insurance – All Dependents	
2	Medical Insurance – All Dependents	
3	Disability Insurance – If Not Retired	
4	Dental Insurance – All Dependents	
5	Optical Insurance - All Dependents	
6	Long Term Care Insurance – If Retired	
7	Umbrella Insurance	
8	Property Insurance – Homeowner/Renters	
9	Auto Insurance	
10	Filed All Bills & Receipts	

WEALTH LEVEL 4 - Look Good On Paper		
#	**Description**	**Deposit**
1	Have A Credit Score Above 760	
2	Have A Secured Credit Cards Only	
3	10% Of Income Invested Upon Payment	
4	Monitor Your Credit Report Monthly	
WEALTH LEVEL 5 - Sustainability		
#	**Description**	**Deposit**
1	Sustainable Power Supply – No Bill	
2	Sustainable Water Supply – No Bill	
3	Recycle & Eliminate Own Waste	
4	Have No Mortgage Or Rent Bill	
5	20-Year Property Tax Funds Reserved	
6	Homestead	
	Total:	

NOTES:____

AFFIRMATIONS:__________________________________

SIGNATURE:________________________ DATE:______________

FINANCIAL CHALLENGES					
#	Description	Hours	Rate	Deposit	Withdrawal
1					
2					
3					
4					
5					
		Total:			

MENTAL CHALLENGES					
#	Description	Hours	Rate	Deposit	Withdrawal
1					
2					
3					
4					
5					
		Total:			

PHYSICAL CHALLENGES					
#	Description	Hours	Rate	Deposit	Withdrawal
1					
2					
3					
4					
5					
		Total:			

SOCIAL CHALLENGES					
#	Description	Hours	Rate	Deposit	Withdrawal
1					
2					
3					
4					
5					
		Total:			

Prodigy Planner Workbook

SPIRITUAL CHALLENGES					
#	Description	Hours	Rate	Deposit	Withdrawal
1					
2					
3					
4					
5					
		Total:			

DAILY SUMMARY			
#	Description	Yesterday's Balance	Add Today's Balance
1	Financial		
2	Mental		
3	Physical		
4	Social		
5	Spiritual		
Monthly Wealth Bonus			
Total			

NOTES:____

____

____

____

____

____

AFFIRMATIONS:____

____

____

____

____

____

SIGNATURE:______________________________ DATE:__________________

FINANCIAL CHALLENGES					
#	Description	Hours	Rate	Deposit	Withdrawal
1					
2					
3					
4					
5					
		Total:			

MENTAL CHALLENGES					
#	Description	Hours	Rate	Deposit	Withdrawal
1					
2					
3					
4					
5					
		Total:			

PHYSICAL CHALLENGES					
#	Description	Hours	Rate	Deposit	Withdrawal
1					
2					
3					
4					
5					
		Total:			

SOCIAL CHALLENGES					
#	Description	Hours	Rate	Deposit	Withdrawal
1					
2					
3					
4					
5					
		Total:			

Prodigy Planner Workbook

SPIRITUAL CHALLENGES					
#	Description	Hours	Rate	Deposit	Withdrawal
1					
2					
3					
4					
5					
		Total:			

DAILY SUMMARY			
#	Description	Yesterday's Balance	Add Today's Balance
1	Financial		
2	Mental		
3	Physical		
4	Social		
5	Spiritual		
Total			

NOTES:____

____

____

____

____

____

AFFIRMATIONS:______________________________________

____

____

____

____

____

____

SIGNATURE:____________________________ DATE:______________

FINANCIAL CHALLENGES					
#	Description	Hours	Rate	Deposit	Withdrawal
1					
2					
3					
4					
5					
		Total:			

MENTAL CHALLENGES					
#	Description	Hours	Rate	Deposit	Withdrawal
1					
2					
3					
4					
5					
		Total:			

PHYSICAL CHALLENGES					
#	Description	Hours	Rate	Deposit	Withdrawal
1					
2					
3					
4					
5					
		Total:			

SOCIAL CHALLENGES					
#	Description	Hours	Rate	Deposit	Withdrawal
1					
2					
3					
4					
5					
		Total:			

SPIRITUAL CHALLENGES					
#	Description	Hours	Rate	Deposit	Withdrawal
1					
2					
3					
4					
5					
		Total:			

DAILY SUMMARY			
#	Description	Yesterday's Balance	Add Today's Balance
1	Financial		
2	Mental		
3	Physical		
4	Social		
5	Spiritual		
Total			

NOTES:______________________________

AFFIRMATIONS:______________________________

SIGNATURE:______________________ DATE:______________

FINANCIAL CHALLENGES					
#	Description	Hours	Rate	Deposit	Withdrawal
1					
2					
3					
4					
5					
		Total:			

MENTAL CHALLENGES					
#	Description	Hours	Rate	Deposit	Withdrawal
1					
2					
3					
4					
5					
		Total:			

PHYSICAL CHALLENGES					
#	Description	Hours	Rate	Deposit	Withdrawal
1					
2					
3					
4					
5					
		Total:			

SOCIAL CHALLENGES					
#	Description	Hours	Rate	Deposit	Withdrawal
1					
2					
3					
4					
5					
		Total:			

Prodigy Planner Workbook

SPIRITUAL CHALLENGES					
#	**Description**	**Hours**	**Rate**	**Deposit**	**Withdrawal**
1					
2					
3					
4					
5					
		Total:			

DAILY SUMMARY			
#	**Description**	**Yesterday's Balance**	**Add Today's Balance**
1	Financial		
2	Mental		
3	Physical		
4	Social		
5	Spiritual		
Total			

NOTES:____

AFFIRMATIONS:____________________________________

SIGNATURE:_________________________ DATE:______________

FINANCIAL CHALLENGES					
#	Description	Hours	Rate	Deposit	Withdrawal
1					
2					
3					
4					
5					
		Total:			

MENTAL CHALLENGES					
#	Description	Hours	Rate	Deposit	Withdrawal
1					
2					
3					
4					
5					
		Total:			

PHYSICAL CHALLENGES					
#	Description	Hours	Rate	Deposit	Withdrawal
1					
2					
3					
4					
5					
		Total:			

SOCIAL CHALLENGES					
#	Description	Hours	Rate	Deposit	Withdrawal
1					
2					
3					
4					
5					
		Total:			

SPIRITUAL CHALLENGES					
#	Description	Hours	Rate	Deposit	Withdrawal
1					
2					
3					
4					
5					
		Total:			

DAILY SUMMARY			
#	Description	Yesterday's Balance	Add Today's Balance
1	Financial		
2	Mental		
3	Physical		
4	Social		
5	Spiritual		
Total			

NOTES:____________________

AFFIRMATIONS:____________________

SIGNATURE:____________________ DATE:____________

FINANCIAL CHALLENGES					
#	Description	Hours	Rate	Deposit	Withdrawal
1					
2					
3					
4					
5					
		Total:			

MENTAL CHALLENGES					
#	Description	Hours	Rate	Deposit	Withdrawal
1					
2					
3					
4					
5					
		Total:			

PHYSICAL CHALLENGES					
#	Description	Hours	Rate	Deposit	Withdrawal
1					
2					
3					
4					
5					
		Total:			

SOCIAL CHALLENGES					
#	Description	Hours	Rate	Deposit	Withdrawal
1					
2					
3					
4					
5					
		Total:			

Prodigy Planner Workbook

SPIRITUAL CHALLENGES					
#	Description	Hours	Rate	Deposit	Withdrawal
1					
2					
3					
4					
5					
		Total:			

DAILY SUMMARY			
#	Description	Yesterday's Balance	Add Today's Balance
1	Financial		
2	Mental		
3	Physical		
4	Social		
5	Spiritual		
Total			

NOTES:____

AFFIRMATIONS:__________________________________

SIGNATURE:____________________ DATE:____________

FINANCIAL CHALLENGES					
#	Description	Hours	Rate	Deposit	Withdrawal
1					
2					
3					
4					
5					
		Total:			

MENTAL CHALLENGES					
#	Description	Hours	Rate	Deposit	Withdrawal
1					
2					
3					
4					
5					
		Total:			

PHYSICAL CHALLENGES					
#	Description	Hours	Rate	Deposit	Withdrawal
1					
2					
3					
4					
5					
		Total:			

SOCIAL CHALLENGES					
#	Description	Hours	Rate	Deposit	Withdrawal
1					
2					
3					
4					
5					
		Total:			

SPIRITUAL CHALLENGES					
#	**Description**	**Hours**	**Rate**	**Deposit**	**Withdrawal**
1					
2					
3					
4					
5					
		Total:			

DAILY SUMMARY			
#	**Description**	**Yesterday's Balance**	**Add Today's Balance**
1	Financial		
2	Mental		
3	Physical		
4	Social		
5	Spiritual		
Total			

NOTES:______________________________

AFFIRMATIONS:__________________________

SIGNATURE:__________________ DATE:__________

FINANCIAL CHALLENGES					
#	Description	Hours	Rate	Deposit	Withdrawal
1					
2					
3					
4					
5					
		Total:			

MENTAL CHALLENGES					
#	Description	Hours	Rate	Deposit	Withdrawal
1					
2					
3					
4					
5					
		Total:			

PHYSICAL CHALLENGES					
#	Description	Hours	Rate	Deposit	Withdrawal
1					
2					
3					
4					
5					
		Total:			

SOCIAL CHALLENGES					
#	Description	Hours	Rate	Deposit	Withdrawal
1					
2					
3					
4					
5					
		Total:			

Prodigy Planner Workbook

SPIRITUAL CHALLENGES					
#	Description	Hours	Rate	Deposit	Withdrawal
1					
2					
3					
4					
5					
		Total:			

DAILY SUMMARY			
#	Description	Yesterday's Balance	Add Today's Balance
1	Financial		
2	Mental		
3	Physical		
4	Social		
5	Spiritual		
Total			

NOTES:____

____

____

____

____

____

AFFIRMATIONS:______________________________________

____

____

____

____

____

____

SIGNATURE:______________________________ DATE:________________

FINANCIAL CHALLENGES					
#	Description	Hours	Rate	Deposit	Withdrawal
1					
2					
3					
4					
5					
			Total:		

MENTAL CHALLENGES					
#	Description	Hours	Rate	Deposit	Withdrawal
1					
2					
3					
4					
5					
			Total:		

PHYSICAL CHALLENGES					
#	Description	Hours	Rate	Deposit	Withdrawal
1					
2					
3					
4					
5					
			Total:		

SOCIAL CHALLENGES					
#	Description	Hours	Rate	Deposit	Withdrawal
1					
2					
3					
4					
5					
			Total:		

Prodigy Planner Workbook

SPIRITUAL CHALLENGES					
#	Description	Hours	Rate	Deposit	Withdrawal
1					
2					
3					
4					
5					
		Total:			

DAILY SUMMARY			
#	Description	Yesterday's Balance	Add Today's Balance
1	Financial		
2	Mental		
3	Physical		
4	Social		
5	Spiritual		
Total			

NOTES:____

AFFIRMATIONS:____________________________________

SIGNATURE:________________________ DATE:______________

FINANCIAL CHALLENGES					
#	Description	Hours	Rate	Deposit	Withdrawal
1					
2					
3					
4					
5					
		Total:			

MENTAL CHALLENGES					
#	Description	Hours	Rate	Deposit	Withdrawal
1					
2					
3					
4					
5					
		Total:			

PHYSICAL CHALLENGES					
#	Description	Hours	Rate	Deposit	Withdrawal
1					
2					
3					
4					
5					
		Total:			

SOCIAL CHALLENGES					
#	Description	Hours	Rate	Deposit	Withdrawal
1					
2					
3					
4					
5					
		Total:			

Prodigy Planner Workbook

SPIRITUAL CHALLENGES					
#	**Description**	**Hours**	**Rate**	**Deposit**	**Withdrawal**
1					
2					
3					
4					
5					
		Total:			

DAILY SUMMARY			
#	**Description**	**Yesterday's Balance**	**Add Today's Balance**
1	Financial		
2	Mental		
3	Physical		
4	Social		
5	Spiritual		
Total			

NOTES:____

____

____

____

____

____

AFFIRMATIONS:_______________________________________

____

____

____

____

____

____

SIGNATURE:_________________________ DATE:_______________

FINANCIAL CHALLENGES					
#	Description	Hours	Rate	Deposit	Withdrawal
1					
2					
3					
4					
5					
		Total:			

MENTAL CHALLENGES					
#	Description	Hours	Rate	Deposit	Withdrawal
1					
2					
3					
4					
5					
		Total:			

PHYSICAL CHALLENGES					
#	Description	Hours	Rate	Deposit	Withdrawal
1					
2					
3					
4					
5					
		Total:			

SOCIAL CHALLENGES					
#	Description	Hours	Rate	Deposit	Withdrawal
1					
2					
3					
4					
5					
		Total:			

SPIRITUAL CHALLENGES					
#	Description	Hours	Rate	Deposit	Withdrawal
1					
2					
3					
4					
5					
		Total:			

DAILY SUMMARY			
#	Description	Yesterday's Balance	Add Today's Balance
1	Financial		
2	Mental		
3	Physical		
4	Social		
5	Spiritual		
Total			

NOTES:____

AFFIRMATIONS:_______________________________________

SIGNATURE:_________________________ DATE:______________

FINANCIAL CHALLENGES					
#	Description	Hours	Rate	Deposit	Withdrawal
1					
2					
3					
4					
5					
		Total:			

MENTAL CHALLENGES					
#	Description	Hours	Rate	Deposit	Withdrawal
1					
2					
3					
4					
5					
		Total:			

PHYSICAL CHALLENGES					
#	Description	Hours	Rate	Deposit	Withdrawal
1					
2					
3					
4					
5					
		Total:			

SOCIAL CHALLENGES					
#	Description	Hours	Rate	Deposit	Withdrawal
1					
2					
3					
4					
5					
		Total:			

Prodigy Planner Workbook

SPIRITUAL CHALLENGES					
#	Description	Hours	Rate	Deposit	Withdrawal
1					
2					
3					
4					
5					
		Total:			

DAILY SUMMARY			
#	Description	Yesterday's Balance	Add Today's Balance
1	Financial		
2	Mental		
3	Physical		
4	Social		
5	Spiritual		
Total			

NOTES:____

AFFIRMATIONS:____________________________________

SIGNATURE:____________________ DATE:____________

FINANCIAL CHALLENGES					
#	Description	Hours	Rate	Deposit	Withdrawal
1					
2					
3					
4					
5					
		Total:			

MENTAL CHALLENGES					
#	Description	Hours	Rate	Deposit	Withdrawal
1					
2					
3					
4					
5					
		Total:			

PHYSICAL CHALLENGES					
#	Description	Hours	Rate	Deposit	Withdrawal
1					
2					
3					
4					
5					
		Total:			

SOCIAL CHALLENGES					
#	Description	Hours	Rate	Deposit	Withdrawal
1					
2					
3					
4					
5					
		Total:			

Prodigy Planner Workbook

SPIRITUAL CHALLENGES					
#	Description	Hours	Rate	Deposit	Withdrawal
1					
2					
3					
4					
5					
		Total:			

DAILY SUMMARY			
#	Description	Yesterday's Balance	Add Today's Balance
1	Financial		
2	Mental		
3	Physical		
4	Social		
5	Spiritual		
Total			

NOTES:____

____

____

____

____

____

AFFIRMATIONS:____

____

____

____

____

____

____

SIGNATURE:____________________________ DATE:________________

FINANCIAL CHALLENGES					
#	Description	Hours	Rate	Deposit	Withdrawal
1					
2					
3					
4					
5					
		Total:			

MENTAL CHALLENGES					
#	Description	Hours	Rate	Deposit	Withdrawal
1					
2					
3					
4					
5					
		Total:			

PHYSICAL CHALLENGES					
#	Description	Hours	Rate	Deposit	Withdrawal
1					
2					
3					
4					
5					
		Total:			

SOCIAL CHALLENGES					
#	Description	Hours	Rate	Deposit	Withdrawal
1					
2					
3					
4					
5					
		Total:			

SPIRITUAL CHALLENGES					
#	Description	Hours	Rate	Deposit	Withdrawal
1					
2					
3					
4					
5					
		Total:			

DAILY SUMMARY			
#	Description	Yesterday's Balance	Add Today's Balance
1	Financial		
2	Mental		
3	Physical		
4	Social		
5	Spiritual		
Total			

NOTES:____

AFFIRMATIONS:____

SIGNATURE:____________________ DATE:______________

FINANCIAL CHALLENGES					
#	Description	Hours	Rate	Deposit	Withdrawal
1					
2					
3					
4					
5					
		Total:			

MENTAL CHALLENGES					
#	Description	Hours	Rate	Deposit	Withdrawal
1					
2					
3					
4					
5					
		Total:			

PHYSICAL CHALLENGES					
#	Description	Hours	Rate	Deposit	Withdrawal
1					
2					
3					
4					
5					
		Total:			

SOCIAL CHALLENGES					
#	Description	Hours	Rate	Deposit	Withdrawal
1					
2					
3					
4					
5					
		Total:			

SPIRITUAL CHALLENGES					
#	**Description**	**Hours**	**Rate**	**Deposit**	**Withdrawal**
1					
2					
3					
4					
5					
		Total:			

DAILY SUMMARY			
#	**Description**	**Yesterday's Balance**	**Add Today's Balance**
1	Financial		
2	Mental		
3	Physical		
4	Social		
5	Spiritual		
Total			

NOTES:____

____

____

____

____

____

AFFIRMATIONS:______________________________________

____

____

____

____

____

____

SIGNATURE:_______________________ DATE:______________

FINANCIAL CHALLENGES					
#	Description	Hours	Rate	Deposit	Withdrawal
1					
2					
3					
4					
5					
		Total:			

MENTAL CHALLENGES					
#	Description	Hours	Rate	Deposit	Withdrawal
1					
2					
3					
4					
5					
		Total:			

PHYSICAL CHALLENGES					
#	Description	Hours	Rate	Deposit	Withdrawal
1					
2					
3					
4					
5					
		Total:			

SOCIAL CHALLENGES					
#	Description	Hours	Rate	Deposit	Withdrawal
1					
2					
3					
4					
5					
		Total:			

Prodigy Planner Workbook

SPIRITUAL CHALLENGES					
#	Description	Hours	Rate	Deposit	Withdrawal
1					
2					
3					
4					
5					
			Total:		

DAILY SUMMARY			
#	Description	Yesterday's Balance	Add Today's Balance
1	Financial		
2	Mental		
3	Physical		
4	Social		
5	Spiritual		
Total			

NOTES:____

AFFIRMATIONS:____

SIGNATURE:________________________________ DATE:__________________

FINANCIAL CHALLENGES					
#	Description	Hours	Rate	Deposit	Withdrawal
1					
2					
3					
4					
5					
			Total:		

MENTAL CHALLENGES					
#	Description	Hours	Rate	Deposit	Withdrawal
1					
2					
3					
4					
5					
			Total:		

PHYSICAL CHALLENGES					
#	Description	Hours	Rate	Deposit	Withdrawal
1					
2					
3					
4					
5					
			Total:		

SOCIAL CHALLENGES					
#	Description	Hours	Rate	Deposit	Withdrawal
1					
2					
3					
4					
5					
			Total:		

Prodigy Planner Workbook

SPIRITUAL CHALLENGES					
#	Description	Hours	Rate	Deposit	Withdrawal
1					
2					
3					
4					
5					
		Total:			

DAILY SUMMARY			
#	Description	Yesterday's Balance	Add Today's Balance
1	Financial		
2	Mental		
3	Physical		
4	Social		
5	Spiritual		
Total			

NOTES:____________________________________

____

____

____

____

____

AFFIRMATIONS:____________________________________

____

____

____

____

____

____

SIGNATURE:____________________ DATE:____________

FINANCIAL CHALLENGES					
#	Description	Hours	Rate	Deposit	Withdrawal
1					
2					
3					
4					
5					
		Total:			

MENTAL CHALLENGES					
#	Description	Hours	Rate	Deposit	Withdrawal
1					
2					
3					
4					
5					
		Total:			

PHYSICAL CHALLENGES					
#	Description	Hours	Rate	Deposit	Withdrawal
1					
2					
3					
4					
5					
		Total:			

SOCIAL CHALLENGES					
#	Description	Hours	Rate	Deposit	Withdrawal
1					
2					
3					
4					
5					
		Total:			

Prodigy Planner Workbook

SPIRITUAL CHALLENGES					
#	**Description**	**Hours**	**Rate**	**Deposit**	**Withdrawal**
1					
2					
3					
4					
5					
		Total:			

DAILY SUMMARY			
#	**Description**	**Yesterday's Balance**	**Add Today's Balance**
1	Financial		
2	Mental		
3	Physical		
4	Social		
5	Spiritual		
Total			

NOTES:____

____

____

____

____

____

AFFIRMATIONS:______________________________________

____

____

____

____

____

____

SIGNATURE:______________________ DATE:____________

FINANCIAL CHALLENGES					
#	Description	Hours	Rate	Deposit	Withdrawal
1					
2					
3					
4					
5					
		Total:			

MENTAL CHALLENGES					
#	Description	Hours	Rate	Deposit	Withdrawal
1					
2					
3					
4					
5					
		Total:			

PHYSICAL CHALLENGES					
#	Description	Hours	Rate	Deposit	Withdrawal
1					
2					
3					
4					
5					
		Total:			

SOCIAL CHALLENGES					
#	Description	Hours	Rate	Deposit	Withdrawal
1					
2					
3					
4					
5					
		Total:			

SPIRITUAL CHALLENGES					
#	Description	Hours	Rate	Deposit	Withdrawal
1					
2					
3					
4					
5					
		Total:			

DAILY SUMMARY			
#	Description	Yesterday's Balance	Add Today's Balance
1	Financial		
2	Mental		
3	Physical		
4	Social		
5	Spiritual		
Total			

NOTES:______________________________

AFFIRMATIONS:______________________________

SIGNATURE:__________________ DATE:____________

FINANCIAL CHALLENGES					
#	Description	Hours	Rate	Deposit	Withdrawal
1					
2					
3					
4					
5					
		Total:			

MENTAL CHALLENGES					
#	Description	Hours	Rate	Deposit	Withdrawal
1					
2					
3					
4					
5					
		Total:			

PHYSICAL CHALLENGES					
#	Description	Hours	Rate	Deposit	Withdrawal
1					
2					
3					
4					
5					
		Total:			

SOCIAL CHALLENGES					
#	Description	Hours	Rate	Deposit	Withdrawal
1					
2					
3					
4					
5					
		Total:			

Prodigy Planner Workbook

SPIRITUAL CHALLENGES					
#	Description	Hours	Rate	Deposit	Withdrawal
1					
2					
3					
4					
5					
		Total:			

DAILY SUMMARY			
#	Description	Yesterday's Balance	Add Today's Balance
1	Financial		
2	Mental		
3	Physical		
4	Social		
5	Spiritual		
Total			

NOTES:____

AFFIRMATIONS:________________________________

SIGNATURE:____________________ DATE:____________

FINANCIAL CHALLENGES					
#	Description	Hours	Rate	Deposit	Withdrawal
1					
2					
3					
4					
5					
		Total:			

MENTAL CHALLENGES					
#	Description	Hours	Rate	Deposit	Withdrawal
1					
2					
3					
4					
5					
		Total:			

PHYSICAL CHALLENGES					
#	Description	Hours	Rate	Deposit	Withdrawal
1					
2					
3					
4					
5					
		Total:			

SOCIAL CHALLENGES					
#	Description	Hours	Rate	Deposit	Withdrawal
1					
2					
3					
4					
5					
		Total:			

SPIRITUAL CHALLENGES					
#	Description	Hours	Rate	Deposit	Withdrawal
1					
2					
3					
4					
5					
		Total:			

DAILY SUMMARY			
#	Description	Yesterday's Balance	Add Today's Balance
1	Financial		
2	Mental		
3	Physical		
4	Social		
5	Spiritual		
Total			

NOTES:

AFFIRMATIONS:

SIGNATURE: DATE:

FINANCIAL CHALLENGES					
#	Description	Hours	Rate	Deposit	Withdrawal
1					
2					
3					
4					
5					
		Total:			

MENTAL CHALLENGES					
#	Description	Hours	Rate	Deposit	Withdrawal
1					
2					
3					
4					
5					
		Total:			

PHYSICAL CHALLENGES					
#	Description	Hours	Rate	Deposit	Withdrawal
1					
2					
3					
4					
5					
		Total:			

SOCIAL CHALLENGES					
#	Description	Hours	Rate	Deposit	Withdrawal
1					
2					
3					
4					
5					
		Total:			

Prodigy Planner Workbook

SPIRITUAL CHALLENGES					
#	**Description**	**Hours**	**Rate**	**Deposit**	**Withdrawal**
1					
2					
3					
4					
5					
		Total:			

DAILY SUMMARY			
#	**Description**	**Yesterday's Balance**	**Add Today's Balance**
1	Financial		
2	Mental		
3	Physical		
4	Social		
5	Spiritual		
Total			

NOTES:______________________________

AFFIRMATIONS:______________________________

SIGNATURE:____________________ DATE:______________

FINANCIAL CHALLENGES					
#	Description	Hours	Rate	Deposit	Withdrawal
1					
2					
3					
4					
5					
		Total:			

MENTAL CHALLENGES					
#	Description	Hours	Rate	Deposit	Withdrawal
1					
2					
3					
4					
5					
		Total:			

PHYSICAL CHALLENGES					
#	Description	Hours	Rate	Deposit	Withdrawal
1					
2					
3					
4					
5					
		Total:			

SOCIAL CHALLENGES					
#	Description	Hours	Rate	Deposit	Withdrawal
1					
2					
3					
4					
5					
		Total:			

Prodigy Planner Workbook

SPIRITUAL CHALLENGES					
#	Description	Hours	Rate	Deposit	Withdrawal
1					
2					
3					
4					
5					
		Total:			

DAILY SUMMARY			
#	Description	Yesterday's Balance	Add Today's Balance
1	Financial		
2	Mental		
3	Physical		
4	Social		
5	Spiritual		
Total			

NOTES:______________________________

AFFIRMATIONS:______________________________

SIGNATURE:______________________ DATE:______________

FINANCIAL CHALLENGES					
#	Description	Hours	Rate	Deposit	Withdrawal
1					
2					
3					
4					
5					
		Total:			

MENTAL CHALLENGES					
#	Description	Hours	Rate	Deposit	Withdrawal
1					
2					
3					
4					
5					
		Total:			

PHYSICAL CHALLENGES					
#	Description	Hours	Rate	Deposit	Withdrawal
1					
2					
3					
4					
5					
		Total:			

SOCIAL CHALLENGES					
#	Description	Hours	Rate	Deposit	Withdrawal
1					
2					
3					
4					
5					
		Total:			

Prodigy Planner Workbook

SPIRITUAL CHALLENGES					
#	Description	Hours	Rate	Deposit	Withdrawal
1					
2					
3					
4					
5					
		Total:			

DAILY SUMMARY			
#	Description	Yesterday's Balance	Add Today's Balance
1	Financial		
2	Mental		
3	Physical		
4	Social		
5	Spiritual		
Total			

NOTES:____

____

____

____

____

____

AFFIRMATIONS:____

____

____

____

____

____

____

SIGNATURE:______________________________ DATE:________________

FINANCIAL CHALLENGES					
#	Description	Hours	Rate	Deposit	Withdrawal
1					
2					
3					
4					
5					
		Total:			

MENTAL CHALLENGES					
#	Description	Hours	Rate	Deposit	Withdrawal
1					
2					
3					
4					
5					
		Total:			

PHYSICAL CHALLENGES					
#	Description	Hours	Rate	Deposit	Withdrawal
1					
2					
3					
4					
5					
		Total:			

SOCIAL CHALLENGES					
#	Description	Hours	Rate	Deposit	Withdrawal
1					
2					
3					
4					
5					
		Total:			

SPIRITUAL CHALLENGES					
#	**Description**	**Hours**	**Rate**	**Deposit**	**Withdrawal**
1					
2					
3					
4					
5					
		Total:			

DAILY SUMMARY			
#	**Description**	**Yesterday's Balance**	**Add Today's Balance**
1	Financial		
2	Mental		
3	Physical		
4	Social		
5	Spiritual		
Total			

NOTES:______________________________

AFFIRMATIONS:______________________________

SIGNATURE:____________________ DATE:____________

FINANCIAL CHALLENGES					
#	Description	Hours	Rate	Deposit	Withdrawal
1					
2					
3					
4					
5					
		Total:			

MENTAL CHALLENGES					
#	Description	Hours	Rate	Deposit	Withdrawal
1					
2					
3					
4					
5					
		Total:			

PHYSICAL CHALLENGES					
#	Description	Hours	Rate	Deposit	Withdrawal
1					
2					
3					
4					
5					
		Total:			

SOCIAL CHALLENGES					
#	Description	Hours	Rate	Deposit	Withdrawal
1					
2					
3					
4					
5					
		Total:			

SPIRITUAL CHALLENGES					
#	Description	Hours	Rate	Deposit	Withdrawal
1					
2					
3					
4					
5					
		Total:			

DAILY SUMMARY			
#	Description	Yesterday's Balance	Add Today's Balance
1	Financial		
2	Mental		
3	Physical		
4	Social		
5	Spiritual		
Total			

NOTES:______________________________

AFFIRMATIONS:______________________________

SIGNATURE:____________________ DATE:____________

FINANCIAL CHALLENGES					
#	Description	Hours	Rate	Deposit	Withdrawal
1					
2					
3					
4					
5					
		Total:			

MENTAL CHALLENGES					
#	Description	Hours	Rate	Deposit	Withdrawal
1					
2					
3					
4					
5					
		Total:			

PHYSICAL CHALLENGES					
#	Description	Hours	Rate	Deposit	Withdrawal
1					
2					
3					
4					
5					
		Total:			

SOCIAL CHALLENGES					
#	Description	Hours	Rate	Deposit	Withdrawal
1					
2					
3					
4					
5					
		Total:			

Prodigy Planner Workbook

SPIRITUAL CHALLENGES					
#	Description	Hours	Rate	Deposit	Withdrawal
1					
2					
3					
4					
5					
		Total:			

DAILY SUMMARY			
#	Description	Yesterday's Balance	Add Today's Balance
1	Financial		
2	Mental		
3	Physical		
4	Social		
5	Spiritual		
Total			

NOTES:______________________________

AFFIRMATIONS:______________________________

SIGNATURE:____________________ DATE:____________

FINANCIAL CHALLENGES					
#	Description	Hours	Rate	Deposit	Withdrawal
1					
2					
3					
4					
5					
		Total:			

MENTAL CHALLENGES					
#	Description	Hours	Rate	Deposit	Withdrawal
1					
2					
3					
4					
5					
		Total:			

PHYSICAL CHALLENGES					
#	Description	Hours	Rate	Deposit	Withdrawal
1					
2					
3					
4					
5					
		Total:			

SOCIAL CHALLENGES					
#	Description	Hours	Rate	Deposit	Withdrawal
1					
2					
3					
4					
5					
		Total:			

SPIRITUAL CHALLENGES					
#	Description	Hours	Rate	Deposit	Withdrawal
1					
2					
3					
4					
5					
			Total:		

DAILY SUMMARY			
#	Description	Yesterday's Balance	Add Today's Balance
1	Financial		
2	Mental		
3	Physical		
4	Social		
5	Spiritual		
		Total	

NOTES:____

AFFIRMATIONS:_______________________________________

SIGNATURE:________________________ DATE:______________

1 Year Completed!

How has this planner helped you so far?

____

____

____

____

____

____

What could have been done to improve your success?

____

____

____

____

____

____

Be sure to order another copy to continue your planner! I hope you found this planner as useful as I did.

- Draven Xarcell Vestatt